D1567001

LOWRIDERS IN
CHICANO CULTURE

LOWRIDERS IN CHICANO CULTURE

From Low to Slow to Show

Charles M. Tatum

 GREENWOOD

AN IMPRINT OF ABC-CLIO, LLC
Santa Barbara, California • Denver, Colorado • Oxford, England

Library of Congress Cataloging-in-Publication Data

Tatum, Charles M
    Lowriders in Chicano culture : from low to slow to show / Charles M. Tatum.
      p. cm.
    Includes bibliographical references and index.
    ISBN 978–0–313–38149–2 (hard copy : alk. paper) — ISBN 978–0–313–38150–8 (ebook)
1. Mexican Americans–California–Los Angeles–Social life and customs–20th century.
2. Lowriders–Social aspects–California–Los Angeles. 3. Lowriders–History.
4. Automobiles–Societies, etc.–Social aspects–California–Los Angeles. 5. Popular culture–California–Los Angeles. I. Title.
F869.L89M575 2011
629.28'72—dc22   2011015376

ISBN: 978–0–313–38149–2
EISBN: 978–0–313–38150–8

15 14 13 12 11   1 2 3 4 5

This book is also available on the World Wide Web as an eBook.
Visit www.abc-clio.com for details.

Greenwood
An Imprint of ABC-CLIO, LLC

ABC-CLIO, LLC
130 Cremona Drive, P.O. Box 1911
Santa Barbara, California 93116-1911

This book is printed on acid-free paper ∞

Manufactured in the United States of America

I dedicate this book to Anne Tatum
with love and appreciation.

Contents

Contents

Preface

When I was first contacted about writing a book on lowrider culture, I responded enthusiastically to this unique opportunity. I have long been interested in popular culture in general and in Chicana/o and Latin American popular culture in particular. As a child growing up in Mexico in the 1940s and 1950s, I read avidly both Mexican and American comic books, acquiring the Spanish-language comic books at newspaper and magazine stands in my hometown of Parral, Chihuahua, and English-language comic books on frequent family trips across the U.S.-Mexico border to El Paso, Texas. As I look back on those many hours spent enjoying the intriguing and engaging content and the excellent graphics of comic books such as *La familia Burrón* (*The Burrón Family*), a comic published in Mexico since the 1930s, as well as *Captain Marvel* and *Superman*, my one regret is that I did not save and preserve the comic books. I imagine that a few of them might have become very valuable as the collection of such ephemeral publications has become increasingly more popular—and more lucrative. To add to this grievous error in childhood judgment, I also read and then passed on to friends my older brother's collection of comic books that he had put away carefully in a sturdy wooden box in our basement. I think he has forgiven me, but I haven't dared to raise the topic these 60 years later.

My interest in comic books and other forms of popular culture became dormant over the next 20 years as I proceeded through high school, college, graduate school, and the first years of establishing an academic career. It was not until the early 1970s during a University of Minnesota, Morris summer study abroad program in Cuernavaca, Mexico when my interest in Mexican comic books was again piqued. An astute and observant student in the program pointed out to my colleague, Dr. Harold Hinds, Jr., and me that he was impressed by how widespread comic books were among Mexican readers, both young and old, who he had seen in the public plazas, around kiosks where comic books were sold, and on the streets of our neighborhood where enterprising youth were renting used comic books by the hour. Our student rightly concluded that comic books could provide a window into a deeper understanding of contemporary Mexican culture. My colleague, a professor of Latin American history, proposed that we integrate comic books into our summer Spanish language and Mexican culture classes, a suggestion I readily accepted.

This initial renewal of my interest in a comic books, a very valuable aspect of Mexican popular culture, led to a research project to coauthor a book on Mexican comic books during the late 1960s and 1970s, a particularly fertile period when many kinds of comic books were being published and read widely by millions of readers each week with the publication of new installments and the passing on to family and friends of old ones. We eventually finished and published the book, *Not Just for Children: The Mexican Comic Book in the Late 1960s and 1970s* (Greenwood Press, 1992), after subsequent summers spent in Mexico collecting representative samples of comic books. We and some of our summer study abroad students spent hundreds of hours rummaging around in dusty used magazine shops in Mexico City until we had amassed sufficient numbers of different categories of comic books—for example, superhero/adventure, romance, Western, family humor, political humor, and police/detective titles.

Seeing the rise of and increasing research interest in popular culture studies, my colleague Harold had also suggested that we cofound and coedit a journal, *Studies in Latin American Popular Culture*, that over the years has published scholarly articles on a wide range of Chicana/o and Latin American popular culture topics such as sports, music, radio, television, the cinema, popular literature, magazines, comic books, food, and secular and religious festivals and celebrations.

The journal, which is now published by the University of Texas Press, has become one of the most important scholarly publications in the rapidly expanding fields of Latina/o and Latin American popular culture, expressive culture, and cultural studies.

My own continuing interest in popular culture crystallized a few years ago when I was asked to write a book on Chicana/o popular culture, *Chicano Popular Culture: Que Hable el Pueblo* (*Let the People Speak*) for a University of Arizona Press series titled "The Mexican American Experience." Research for the book, which was published in 2001, involved areas of expressive culture such as music, cinema, newspapers, radio, television, popular literature, art, celebrations, and other popular traditions including a section on lowrider culture.

For many years, I have had an interest in lowrider culture, particularly the social and group dynamics of lowrider clubs and gatherings as well as the elaborate designs and murals displayed on lowrider vehicles. I have been fortunate to live in Tucson, Arizona, an urban community that hosts an annual "Tucson Meet Yourself" festival, which brings together over a three-day period a wide variety of ethnic, racial, and national groups who celebrate proudly their respective cultures through food, exhibits, costumes, and performances. An important part of the festival has been the lowrider vehicles exhibit, where owners are readily available to answer questions about different aspects of lowrider culture. Dr. Celestino Fernández, a colleague at the University of Arizona, was responsible for many years for coordinating this important part of the festival, drawing on his knowledge of lowrider culture and research on other forms of Chicana/o popular culture such as *corridos* (ballads). In addition to the festival, Tucson periodically holds lowrider shows that afford local lowrider owners the opportunity to exhibit the best of their cars, trucks, and bicycles for enthusiastic crowds of aficionados. These local events and some published research by scholars formed the basis of the short section on lowrider culture included in my 2001 book.

Doing research for an entire book on lowrider culture has required a very different approach. Again, I was able to draw on the scholarly resources I had used before as well as on some more recent research, including a doctoral thesis and a popular book on lowrider culture. However, I found that in order to do justice to the topic of lowrider culture, it was necessary to discuss its various aspects within its broad sociocultural context. Consequently, I did extensive research in relevant areas of history, art, music, media, and language. My research also involved attending large lowrider super shows in order to get a firsthand experience—a flavor—of the multifaceted aspects of these shows including the vehicle exhibits, the participants, the fans, the vendors, the pageantry, and the various competitions. This also allowed me and my wife, Anne, who accompanied me, to take photographs. Fortunately, she is a much better photographer than I am, with a great eye for detail and composition. This book is dedicated to her.

There are still many skeptics among my colleagues in the humanities and the social sciences who doubt that the study of popular culture is worthy of serious academic research, but there are many more, especially younger colleagues, who are very comfortable with popular culture studies, which slowly have transformed over the past two decades into cultural studies, a thriving area of interest of serious scholarly consideration that has led to a commensurate surge in journals and books. As I like to tell curious and sometimes skeptical friends and colleagues who ask why I have chosen to engage in this kind of research and writing, we are surrounded daily during the hours we are awake by popular culture: television and radio, newspapers, electronic and print advertising, whole sections of book stores, magazines at the supermarket, music on our hand-carried smart phones and iPads, websites whenever we use Google or another search engine, and on and on. By studying popular culture we can learn a great deal about ourselves and others that may not be readily apparent. Popular culture is a window, one of many, on different facets of the culture in which we live and thrive. The study of lowrider culture provides such a window on an important aspect of U.S. car culture in general and Chicana/o culture in particular. I have written this book not as a heavily footnoted academic monograph laden with specialized jargon but with the general reader in mind, the reader who needs no specialized knowledge of the topic but who might be curious to learn more about lowrider culture, which is a multifaceted and fascinating cultural phenomenon that has thrived in the United States since the 1950s and more recently in some foreign countries.

For the reader would like to learn more about the complexities popular culture and the critical approaches than have been used to study it, please see the "Further Readings" section at the end of the Preface. These resources will, in turn, lead the reader more deeply into the various methodologies that scholars from different academic fields—for example, history, anthropology, cultural studies, art, music, sociology, political science, and literature—use to provide nuanced views of popular culture.

FURTHER READING

Fiske, John. *Reading Popular Culture*. Boston: Unwin and Hyman, 1989.

Gaspar de Alba, Alicia, ed. *Velvet Barrios: Popular Culture & Chicana/o Sexualities*. New York: Palgrave Macmillan, 2003.

Strinati, Domic. *An Introduction to the Theories of Popular Culture*. 2nd ed. London and New York: Routledge, 2004.

Tatum, Charles. *Chicano Popular Culture: Que Hable el Pueblo*. Tucson: University of Arizona Press, 2001.

1

The History and Evolution of Lowrider Culture

THE HISTORY OF THE AUTOMOBILE

The car is central to lowrider culture, and to understand and appreciate this popular cultural phenomenon it is important to situate it within the context of the history of automobiles in general and the history of automobiles in the United States in particular. An essential characteristic of an automobile is that it has a self-contained motor. Vehicles with motors can be traced to at least the early part of the nineteenth century when a steam-powered vehicle known as the "Puffing Devil" was designed. Because the boiler in which steam was produced was very large and cumbersome and required frequent water stops so that it could be fueled, the steam-powered automobile was never very popular. It was soon replaced later in the nineteenth century by vehicles with electric motors and internal combustion engines—engines in which a combination of air and fuel are combined in a combustion chamber to produce energy. The first successful internal combustion engine was fueled by a mixture of oxygen and hydrogen. In 1885, a German engineer named Karl Benz designed the first gasoline-powered internal combustion engine; he is generally recognized to be the father of the modern automobile. Diesel-powered cars would later be produced by companies such as Peugeot in France and Mercedes-Benz in Germany.

Although automobiles were made available for purchase by the public in France and Germany before they were in the United States, it was an American who, in 1914, successfully started mass-producing automobiles. Henry Ford began using a factory assembly line on which auto workers were responsible for only a specific aspect of the assembly of a car. He was so successful in designing and implementing efficient ways of producing cars—including the use of quick-drying black car paint—that the United States soon began to dominate the automobile industry worldwide. The Ford Motor Company produced thousands of black Model T Fords—and later, in 1928, Model A Fords—before other American and European companies adopted key aspects of assembly line production.

The companies that prospered soon began to successfully compete with Ford by offering consumers more variety such as different car colors and models. For example, Alfred P. Sloan of General Motors, a leading competitor to Ford, anticipated that consumers were growing tired of the sameness of Model T and Model A Fords and that they would respond enthusiastically to the greater variety of cars produced in his factories.

Cars Built for Speed

At the same time that automobile companies were offering consumers more variety in style, models, colors, and options, they were responding to buyers' demands that cars go faster and that they reflect greater consumer individuality. These two ends were achieved as companies as well as owners themselves began to modify, customize, and personalize their vehicles. From the very beginning of the era of his mass-produced cars, Henry Ford promoted Model T Fords that went faster than the regular assembly line product. His company's Model Ts set many speed records, a feat achieved by modifying standard engines. Later, the Chevrolet brothers in France designed a special engine for Model Ts that was wildly popular among consumers who took pride in their speedsters. Speed was also achieved by stripping down Model Ts and other models to make them lighter and more aerodynamic. Professional and amateur race car drivers would race their modified cars on dirt ovals, board tracks, and even city streets throughout the United States. Car races and speed record events soon became very popular in cities and towns wherever a well-constructed or improvised racing venue could be found.

During the years of the Great Depression of the late 1920s and the 1930s, young men and a few women (including a few Mexican American youth from the urban neighborhoods in cities such as San Antonio and Los Angeles) who were unable to afford more expensive speed-designed cars produced by car companies would buy older and more affordable Model Ts and Chevrolets that they would convert into what came to be known as the first hot rods. These owners would commonly do the mechanical modifications themselves, often using junkyard parts. They would also carefully paint and then decorate their stripped-down cars with racing stripes and other designs.

Southern California began to emerge as the unofficial capital of a regional hot rod culture, due in part to the proximity of large, flat, hard-packed dry lake beds to Los Angeles where hot rodders could race their cars. In the 1930s, hot rodders began to organize themselves into clubs, an important step meant to dispel the notion that they were members of youth gangs who engaged in crime. Decades later, lowriders in many cases would also create car clubs for essentially the same reason (See Chapter 7, "Lowrider Clubs").

Custom Cars

At the same time that the hot rod craze took root in Southern California, another trend in automobile modification was taking place: the custom car designed for exhibition at car shows and for cruising city streets where speed was not a concern. Individual car owners began to customize vehicles such as Fords, Chevrolets, Mercuries, Cadillacs, and Buicks by lowering the cars to the ground; "chopping" or lowering their tops; painting them with deep and dark tones; decorating them with intricate artistic designs; replacing seats, dashboards, steering wheels, and so forth; and outfitting them with plush interiors. One very well-known customizer was Harry Westergard from Sacramento, who as early as 1938 began modifying cars for himself and later for other owners such as George Burris, a Northern California piano player who would himself turn to customizing cars in the late 1940s and early 1950s in North Hollywood. Burris recognized that he could turn the burgeoning popularity of customized cars among Hollywood movie stars and other celebrities into a solid business enterprise. He and other customizers modified cars to enhance their looks and to provide smoother rides. They had little interest in equipping their customized cars with powerful motors built for speed, a high priority for hot rodders. By the late 1930s, the custom car and the hot rod styles had gradually developed into two very different popular automobile sub-cultures based mainly in Southern California. The hot rod was designed primarily for speed and racing, but the custom car was modified primarily to achieve a specific style, with the goal of showing off the vehicle by traveling slowly down city streets. The customized cars were commonly described as "low and slow," the very look that would later be associated with the vehicles that, beginning in the 1950s, would be referred to as "lowrider" cars, and whose owners, like the owners of the Westergard- and Burris-designed cars, were not at all interested in powerful motors and speed. The first lowrider cars evolved out of the custom car subculture (Ganahl 2000, 13–15).

When the United States entered World War II on December 7, 1941 (the date of the Japanese bombing of Pearl Harbor in Hawaii), the modification of cars was severely curtailed, and it would not resume until after the war ended in 1945. Civilian car production was drasti-cally reduced as automobile assembly lines were converted to the war effort with the production of jeeps, tanks, and other mechanized vehicles destined for the European and Pacific theatres. The rationing of crucial materials, including car parts and rubber for tires, had a negative impact on the building of hot rods and custom cars. But the most important factor that brought most of this activity to a halt was that thousands of young custom car and hot rod owners, including Mexican Americans, volunteered or were drafted into the U.S. Armed Forces and sent to Europe or to the Pacific.

The war ended in 1945, and many thousands of veterans returned to the United States to continue their lives as civilians. The economic prosperity of the post–World War II years contributed to a boom in civilian automobile manufacturing and a corresponding flooding of the used car market. Even before the war, Los Angeles had become a major center for heavy industry, including the automobile industry. In the 1930s, Ford, Chrysler and General Motors had established assembly plants, as had tire companies such as Goodyear, Goodrich, Firestone, and U.S. Rubber. Car parts companies had also established their own plants. Los Angeles was already beginning to seriously com-pete with Detroit as a major new car manufacturing and assembly center, and after 1945 it became the second most important center in the United States. This was very significant in solidifying Southern California as a region where the car was rapidly becoming central to the lives of working- and middle-class Americans of all national and ethnic backgrounds.

THE COMMUNITY OF EAST LOS ANGELES AS A CENTER OF POST–WORLD WAR II LOWRIDER CULTURE

Since the late nineteenth century, Los Angeles has had the largest concentration of Americans of Mexican descent of any city in the United States, and East Los Angeles (East L.A.) generally is recognized to be the most important urban barrio (the term commonly used for neighborhoods with a majority Mexican American population) in the Southwest. Los Angeles was originally one of the many missions (e.g., San Diego, San Clemente, San Luis Obispo, San Jose, and San Francisco) established by the Spanish Crown and the Catholic Church along the coast of California as early as the eighteenth century. It remained a small pueblo consisting mainly of wealthy land-owning *Californios* (Californians of Spanish and, later, Mexican descent) who farmed and ranched the areas on the periphery of what is today's downtown Los Angeles using cheap Mexican laborers who, after Mexico's independence from Spain in 1821, had migrated north from Central Mexico. After 1848, a dramatic shift in land ownership occurred as *Californios* lost their lands to the newly arrived and increasingly powerful Anglo-American businessmen and bankers.

With the growth in economic power, European Americans began to dominate Los Angeles's municipal government; by the 1860s, they controlled the city council, even though Mexican Americans and, to a lesser extent, Chinese immigrants vastly outnumbered Anglo-Americans. City councilmen sold off much of the land on the periphery of downtown that before 1848 had been owned by the Spanish-speaking population. The sale of lands to the highest bidder coupled with the increasing demand for cheap labor forced Mexican Americans and Mexican and Chinese immigrants to live in squalid conditions in slums only blocks from downtown Los Angeles's increasingly prosperous business and residential centers. An ethnic consciousness began to develop among members of the Mexican American community. This was reflected in the publication of several Spanish-language newspapers and in the founding of mutual-aid societies (*mutualistas*) that offered loans and medical and life insurance to their members. The European American population increased rapidly during the late nineteenth century. The number of small businesses, department and other stores, movie houses, and restaurants increased rapidly forcing out Mexican Americans in the downtown district. The *Los Angeles Times*, under its owner Harry Chandler, who was involved in real estate speculation, became a major booster for Los Angeles's rapid growth and prosperity (Acuña 1984, 6–8).

During the early years of the twentieth century, Los Angeles's Mexican American population began to leave the downtown area and to relocate to the east, across from the Los Angeles River, on land that was affordable. The shift of this population to the east was accelerated when, at the beginning of the Mexican Revolution in 1910, thousands of Mexicans fled Mexico to temporarily or permanently establish a new home in cities across the United States, especially Los Angeles. Mexican American–dominated communities sprung up in the Belvedere area east of the river. Shanty towns also were created on the outskirts of established eastside towns such as Whittier, Montebello, and El Monte. El Hoyo Maravilla was one of the first identifiable Mexican American settlements within the area increasingly identified as East Los Angeles. Boyle Heights, another town east of the river that had been predominantly Anglo-American, began to change in the 1930s as more Mexican Americans from other parts of the Southwest and Mexican immigrants settled there. It would become solidly Mexican American in the post–World War II years. As early as 1925, and again in 1931, Mexican American leaders tried unsuccessfully to have East Los Angeles incorporated, which would have given the area a tax base and political representation. East Los Angeles remains unincorporated even today (Acuña 1984, 9).

The World War II period (1941–1945) brought about great changes in American society as the citizenry mobilized to fight a massive war on two fronts: Europe and the Pacific. The United States officially declared war on Japan and Germany after the Japanese air force bombed Pearl Harbor, a large naval base close to Honolulu, on December 7, 1941, sinking many of the U.S. Navy Pacific Fleet aircraft carriers, destroyers, and other ships and resulting in the deaths of thousands of military personnel and some civilians. Millions of young Americans, including Mexican Americans, volunteered for military duty.

Growth of the East Los Angeles Barrio after World War II

Los Angeles grew rapidly during the post-war period as veterans and nonveterans and their families moved there to live and work in the city's expanding commercial and manufacturing sectors. The Mexican American population of Los Angeles County had increased to over 600,000 by 1959. Powerful downtown commercial interests came together to formulate what was called the Greater Los Angeles Plan. One of the primary goals of the plan was to build more commercial buildings and higher-cost housing in the central downtown area. This resulted in the displacement of lower-income Mexican Americans and

African Americans to areas where land was less expensive and housing more affordable, the former group settling in East Los Angeles and the latter group in South Central Los Angeles.

As East Los Angeles grew, problems that were common in other urban concentrations appeared there as well. One of these problems was the growth in the number of youth gangs. Working with the Los Angeles County Sheriff's Department, eastside Mexican American leaders developed a strategy to bring existing hot rod car and lowrider clubs together into a federation to help deal with the gang problem. The car clubs in East Los Angeles, which included both men and women, became active in community events such a Christmas give-away project. Also, the East Los Angeles Youth Council and the Catholic Youth Organization became active in recruiting new members to encourage them to become engaged in productive community events instead of gang activities (Acuña 1984, 49).

Although the barrio of East Los Angeles, due in part to its unincorporated status, continued to suffer from poor housing, poor health services, and a host of infrastructure problems, it had some effective political representation. Perhaps the best-known leader was Edward R. Roybal, who represented eastside interests. Roybal was elected to the Los Angeles City Council in 1949, the first Chicano to serve on this powerful body in 80 years. He often opposed other members of the council, finding himself a lone voice when the interests of Mexican Americans were not being served by the council. One such issue was the battle over Chávez Ravine, the home to thousands of Mexican Americans and Mexican immigrants who lived in low-cost housing and had easy access to downtown and manufacturing jobs. The city council ceded a large track of land that encompassed most of the area to Brooklyn Dodgers owner Walter O'Malley so that he could have a stadium built for his Brooklyn Dodgers, whom he wanted to relocate on the West Coast. The ceding of land displaced many Mexican American and Mexican families despite the best and persistent efforts of Roybal to block the council's actions. He engaged in many similar issues with the council until he ran for Congress and was elected to the House of Representatives in 1933, where he served for 30 years.

Los Angeles and the Beginning of Lowrider Culture

Beginning in the late 1940s, Los Angeles underwent a rapid transformation with the development of huge housing construction projects in the suburbs driven by the urgency to accommodate the burgeoning demand for housing generated by returning veterans. This led to a greater dependence on cars to transport suburbanites to from their new homes to their jobs, and this in turn led to the expansion of the freeway system all across the Los Angeles area. The general prominence and importance of the car to a large percentage of Los Angeles's population spurred a renewed interest and vigor among custom car and hot rod owners, who now had available to them a bonanza of cheaper used cars for those who could not afford the latest models. The custom car craze that had temporarily come to halt during the war years continued after 1945 in a robust way, energized by those who had discretionary income available to invest in modifying automobiles.

Thousands of Mexican American veterans either returned to the Los Angeles area or moved there from all over the Southwest in search of better-paying jobs in the city's rapidly expanding industrial sector. Although it was not just veterans who bought cars in the few years following the end of the war, many veterans did so. A factor that was particularly important to the Mexican American veterans' ability to own new and secondhand cars for the first time was a $20 weekly benefit that all veterans began to receive after 1945. This extra income gave Mexican American veterans a sufficient margin in their total income to be able to afford cars, and in this way they were able to avoid a higher new car payment and the relative difficulty of securing a loan for a new car. Many of these first-time car owners had acquired advanced mechanical skills during their years of service in military vehicle motor pools, aircraft repair shops, and navy shipyards. They were able to apply these skills in customizing their recently purchased used vehicles.

The ownership of mechanically sound and reliable used cars was also important to the rapidly growing Mexican American migrant worker population. In a 1980 interview with *Lowrider* magazine, the well-known Chicano farm-worker labor organizer and leader César Chávez emphasized how important it was to have a functioning car in order to move families around from one rural location to another in order to take full advantage of work in the agricultural fields picking cotton, lettuce, vegetables, and fruit. Reliable cars were also essential to Mexican American workers in order to commute from home to well-paying manufacturing jobs in the Los Angeles area. Compared to the general population, there were unfortunately only a handful of Mexican Americans who were fortunate to secure these jobs.

In Los Angeles's Mexican American barrios, custom car enthusiasts in the late 1940s and early 1950s preferred the 1939 Chevrolet Deluxe, the 1948 Fleetline, the 1950 Chevrolet hardtop, and the 1949 and 1950 Mercury; these models lent themselves to customizing. Small tires were used in order to lower the cruisers a few inches from the ground. Small tires had the additional advantage that they were less expensive than the racing tires favored by hot rodders and customizers who had more discretionary income to spend on their hobby. The lowering of a vehicle was also achieved at this time by cutting the suspension coils and by placing heavy objects such as cement bags or bricks in the trunk. Owners would typically visit junkyards in their vicinity to find spare car parts such as hubcaps, bumpers, grilles, and transmissions. Mexican American veterans with ironworking or welding experience gained during their military service were in great demand, putting their skills to work to strip cars and rebuild them to different specifications. It was not uncommon for these skilled craftsmen to build their own parts in a way that enhanced their own pride and at the same time helped distinguish one car from another (Penland 2003, 13).

Painting was one of the other essential skills that Mexican Americans had honed during their military service. While this skill was important in general in developing unique customized paint jobs, a particular use of Navy gray primer paint to cover up rust spots became very popular in San Diego, a major Navy port. Owners would sand the rust spots, patch the holes with a compound, and paint the entire car with several coats of primer that had rust-resistant qualities and that would harden so that the entire surface of the car was uniform (see Chapter 4, "Art").

Many Mexican American veterans who had already acquired basic skills during their military service found well-paying jobs in the newly established automotive industry in Los Angeles in the 1950s. The automotive industry also attracted Mexican American families from all over California as well as Arizona, New Mexico, and Texas. Many families moved permanently to the Mexican American barrios of Los Angeles, especially East Los Angeles, while others came only as temporary workers. Years later, when the automotive industry in Los Angeles fell on hard times, many of the temporary workers and their families moved back to the cities and towns from which they had relocated. Importantly, the automotive workers took with them their professional skills of basic automotive engineering and paint and body work acquired in the factories, and they began applying these skills as mechanics and skilled craftsmen back home. This migration back to other locales also served to give a big boost to the spread of the lowrider subculture so important in Southern California to other areas of the country.

Cruising on an East L.A. street. (AP Photo/Reed Saxon)

LOWRIDER CULTURE IN THE 1950s

Although the term *lowrider* was still not commonly used in the early 1950s, much of the activity which was later associated with lowrider culture was common at that time. For example, East Los Angeles groups of low and slow cruiser owners began in the early 1950s to organize themselves into clubs with names like the Honey Drippers, the Pan Draggers, the Street Scruppers, the Cut Outs, and the Renegades. Club members would congregate and cruise down certain well-known Los Angeles locations such as the Miracle Mile in West Los Angeles, Olvera Street, and especially Lincoln Park, which featured carnival-type rides and taco and *raspada* (flavored ice) stands. The Park also provided live music, including traditional Mexican *mariachi* music, and dancing in the evenings under the stars (Penland 2003, 14–15).

Lowrider club members also would drive longer distances from their barrio homes to places like the rivers near Pico Rivera, Cabrillo Beach, and Long Beach. Cruiser owners would use the streets and the places where they congregated to show off certain features of their cars, especially how low they were to the ground, the paint jobs, and decorative elements such as hubcaps, spotlights, grilles, and fenders. In the early 1950s, Larry Watson was in great demand as a painter of low and slow cruisers. He had his own car, a professionally painted Chevy that he took out cruising with others in the low and slow crowd. Eddie Martínez was a top-notch Los Angeles upholsterer whose services were becoming progressively more desired as car owners began to put greater emphasis on the interiors of their cars. Across the California border in Tijuana, upholsterers were able to provide basic interior upgrades. More and more California Mexican American and Tijuana Mexican upholsterers soon learned to provide much more sophisticated and expensive options to owners.

By the mid-1950s, a string of Clock Drive-Ins in Los Angeles communities such as Bellflower, Pasadena, and Long Beach prospered in part because some cruisers and other custom car owners needed locations to show off their paint jobs, decorative additions, and interiors. The bright lights that typically lit up these venues were ideal for highlighting the various paint hues and decorative details. Later, when the Clock Drive-In chain was acquired by A&W, cruisers started hanging out at Harvey's Broiler and at other drive-ins in the Los Angeles area (Penland 2003, 15–16).

It was not until the late 1950s that the low and slow cruisers began to be systematically harassed by law enforcement officials, especially traffic policemen, in the Los Angeles area. This behavior was a continuation of decades of animosity between Mexican American communities and the media, public officials, and law enforcement that had peaked during World War II. The pretext for stopping a cruiser was that it was too low and causing damage by scraping the paved or cemented surface of a city street. There was growing public concern and media coverage of the long lines of Mexican American–owned vehicles cruising slowly up and down Whittier Boulevard in Los Angeles and the main streets of other cities such as San Diego and Long Beach. Media coverage suggested that the cruisers were gangs of roving criminals threatening white residents. Although it is probably true that there were some gang members among the lowriders, the media coverage grossly exaggerated these claims to the point of causing a public outcry. Pressure on politicians resulted in the California legislature passing a law in 1959 prohibiting the use of any vehicle with any part of it below the rim base.

This law led to the development of hydraulics, an ingenious device that low and slow cruiser enthusiasts began to install in their cars. Although hydraulics had been used in standard car models before, it was the low and slow cruiser crowd who spread their popularity in Southern California. According to one account it was Ron Aguirre and his father Louis who first installed a hydraulic system on a 1957

Corvette that was well known in the Los Angeles area as the "X-Sonic." After being harassed repeatedly by traffic cops for driving an illegally lowered car on city streets, Ron and his father are said to have gone Palley's Surplus in Los Angeles to buy used hydraulics found originally on the wings of B-52 bombers. They then ingeniously modified and installed the hydraulics on the Corvette—not a typical model preferred by cruiser owners—giving the driver the ability to raise and lower the vehicle at will. Ron would then raise the car a few inches whenever he encountered a traffic cop and then proceed to lower it once he was in the clear. The hydraulic-equipped Corvette was featured at the 1958 Long Beach Memorial Day car show where thousands of people were said to have witnessed the rapid raising and lowering of a custom car for the first time. Soon after the Long Beach show, Ron and Louis Aguirre set up their own business installing used hydraulic systems in cars throughout the Los Angeles area, including the vehicles owned by established customizers such as George Burris and Larry Watson. More importantly, cruisers from local custom car clubs began to patronize their business (Penland 2003, 16, 19).

Originally the cars with newly installed hydraulics were mainly show-quality customs built to be displayed at car shows. Hydraulics were too expensive for the average street cruisers. However, this changed over the next few years when other talented mechanics set up their own hydraulic-installing businesses that made this mechanical innovation less expensive and therefore available to a greater number of cruiser owners.

LOWRIDER CULTURE IN THE 1960s

Some say that the introduction of hydraulics signaled the beginning of the use of the term *lowrider*. Others associate the term with the lowered front seats that characterized many of the cruisers; drivers could barely see above the steering wheel as they cruised slowly down city streets. The mainstream automotive press probably did not begin to use the term until about 1966.

The speculations about the origin of the term are very difficult to tie down and to carefully and reliably document, but what is known is that the mechanical innovation of hydraulics as well as the lowered front seats came to be associated widely from the mid-1960s on with the lowrider culture of today. Today, lowrider vehicles are customized cars, bicycles, tricycles, motorcycles, trucks, and vans that have been altered in the lowrider style, which may include the following elements: the lowering of the vehicle; the addition of accessories; the use of hydraulics and plush interiors for cars, trucks and vans; elaborately painted vehicles; the refurbishing of a vehicle's interior including its upholstery, and the addition of decorative art on the exterior of the vehicles.

The 1960s can be viewed as a transitional decade for lowrider culture. Hot rod clubs such as the Roadrunners, the Challengers, and the Tridents still predominated and were largely responsible for organizing car shows in the Los Angeles area. Although some of the owners still lowered their cars with a combination of cut suspensions and cement bags and bricks in the trunk and adding features such as rims and tires, their car motors were still very large and designed for speed. Speed was not a characteristic of typical lowrider cars, whose owners much preferred cruising very slowly down main streets so that the cars' mechanical and decorative alterations could be fully viewed and appreciated.

Newly organized lowrider clubs increasingly brought out their customized low and slow cars to cruise some of Los Angeles's busiest main streets like Tweedy Boulevard in Southgate, Van Nuys Boulevard in the San Fernando Valley, and Whittier Boulevard in East Los Angeles. One of the attractions of streets like Whittier was that the glass-fronted stores all along the cruising route reflected the drivers in lowered seats as they carefully and proudly paraded their low-slung cars with their striking paint jobs and other distinctive features (e.g., wheel covers, "pipes," and spotlights) back and forth from one point to another (Penland 2003, 20).

Mexican American clubs preferred the segment of Whittier Boulevard that ran through East Los Angeles, which had become California's largest and most vibrant Mexican American barrio. One of the first clubs, the Imperial car club, preferred lowered 1957 Chevys, according to the club's first president, Armando Valadez, an employee at a local Chevrolet agency. He organized a group of friends to form the club, which met regularly at a Shell station to exchange car ideas and to scope out the local social scene before cruising down Whittier. In order to avoid problems with the local police and business owners along the route, the club would obtain a parade permit. By the mid-1960s, other recently organized Mexican American car clubs (e.g., In Crowd, Dirty Boys, Orpheus, New Life, Sons of Soul, East Crowd) were also cruising Whittier Boulevard. The clubs would typically park their cars in a designated parking area to display their vehicles and their club plaques for spectators to admire. In a spirit of mutual trust and respect, clubs would often exchange cars and plaques as they cruised East Los Angeles and other sites such as Griffith Park, Chávez Ravine (today

Residents demand that East L.A. be made an official municipality. (AP Photo/ Reed Saxon)

the home of Dodger Stadium), Downey, Van Nuys, and the Pacific Highway in Long Beach (Penland 2003, 27).

The Mexican American clubs would often hang out and party with the Anglo-American clubs like the Night Owls, Majestics, and Tridents in areas such as Long Beach where there were few Mexican Americans. Crenshaw Boulevard in South Central Los Angeles was another favorite caravan route for low and slow cruisers by the mid-1960s. It also had the added attraction of having several hydraulics-installation businesses. Crenshaw Boulevard was also popular with young African American lowriders.

Throughout the 1960s, lowrider clubs enjoyed steady growth in and around Los Angeles, with a corresponding increase in the number of businesses that provided different services such as hydraulics, interiors, body work, and painting and decorative embellishments such as pinstriping and traditional figures (e.g., Aztec warriors and maidens, the Virgin of Guadalupe). And although lowriding was becoming increasingly popular and accepted in the Mexican American barrios, it was still viewed with suspicion by the police and the established media. Also, most of the large, well-financed commercial custom car shows still would not accept lowrider cars as entries, ostensibly because they did not conform to any of the established custom car categories.

However, it is reasonable to speculate that their exclusion was probably due to the negative stereotyping that the largely Anglo-American organizers attributed to lowriders as rowdy and violent. Finally, after years of trying, a 1963 Chevrolet Impala was accepted by a major 1968 Long Beach car show. To the surprise of many, the "Gypsy Rose" took a first place in its category.

The "Gypsy Rose" became, in at least two of its incarnations, probably the most famous lowrider car since the late 1960s. The January 1997 20th anniversary issue of *Lowrider* magazine devoted a special section to this car. Jesse Valadez, past president of the Imperials club of East Los Angeles, owned both the original 1963 Chevrolet Impala and its successor, a 1964 Chevrolet Impala. The later version gained additional fame when it was featured in 1974 on the NBC comedy show "Chico and the Man" (*Lowrider* January 1997, 21–22).

The Watts Uprising and Lowrider Culture

On August 11, 1965, the Los Angeles neighborhood of Watts erupted into one of the worst violent urban uprisings to occur in any U.S. city before or since, with the possible exception of the 1992 riot in South Central Los Angeles associated with the brutal police beating and arrest of Rodney King, an African American. The African American community of Watts had for many years complained about police harassment and brutality. In 1965, sparked by the aggressive arrest of three members of an African American family by members of the Los Angeles Police Department after a traffic violation, the largely African American community rioted for six days, leaving $40 million in property damage and countless injuries among civilians, the police, and the California National Guard.

EAST LOS ANGELES DURING THE TURBULENT 1960s AND 1970s

The tragic loss of lives and property that occurred in Watts in 1965 was not an isolated event; it was part of a pattern of urban uprisings that occurred across the United States from the mid-1960s through the early 1970s. The backdrop for these violent upheavals that pitted marginalized African American and Mexican American urban populations against what they considered repressive law enforcement agencies was the combination of social forces that would significantly alter the lives of millions of Americans.

The 1960s brought about a dramatic shift in Mexican American politics with the rise of the Chicano movement, a confluence of social and political forces that ranged from the César Chávez and Dolores Huerta–led unionization of farm workers in the fields of California and later throughout the Southwest; the Crusade for Justice, an urban justice movement founded in 1966 by Denver activist Rodolfo "Corky" González; the 1968 and 1969 public school walkouts and demands by high school and college students for curricular reform and the establishment of Chicano Studies programs; and the 1970 National Chicano Moratorium Against the Vietnam War.

University and high school students, community activists, and others began to self-identify as "Chicanos," which signified that they proudly embraced the concept that they were partially of Mexican Indian origin. The term *Chicano*, which had in previous decades been used derogatorily by middle- and upper-class Mexican Americans to label and separate themselves from recently arrived, poor, and relatively uneducated Mexican immigrants, became, from the mid-1960s on, a term denoting pride in one's mestizo ancestry.

The concept of "Aztlán" accompanied that of Chicano. Aztlán denoted a homeland for Americans of Mexican descent that encompassed the territories that Mexico ceded to the United States in 1848 at the conclusion of the Mexican-American War: California, Arizona, New Mexico, Texas, and parts of Nevada, Colorado, and Wyoming. To believe in Aztlán was to express a desire to reclaim this lost homeland, not in a strict legal sense for most Chicanos, but certainly in a spiritual and cultural sense.

The American intervention in Vietnam in the early 1960s followed by the escalation of this conflict in the mid to late 1960s produced a mass anti–Vietnam War movement across the United States. The increasing disillusionment with the war spread to barrios throughout California and the Southwest where parades and demonstrations against the war became more frequent. The East Los Angeles barrio was a major site for Mexican American protests that culminated with a huge demonstration, organized by the National Chicano Moratorium committee, at Laguna Park on August 29, 1970. Approximately 20,000 to 30,000 people from East Los Angeles as well as from throughout California and the Southwest gathered at this park to protest. According to eyewitnesses, also present were a large number of Los Angeles Sheriff's Department deputies and other law enforcement personnel. Skirmishes broke out between them and some protest participants, resulting in the clearing of the park and the arrest of many participants, some of them beaten and gassed. Perhaps the most tragic occurrence of the protest and its aftermath was the death of Rubén Salazar, a prominent Chicano journalist from Los Angeles; he was reportedly hit in the head by a tear gas canister while seeking refuge in an East Los Angles café. Laguna Park and many other events in East Los Angeles and in cities such as Albuquerque, Denver, and San Francisco galvanized the Mexican American community throughout the United States against the Vietnam War.

The events in Watts and in East Los Angeles heightened tensions in other ethnic minority communities in Los Angeles, including South Central Los Angeles, where an atmosphere of extreme tension between the local population and the police also existed. The increased presence of law enforcement officials created more incidents and confrontations on Crenshaw Avenue between the caravans of cruising drivers and the police. The police and some of the Los Angeles media used the term *lowrider* in a derogatory way by associating it with gang and criminal activity not only among Mexican American but also African American youth in Watts and South Central. Ironically, the more powerful gangs became in Los Angeles's minority neighborhoods, the more young Mexican Americans organized themselves into lowrider clubs as a way to legitimize and differentiate themselves from the criminal activities of gangs (Penland 2003, 26).

As lowriding became very well established in the Los Angeles area in the 1960s, it was beginning to take root in other California cities such as San Diego, San Francisco, and especially San Jose. It was also spreading outside of California to cities like El Paso, Phoenix, San Antonio, Albuquerque, and the small New Mexico city of Española. Initially, it was young Mexican American residents of these communities who had relatives and friends in Los Angeles involved in lowrider activities. The residents of these cities would visit their relatives and friends in Los Angeles or would be visited by them in their home cities.

San Jose was the most important city in Northern California for lowriders, mainly because it had a large and dynamic Mexican American population that supported lowrider activities. Lowriders in San Jose seemed to be more developed and more active politically than their counterparts in Southern California, perhaps because of the city's proximity to San Francisco and the University of California at Berkeley, where different groups of political activists had been active even before the decade of the 1960s. San Jose lowriders began to participate in protest marches against the Vietnam War and protests over other issues such as police harassment, not only within their own locale but throughout the Bay Area of Northern California.

Los Angeles Lowriders and the Whittier Avenue Confrontations

One of the factors that led to greater involvement of a few Los Angeles lowriders in political protest in the late 1960s was linked to the community-based activism of UCLA and other area Chicano and Chicana university students. For example, the discovery by UCLA students of an economist's 1967 report, "Business and Mexican-American Relations in East Los Angeles," revealed that most of the businesses in East Los Angeles—including those along Whittier Boulevard, a favorite lowrider route—were owned by non-Chicanos who did not reside in the Chicano barrio. The report concluded that the presence of law enforcement along, for example, Whittier Boulevard, could be attributed to pressure by outside business owners to protect their property. There had for several years been numerous instances of the police stopping, citing, and harassing lowriders for minor traffic infractions. There had also been some beatings by the police that had raised the ire of East Los Angeles residents. The combination of the heavy police presence along Whittier Boulevard and the publication of the results of the report led to a mass protest demonstration on July 3, 1968, on Whittier Boulevard at which some lowriders, student activists, and community members joined together to protest. Violence broke out that resulted in the breaking of car windshields, the smashing of glass storefronts of some businesses along the Boulevard, and some looting. Many protesters were arrested after police called for reinforcements. Six of those arrested supposedly hung themselves in their jail cells. This event led to three nights of riots along Whittier Boulevard and elsewhere in East Los Angeles. The police and the media placed responsibility for the rioting and property destruction squarely on the shoulders of the lowriders, who were portrayed as common thugs and members of violent gangs. Los Angeles authorities prohibited any further cruising on Whittier Boulevard (Penland 2003, 37–38).

Like members of any group, lowriders did not all share the same political views. Some were apolitical; some preferred to separate themselves from the political activism of the university students and progressive community leaders; others began to become more involved in political activities in East Los Angeles. Many in this last group also proudly displayed symbols of ethnic pride on their vehicles. Protests against the police presence and the barricading of Whittier Boulevard continued even as lowriders sought out other venues to continue cruising in their low and slow vehicles. Importantly, following the example of the students and community activists, many rival lowrider clubs came together to form an organization, the

Federation of Lowriders, to more effectively express their concerns about police harassment and to press their legitimate demands to have Whittier Boulevard reopened, invoking the Constitutional guarantee of free assembly. The Federation took a leadership role in organizing community events and in sprucing up the streets and removing graffiti from the walls of businesses. The Federation also tried to create a dialogue with law enforcement officials, but this initiative ultimately failed.

During much of 1970s, Whittier Boulevard would remain barricaded on weekends except for some periods when law enforcement officials would temporarily relax their ban on cruising. Lowriders naturally turned to other routes. For example, some East Los Angeles lowrider clubs like the Imperials and Groupe cruised Santa Monica Beach, Elysian Park, and the cliffs in Huntington Beach. Crenshaw Boulevard became the most popular alternative to Whittier. Throughout the decade of the 1970s, lowriders would congregate along this route on the weekends to show off their paint jobs and interiors, but especially their hydraulics. They would also park to exchange news about parties and lowrider events at restaurants such as Jack in the Box, Stops, and Church's.

Crenshaw became the venue for a new lowrider craze, that of "dancing," where car owners would face each other front bumper to front bumper to manipulate their hydraulic systems up and down, almost like two dancers challenging each other's latest dance moves. Hydraulic systems were becoming increasingly more sophisticated and popular, leading to the opening of many new hydraulics specialty shops in Los Angeles, Sacramento, and the Bay Area. Wire wheels also came into fashion, and this stimulated the establishment of more specialty shops (Penland 2003, 25).

Club membership went through periods of highs and lows in the Los Angeles area and throughout California during the 1970s. Some old clubs almost died off and then bounced back under new leadership, some clubs consolidated to form larger organizations, and new clubs were created. Whittier Boulevard was again closed in the late 1970s because law enforcement continued to make the claim that gang activity and violence were directly related to cruising on East Los Angeles's main street.

The closing of Whittier Boulevard in the late 1970s brought adversarial tensions between lowriders and the Los Angles County Sheriff's Department to their highest point. Roberto Rodríguez, who was then a reporter for *Lowrider* magazine, recounts how he was almost killed by sheriff's deputies on Whittier Boulevard on March 23, 1979. He had been taking photographs of the cruising on the avenue and had witnessed and attempted to photograph what he describes as the beating of an innocent and defenseless individual by the Special Enforcement Bureau of the Los Angeles County Sheriff's Department. He does not deny that there had been "troublemakers" on the avenue for most of the 1970s, but he claims that law enforcement's crackdown on lowriders gave sheriffs free rein to consider all Mexican Americans on the avenue suspect. Rodríguez was attacked by deputies, had his camera and film confiscated, sustained serious head injuries requiring several days of hospitalization, and faced criminal charges for attacking the very deputies who had injured him. He later brought a criminal suit against the Sheriff's Department to clear his name; he won his criminal trial won more than seven years later. Rodríguez describes the night of the violent confrontation: "As a result of the incident, 538 people were arrested, countless individuals were beaten and harassed, the Boulevard was shut down, and by the end of the weekend, Whittier Boulevard in East L.A. resembled a war zone" (Rodríguez 1997, 5).

LOWRIDER CULTURE IN THE 1980s

Lowriding in California and throughout the Southwest in general enjoyed a kind of renaissance in the late 1970s and the early 1980s due to a confluence of factors. The founding of *Lowrider* magazine in 1977 was a significant contributor to this renewed interest in lowriding. The magazine's subscribership increased to over 100,000 by the early 1980s, and the popularity of lowriding among its readers grew accordingly. The magazine gave coverage to local and regional club activities and shows across the United States. It also highlighted some of the early custom cars, hot rods, and lowriders from the post–World War II era through the 1960s. The appearance of lowriders and their cars in feature films and on television programs also sparked interest, although some of the portrayals of lowriders were decidedly negative. Other media such as radio and the record industry also contributed to a new wave of interest (See Chapters 3 and 5, on media and music, respectively).

At the same time that lowriding was booming elsewhere, it began to wane in the mid-1980s in East Los Angeles where it had originated. While lowrider clubs in some other cities in California and across the Southwest were able to come together to form alliances to combat police harassment, the clubs in East Los Angeles were not successful in doing so, due mainly to the rivalries and the antagonism that had existed among the clubs for many years. The lack of effective organizing stymied attempts to pursue legal means to have Whittier Boulevard reopened to cruising on a permanent basis. Most of the hydraulics-installation businesses across Los Angeles closed their doors, club membership dropped, and *Lowrider* magazine subscriptions in the Los Angeles area reached new lows.

One of the few positive indicators of continued interest in lowriding was the success of the large car shows. These shows served to shift the emphasis for lowrider clubs and owners away from cruising and toward the production of award-winning show vehicles. Another positive sign for lowriding in general was the integration of the African American and Chicano cruising scene on Crenshaw Boulevard (See Chapter 8, "Lowrider Shows").

LOWRIDER CULTURE IN THE 1990s

Lowriding in Los Angeles finally began to show signs of recovery in the late 1980s and early 1990s with the reopening of hydraulics shops, the resurgence of traditional clubs, and the creation of new ones. Mexican American and African American print and electronic media and films in addition to some mainstream media went a long way to raise the profile of lowriding in the American imagination. The first major lowrider show in several years was held at the Long Beach Arena in 1989, and this seemed to give new life to shows as far away as San Diego and Fresno. Throughout the 1990s, more and more professionals, such as lawyers, police officers, and doctors, joined lowrider clubs, giving them—at least for the mainstream media—a patina of respectability not afforded to them before. These new members' higher salaries allowed them to spend more on their cars. Their primary interest was exhibiting their cars at shows rather than cruising city streets.

Lowriders who were unable to afford the classic and more expensive lowrider cars such as Chevrolets, Fords, and El Caminos turned to less expensive cars made by foreign car companies. Japanese-made Hondas, Toyotas, and Nissans became very popular and eventually began appearing in car shows under a new category called "Euro" (although the vast majority of cars were not European made). A 1994 Honda Civic, "Orange Passion," owned by an individual from Hawaii caused a sensation because of its decorative embellishments when it was shown at a car show (Penland 2003, 138).

Lowrider trucks have always been part of lowrider culture, and although they are far less common than cars, they have been part of the cruising caravans in California and in other states. Like cars, trucks have been outfitted with hydraulics systems and other accessories. Their exterior paint jobs and designs and their interiors have been just as elaborate and innovative as those of cars. Trucks have been shown at lowrider car shows almost from the beginning. These vehicles have had an additional advantage over cars: the truck beds could also be outfitted with hydraulics, allowing the beds to be lifted dramatically several feet into the air.

Bicycles have been an important part of lowrider culture since the 1960s. They have always provided an opportunity for children and younger adults to participate in lowrider culture well before they have received their driving licenses or have had the financial means to buy cars and trucks. Schwinn bikes were very popular in the 1960s, when this bike company came out with the 1963-1/2 Sting Ray, a model with a spring front fork, banana seat, and high handlebars, some of the characteristics of lowrider bikes. George Burris modified this model for the "Munster" television show by adding, among other accessories, a gold-painted chain frame and an upholstered seat. This popular television series served to give the lowrider bike legitimacy among its young viewers regardless of ethnicity or racial background. To make bikes more like lowrider cars, some young owners would bend the front fork even more and would add chrome. From the late 1970s on, it was common for modified and customized bikes to be exhibited at events along with lowrider cars and trucks. Very soon afterward, a special bike category was created at lowrider car shows. *Lowrider* magazine began to include a special section on bikes in the 1980s. In response to reader demand, in 1993 a separate magazine, *Lowrider Bicycle*, began to be published. Like cars and trucks, customized bicycles today frequently require a substantial monetary investment. Like other lowrider vehicles, lowrider bicycles became popular across the United States as well as abroad in countries such as Japan, Germany, England, Guam, Canada, and New Zealand.

LOWRIDING IN TEXAS

Low-slung cars were seen in along the south Texas-Mexico border as early as the 1940s. However, lowriding did not become firmly established in Texas until the 1960s in locales such as San Antonio, Dallas-Fort Worth, Del Rio, and El Paso. Lowriding was still such as novelty in Texas in the 1960s that it is said that in El Paso one weekend, a few lowriders cruising in the vicinity of a favorite lowrider park were mistaken by the police for a funeral procession and were given a police escort. When they realized their mistake, the police ticketed the lowriders.

Lowrider clubs did not come into existence in Texas until the 1970s, but then they proliferated throughout the state. Like their counterparts in other Southwestern states, Texas lowrider clubs sometimes became involved in serious political protests that were an outgrowth of the Chicano movement. For example, the Odessa, Texas lowrider club, Taste of Latin, took on a leadership role in 1975 in mobilizing the city's Chicano community to speak out against suspected police complicity in the death of a Chicano after his arrest. A branch of this lowrider club participated in voter registration drives in Corpus Christi and elsewhere in Southeast Texas during an active phase in the late 1970s of the Southwest Voter Registration and Education Project, which Chicano activists had founded to support progressive municipal and state political candidates. In the 1970s and the 1980s, umbrella organizations of lowrider clubs sprung up in large cities such as Houston, San Antonio, Dallas, Fort Worth, and El Paso. Anticruising laws were never a major problem for Texas lowriders, perhaps because they were well organized and generally cooperated with law enforcement authorities. For example, the Austin Lowrider Association helped avert a major confrontation with city police by issuing identification cards to their members certifying they were not local gang members. *Lowrider* magazine helped give a boost to the already dynamic Texas lowrider scene by covering local events and clubs in the late 1970s and early 1980s and by sponsoring its first major car show in San Antonio in 198 (Penland 2003, 29–31).

LOWRIDING IN NEW MEXICO

Lowriding in New Mexico is synonymous with Española, a small city within an hour's drive to the northwest of Santa Fe. It is often identified by proud local lowriders as the "Lowrider Capital of the World," and although there is probably proportionately more lowriding activity per capita in Española than any other place in the United States, this lofty title is often disputed by lowriders in Los Angeles. Observers claim to have seen lowriders in Española as early as the 1950s. Hydraulics did not appear there until the late 1960s, somewhat later than they had in the Los Angeles area. The first lowrider show in New Mexico was held in Española in 1975, an event which probably enhanced its reputation as a center for lowrider culture. During the past few decades, lowrider clubs in Española, like many clubs elsewhere, frequently have sponsored benefit car shows for local charities as a way of counteracting their negative image that the clubs are gang related. It is significant that in 1992 a lowrider car, a 1969 Ford LTD named "Dave's Dream," owned by Leroy and Dennis Martínez, was inducted into the automobile collection of the Smithsonian Museum in Washington, D.C. Today, the lowrider tradition continues to be very strong in Española.

New Mexico's first full-sized car show was held in Albuquerque in 1980, organized by the Latin Pride club to raise money for the reconstruction of the San Martín de Porres church, an Albuquerque landmark that had been destroyed by fire. The Catholic Archbishop of Albuquerque rode in a caravan from the site of the lowrider show to the church. Lowrider clubs, principally in Albuquerque but also in other cities, organized a loose confederation, the New Mexico Lowrider Association; in the early 1980s it sponsored shows and other activities. Like East Los Angeles, South Central Los Angeles, and many other cities across the Southwest, Albuquerque has its main lowrider cruising route, a portion of Central Avenue that runs through the Mexican American neighborhoods. And like other cities, the route became contested territory when the police tried to shut it down. Despite sporadic efforts to shut down Central Avenue, at least part of it remains today as a preferred cruising route.

LOWRIDING IN ARIZONA

In Arizona, lowriders began cruising Central Avenue in South Phoenix and South Main in Tucson in the early 1960s. It is thought that the first car club was organized in the early 1970s, with many to follow in rapid succession. The first hydraulics-installation business, House of Hydraulics, was opened in the late 1970s. The first lowrider show in Arizona was held in 1978 on the grounds of the Gila River Indian Reservation, a few miles south of Phoenix, when organizers were unable to secure a site within the city limits. This first show was attended by lowriders from Phoenix, Tucson, and Yuma. The Arizona Lowriders Association (ALA) was organized in 1979 in order to protest police harassment of lowriders when the police department attempted to shut down Central Avenue. The ALA, along with other organizations, then successfully fought attempts by the Arizona Sate Legislature to ban hydraulics and altered suspensions during its 1982 session. For several years, in the 1980s, Phoenix became the site of the lowriding world's biggest and most prestigious "Super Shows." Phoenix is today considered to be one the most important sites for large and well-attended annual lowrider shows sponsored by *Lowrider* magazine and usually held in the fall.

LOWRIDING IN COLORADO

Lowriding was common by the late 1960s in Denver, where low and slow cruisers could be seen on any given night on 38th Avenue. Similar to Los Angeles and other cities in the Southwest, anti-lowrider opposition surfaced in Denver in the late 1970s. The established local media and law enforcement officials claimed that lowrider clubs were controlled by gangs and that criminal activity was linked to club activities, especially cruising. The police barricaded and shut down 38th Avenue at different times during the late 1970s, and then on September 19, 1980, Denver law enforcement officials arrested over 130 lowriders. Activist lawyers intervened on behalf of the lowriders, the mass arrests were declared illegal, all charges against the lowriders were dropped, and 38th Avenue was reopened. A large lowrider car show was held in 1983 in Denver's large National Western Complex, a coup considering how opposed city officials had been to the clubs a few years before. Large shows were later held in Colorado Springs and Pueblo, where lowriding was becoming increasingly more popular. Today, *Lowrider* magazine and local sponsors hold annual shows in Denver and Pueblo.

Although lowrider shows, clubs, and activities are most commonly located in California and in other states of the Southwest, lowrider culture has spread to other regions the United States. For example, in the 1990s, the Eternal Rollerz Car Club was founded in Lowell, Massachusetts, which soon became a center for lowrider activity across New England. In addition to regular coverage of lowrider activities in California and the Southwest, *Lowrider* magazine occasionally features lowrider clubs in the Midwest, the Northeast, and the Southeast. For example, the June 2008 issue of *Lowrider* magazine included a short report and photos of the Drastic Auto Club of New York,which was established in 1994. The club sponsors an annual barbecue where members are encouraged to make contributions in support of the homeless.

LOWRIDER CULTURE OUTSIDE OF THE UNITED STATES

Baseball, our national pastime, was introduced by the U.S. military in Japan and Europe during the post–World War II period when large numbers of military personnel were stationed in these countries as part of the occupation forces. The U.S. military has continued to have a strong presence in Japan and Europe over the past few decades. Not surprisingly, as the overall number of Mexican American military

A Japanese lowrider. (AP Photo/Koji Sasahara)

personnel has increased, their cultural presence and influence has been more strongly represented abroad, including the urban subculture of lowriding. Japan is the country that has most enthusiastically embraced lowriding. *Lowrider* magazine had established its presence in Japan by the mid-1980s, shipping thousands of back issues to venues in Okinawa and other cities. There is today a Japanese version of *Lowrider* magazine and many lowrider clubs. Japanese low and slow car owners originally obtained hydraulics and other mechanical accessories through mail order, but today hydraulics-installation shops prosper in Okinawa, Yokohama, Osaka, and Tokyo. Lowriders began making inroads at the large annual Japanese car shows in the early 1990s, and there were so many cruisers on the streets in Yokohama that in 1991 that city passed an antihydraulics law. *Lowrider* magazine cosponsored its first Super Show in Osaka in 1993, and it has continued to do so since then.

The National Lowrider Club Registry was created in 1996, and, despite its title, the organizers intended to make their reach global, or at least extend to the three continents—North America, Asia, and Europe—where different levels of lowrider activity already existed. Diplomats-Bristol, founded in 1997, was the first British club to sign up for the registry. There has also been sporadic lowrider activity in

Germany, Australia, and Thailand. Eternal Rollerz Car Club of New England has chapters in Germany and Australia, where small groups of club members and fans gather to show their cars or to cruise. Closer to the United States, Tijuana has for several decades been the center for Mexican lowriding; today, there are over 20 clubs that are members of the Tijuana Lowrider Council (Penland 2003, 136).

LOWRIDER CULTURE TODAY

Today, lowrider culture seems to be thriving due in large measure to the popularizing influence that publications such as *Lowrider* magazine, *Lowrider Bicycle*, *Lowrider Arte*, and *Street Low* have had. Another very significant factor contributing to the spread of lowrider culture across the United States and abroad is the Internet. The magazines mentioned above all have online websites that are regularly updated to carry news of events, vehicles, people, and products. There are also literally hundreds of lowrider videos, movies, music, and photos available on sites such as YouTube. Lowrider culture has evolved and changed over the past few decades, but it still continues to be a vital part of urban Chicano popular culture (see Chapter 3, "Media").

FURTHER READING

Acuña, Rodolfo. *Community under Siege: A Chronicle of Chicanos East of the Los Angeles River, 1945–1975*. Los Angeles: UCLA Chicano Studies Research Center Publications, 1984.

Donnelly, Nora. *Customized: Art Inspired by Hot Rods, Low Riders and American Car Culture*. Boston: Harry N. Abrams, Inc. in association with the Institute of Contemporary Art, Boston, 2000.

Franz, Kathleen. *Tinkering: Consumers Reinvent the Early Automobile*. Philadelphia: University of Pennsylvania Press, 2005.

Ganahl, Pat. "The Hot Rod Culture." In *Customized: Art Inspired by Hot Rods, Low Riders and American Car Culture,* edited by Nora Donnelly, 13–15. Boston: Harry N. Abram, Inc., in association with the Institute of Contemporary Art, Boston, 2000.

Lowrider, February 1997, 14.

Penland, Paige R. *Lowrider: History, Pride, Culture*. St. Paul, MN: MBI Publishing, 2003.

Rodríguez, Roberto. *Justice: A Question of Race*. Tempe: Bilingual Review Press, 1997.

Volti, Rudi. *Cars and Culture: The Life Story of a Technology.* Westport, CT: Greenwood Press. 2004.

2

Pachucas/os, Zoot Suiters, and Cholas/os in Lowrider Culture

Pachucas/os and zoot suiters have played important and diverse roles in lowrider culture from the from the very beginning of low and slow cruising on the city streets of East Los Angeles and other Southwestern cities. *Lowrider* magazine helped to keep before its readers the images and lore of pachucas/os and zoot suiters by including a "Lowriders Pasados" (Lowriders from the Past) section in the first few years of its publication, continuing to use pachuco *caló* (slang) throughout its pages, publishing stories related to pachucos and zoot suiters, and carrying ads advertising zoot suit clothing and accessories. At the same time, *Lowrider* magazine and other lowrider publications such as *Lowrider Arte* also started featuring chola/o-related stories on, for example, tattoos. These publications have also included ads for clothing and accessories generally associated with cholas/os, an advertising strategy that has become increasingly more common in the past few years in order to attract and hold new readers. Lowrider shows today frequently hold zoot suit competitions, and clothing vendors at these shows frequently display zoot suits and accessories and also some chola/o-related accessories such as hats that are popular with mainly younger lowrider fans.

HISTORY OF PACHUCAS/OS

Pachuco is an elusive term that has no equivalent in English, and the precise origin of the word is not known. In general, *pachucas/os* refers to young working-class Mexican Americans—*pachucos* referring to men and *pachucas* to women—who lived in urban barrios (the name given to urban neighborhoods heavily populated by Mexican Americans) throughout the Southwest during the late 1930s to the 1950s. Not all Mexican American youth who lived in barrios were pachucas/os, and those who self-identified as pachucas/os were not exclusively working class or lived in barrios. *Pachuca/o* is a term of self-identification that a segment of the young Mexican American population used to distinguish itself from others in their own communities as well as from Anglo-Americans. The term is often associated with *caló*, a version of Spanish slang, and the "zoot suit," the exaggerated dress worn by at least some pachucas/os on the street and at public events and private celebrations.

Many contemporary accounts of pachucas/os agree that they origi-nated in San Antonio, El Paso, Tucson, and Los Angeles in the late 1920 and early 1930s partly as a result of the increased tensions between these cities' European American population and the young, first-generation children of the thousands of impoverished Mexican immigrants who had fled across the U.S.-Mexico border to escape the general chaos and economic straits of the Mexican Revolution, a country-wide war that engulfed Mexico in violence for over ten years beginning in 1910. During this period, armies waged war on each other and on the civilian population, causing many to flee for their safety to the United States.

The newly arrived immigrants settled in cities in the Southwest, and very soon, especially when their children began attending public schools, resentment towards them increased among Anglo-Americans as well as multigenerational middle- and upper-class Mexican Americans. In Tucson, for example, the crash of the stock market in 1929 and the beginning of the Great Depression led to massive job losses, which in turn became the source of great resentment towards Mexican Americans in general, especially the recently arrived immigrants. The massive deportations of Mexican-descent citizens and noncitizens alike in the 1930s was a tragic manifestation of this anti-Mexican sentiment in Tucson and other cities of the Southwest.

Partially in response to the discrimination that resulted from this resentment, young first-generation Mexican Americans and Mexican nationals joined neighborhood or pachuca/o clubs as a way of maintaining group solidarity and self-protection. This occurred in Spanish-speaking enclaves such as the west side of San Antonio; Chihuahita and El Segundo Barrio in El Paso; El Hoyo, Barrio Centro, and Barrio Libre in Tucson; and Maravilla, Alpine, Happy Valley, Palo Verde, and other barrios in Los Angeles. A few of these clubs engaged in gang activities including petty criminality.

Sociologists, linguists, psychologists, and others who have studied the pachuca/o phenomenon sometimes associate it with crime and juvenile delinquency and sometimes with an expression of heroic cultural and class resistance to the established norms of social behavior. "From the beginnings the Pachuco has been a character endowed with mythic dimensions, a construct of fact and fiction, viewed with both hostility and curiosity, revulsion and fascination" (Madrid-Barela 1973, 31).

CALÓ

Much like the various positive and negative values assigned to pachucas/os, caló, the language spoken by those who identified themselves as pachucas/os, has been described since the 1930s in ambivalent ways. For some, it was an argot or secret language that was spoken by young Mexican American criminals who were members of violent gangs that roamed the barrios of cities in the Southwest, carousing, stealing, and generally creating havoc among the law-abiding resident population. To others, caló was simply a form of hybrid speech that was used by pachucas/os to express group solidarity and cultural pride in being different from other Mexican Americans as well as Anglo-Americans. Linguists who have studied this language phenomenon have disagreed not only on who has historically spoken caló but the reasons they have done so. One scholar believes that caló can be traced back as far as the language spoken centuries ago by European gypsies, whose language has variously been identified as *calé, romano, zincalé*, and *calogitano*, which included elements of mutilated French, English, Italian, Latin, Greek, Hebrew, and medieval Moorish. The language spoken by Spanish gypsies came to the Americas as early as the sixteenth century as a slang or dialect along with the standard Spanish spoken at the time. According to this version of the origins of caló, it then underwent additional changes before, centuries later, finding its way to the American Southwest (Rosensweig 1973, 12).

Caló words or phrases that are likely to appear in lowrider publications such as *Lowrider* magazine or to be heard among lowriders at shows and at other public places are: *ranflas* (lowered cars); *firme carruchas* (solid or cool cars); *A.T.M./a toda madre* (fantastic, out of sight, cool); *bomba* (a lowrider car or truck from the 1930s to the mid-1950s); *borlo* (dance or dance party); *Vamos al borlo* (Let's go to the dance); *calcos* (shoes); *chuco* (an abbreviation of *pachuco* that also means "from El Paso," which, according to some, was the site of the first pachucos); *chota* (cops); *ése/ésa* (that boy/ that girl); *no te esponges* (don't get angry); *filero* (knife); *guisa* (woman, girlfriend); *jaina* (woman, honey, girlfriend); *mono* (movie); *mota* (marijuana); *naranjas* (no way.); *nel* (no); *pestañear* (to sleep); *¿Qué onda?* (What's up?); *refiner* (to eat); *ruca* (girlfriend); *Sancho* (boyfriend on the side); *tacuche* (zoot suit and fancy clothing); *wilo* (skinny); and *yonka* (bike).

A recent study describes caló as a dynamic and ever-changing language that consists largely of innovative vocabulary items. Rhythm and intonation also play important roles. The vocabulary comes from both English and Spanish sources, and the new words that continue to be incorporated into caló reflect how arbitrary the sound and its intended meaning might be. Often a word has a different meaning depending on where it is spoken within a sentence and its similarity in sound with another word like, for example, *simón* for *sí* (yes). Also common is the phrase *simón que sí*, which is uttered for emphasis. Examples of caló words that are borrowings from English, that is words similar to words in English, are *birria* (beer); *whatchar* (to watch) and the phrase *Ay te watcho* ("I'll see you later."); *biles* (bills); *waifa* (wife); and *clica* (clique or gang). Sometimes caló words bear no similarity to words either in English or Spanish, such as *chale* (no way); *con safos* (nobody can mess with this.); and *swata* (idiot) (Martínez 2006, 71–74).

Although caló is not spoken by as many people today as it was during the 1930s, the 1940s, and more recently during the height of the Chicano movement from the mid-1960s to the early 1970s, it is still popular among some Spanish speakers in the Southwest. It is found in written form in the pages of *Lowrider* magazine and other lowrider publications. Caló has also been preserved in works of prose, drama, and poetry by Chicana/o writers as well as in films. For example, in the 1970s two Tucson-based Chicano novelists, Aristeo Brito and Miguel Méndez, have long sections of caló dialogue spoken by characters in their works, respectively *El diablo en Tejas* (The Devil in Texas) and *Peregrinos en Aztlán* (Pilgrims in Aztlán).

ZOOT SUITERS

Much like the different theories about pachucas/os and caló, there are different versions about the origins of the zoot suit. The main source of controversy resolves around the popular claim that it is exclusively or primarily a Mexican American phenomenon. Although it is true that the zoot suit continues to be an important part of contemporary Chicana/o popular culture, mainly due to the persistence of the zoot suit's popularity among lowriders and it regular appearance in movies and television programs, its history is rooted in East Coast African American culture of the pre–World War II era.

Some fashion historians claim that the zoot suit was inspired by Clark Gable, the dashing, handsome, and hugely popular movie actor who starred as Rhett Butler, the major male role in the 1939 movie *Gone With the Wind*, one of the most popular U.S. movies of all time. Gable appeared in long coattails, an essential characteristic of the zoot suit. Some scholars think that another characteristic, the baggy pants, was popularized by the popular singer Frank Sinatra, who often wore loose pants when he performed. Others argue that the Mexican comic film actor Tin Tan, who wore a zoot suit in several of his late-1930s and early-1940s movies, was the true inspiration for the fashion. His movies frequently played to packed movie audiences in theaters throughout the Southwest that catered to Spanish-speaking Mexican American and Mexican immigrant audiences. Although he may not have created the style, the popular African American jazz artist Cab Calloway undoubtedly helped the fashion spread among males of all ethnicities who wanted to cultivate a "cool" style (Alvarez 2008, 83–84).

The *New York Times* reported in the summer of 1943 that Clyde Duncan, an African American restaurant worker from Gainesville, Georgia, had invented the first zoot suit. According the newspaper report, several years before, in the late 1930s, Duncan had had one of his regular men's suits popular at the time altered in an exaggerated and baggy style. He apparently ordered the suit from Frierson-McEver's department store, which in turn had the Globe Trading Company in Chicago tailor the suit. The zoot suit quickly became popular in South Georgia among young African American males who referred to the suit as the "Killer Diller" (*New York Times* June 11, 1943, 74).

The popularity of the zoot suit spread quickly to Mississippi, Alabama, and New Orleans, and then to Harlem, the predominantly African American section of New York City. According to several media accounts, the zoot suit style was then widely and rapidly diffused from there across the Midwest and the Southwest to cities such as El Paso

Zoot Suiters in the 1940s. (AP Photo)

and Los Angeles, where many young Mexican American, caló-speaking pachucas/os (and also young Anglo-Americans, African Americans, Filipino Americans, and Japanese Americans) adopted the style.

The basic zoot suit men's fashion (often referred to as "drapes") consists of a long coat that is several inches longer than a business suit coat, sometimes reaching as low as the knee, and that usually has exaggerated padded shoulders, and high-waisted pants that fit loosely, sometimes ballooning just above the knee, and pegged or severely tapered at the ankle or cuff. Zoot suit accessories include a gold-like long watch chain that almost touches the floor; a flat hat that sometimes is adorned with a feather; and long, thick-soled shoes with pointy toes. The most popular zoot suit colors on the East Coast were bright red, blue, and yellow. In Los Angeles, the most popular colors were white, dark brown, or black.

THE PACHUCA

Many accounts of the history of pachucos, caló, and zoot suits focus heavily on young Mexican American males who embraced the lifestyle,

"Yeah, everything was brown. And the coat came down to here [pointing to the knees], right down to here. And the silver chain from the pocket, and the wide, like a pancake, hat, with a real wide brim. If you were short, you would look like a thumbtack! And we used to dress up like that to go to the dances. All of us. All wear the same thing. With the big chain, we'd twirl the chain" (Alvarez 2008, footnote 22).

but they generally ignore that it was also popular among young Mexican American women. Pachucas, who often accompanied their male counterparts on the streets, at dances, and at public events, developed their own unique style that was every bit as distinctive as that of the pachuco. According to Catherine R. Ramírez, "Pachucas teased their hair into high bouffants (called 'rats') and wore what was considered excessive makeup. They usually donned short skirts and long coats . . . and some wore the masculine version of the zoot suit (complete with 'punjab' pants and 'finger-tip' coats)." (The pachuca is discussed in greater detail in Chapter 6, "Women in Lowrider Culture.") (Ramírez 2008, 2).

THE PUBLIC PERCEPTION OF PACHUCAS/OS AND ZOOT SUITERS

After the bombing of Pearl Harbor in 1941, followed soon after by the United States's declaration of war on the Japanese and their allies the Germans, American newspapers and other media began a systematic campaign of vilifying not only the Japanese population of Japan and the Japanese military, but also Japanese Americans, most of whom lived in California. Partially in response to the mass hysteria generated by the media, the administration of President Franklin D. Roosevelt decided that the loyalty of Japanese Americans could not be relied on and that it was important to lessen the threat that this minority population might pose. Civilian and military authorities believed that if the Japanese military tried to invade the West Coast, Japanese Americans might aid and abet the invasion. Consequently, it was decided that the Japanese American population should be removed from their homes and placed in internment camps for the duration of the war. Many U.S. citizens protested this massive disruption of many thousands of lives based on collective suspicion and guilt by association. Civil libertarians at the time condemned this government action by pointing out that many young Japanese Americans volunteered to serve in the military and fought bravely to defend their country against the ravages of German Nazism and Japanese fascism.

The overreaction to the perceived threat of Japanese Americans spilled over to other groups, especially Mexican Americans, who became during the war period a major scapegoat group once Japanese Americans were removed to internment camps. Many clashes occurred in Los Angeles between Anglo-Americans and Mexican Americans, incidents that prominent media outlets such as the *Los Angeles Times* invariably blamed on the latter group. This major newspaper exerted a tremendous influence on public opinion. It changed its coverage of Mexican Americans during the war years, shifting away from glorifying the mythical past of "old California" Spanish culture to a very negative portrayal of Mexican Americans, often falsely and inaccurately associating this Spanish-speaking community with delinquency and criminality. One of the newspaper's major strategies in vilifying the Mexican American population was to focus on pachucas/os, especially those who dressed in public as zoot suiters. The communities east of the Los Angeles River were the "targets of [the newspaper's] racist reports that made East Los Angeles the symbol of the pachuco, the Mexican-American gang member" (Acuña 1984, 6–8).

One of the issues that the *Los Angeles Times* and other Los Angeles newspapers focused on in order to turn public opinion against the zoot-clad pachucas/os was their obvious display of flamboyant dress. In March 1942, the War Production Board (WPB), based in Washington, D.C., issued Order L-224, which set limits on the amount of fabric used in the manufacture of men's suits and all clothing containing wool. In the same month, the WPB issued a second order, L-85, which set restrictions on women's clothing. From the beginning of the war, Americans had been urged by federal officials to sacrifice in certain areas of consumption including fashion, automobiles, petroleum products, and certain foods in order to make materials like fabric, steel, gasoline, rubber, and dairy-derived products available to the military and to the rapid expanding war manufacturing sector that had geared up to produce uniforms, combat boots, tanks, jeeps, airplanes, and ships.

The amount of fabric used in zoot suits exceeded that of the traditional business suit, which led newspapers to accuse zoot suiters of defying Orders L-224 and L-85 and accusing them of engaging in un-American, antipatriotic, and even traitorous activities. Scholars who have studied newspaper coverage of the pachucas/os and zoot suiters have identified the focus on clothes as part of an a orchestrated campaign to identify young Mexican Americans, Japanese Americans, and others as lazy and self-indulgent draft dodgers. In fact, many young people who sported zoot suits were actively serving in the military or working in war-related industries. Dressing up in their zoot suits was an escape from the rigors of military and work life and very much a weekend or leave activity.

The Sleepy Lagoon Case

The so-called Sleepy Lagoon case became an emblem in Los Angeles and throughout California of both mass paranoia and media irresponsibility, especially in the media's focus on Mexican American youth. In August 1942, the body of an adolescent Chicano was found on a road in the south-central part of the city, close to the Sleepy Lagoon, a popular party spot for young Mexican Americans. The police rounded up and interrogated over 600 Mexican Americans who were in attendance at a party the night the murder victim was discovered. The police eventually charged and brought to trial over twenty young defendants, many of them dressed in zoot suits, normal party attire for many young Mexican Americans. Henry (Hank) Leyvas, one of the defendants, had taken his girlfriend to the Sleepy Lagoon party. Chicano dramatist Luis Valdez would base his 1978 play *Zoot Suit* on the Sleepy Lagoon Case. Henry (Hank) Reyna, the character of the lead defendant in the play, was based on Leyvas. The play, and the movie based on the play and using the same title, was enthusiastically received by lowriders and popularized by *Lowrider* magazine.

Prior to the Sleepy Lagoon incident, the local media had frequently portrayed zoot suiters as delinquents; the fashion and the behavior became synonymous among a large segment of the Anglo-American reading public. During the first week of the trial, the prosecution did not allow the defendants to sit with their legal counsel, nor were they permitted to get haircuts or change out of the zoot suits in which they had been arrested. A large part of the prosecution's case was the portrayal of the defendants as genetically inferior by linking them, racially, with Asians in general and with Japanese Americans in particular. The defendants were eventually convicted on several charges, including first-degree murder, second-degree murder, and lesser charges, but then, very soon after, all defendants were acquitted and exonerated when a Court of Appeals overturned the original court's findings and convictions.

The Zoot Suit Riots

Not long after the Sleepy Lagoon trial and acquittals, a large disturbance occurred in Los Angeles, usually referred to by the local press as the "Zoot Suit Riots," which took place between June 3 and 15, 1943. Many Army, Navy, and Coast Guard bases were located in the Los Angeles area, some of them close to Mexican American barrios such as East Los Angeles. As in other cities where military installations and civilian populations were in close proximity, some clashes had taken place between servicemen and civilians, including Mexican Americans. Media outlets such as the *Los Angeles Times* had run a series of stories identifying the civilians as zoot suiters, thereby significantly adding to the tensions between military personnel and Mexican American barrio residents. Although teenage delinquency was widespread and on the rise among all groups (e.g., Anglo-American, African American and Mexican American) during World War II, in Los Angeles, the local press and some law enforcement officials reduced delinquency and its various criminal activities a "Mexican problem," and more specifically a "zoot suiter problem."

Finally, on successive nights in early June of 1943, large bands of soldiers and sailors in Los Angeles and in other Southern California cities began roaming through the downtowns and Mexican American barrios like East Los Angeles, accosting and assaulting individuals and small groups of young Mexican Americans, some dressed in zoot suits, others who were not. The Navy's own characterization of the bands of servicemen attacking civilians was that military authority and discipline had broken down (Mazón 1984, 17–18).

Military authorities had attempted to warn their servicemen not to engage in this kind of mob activity, but the warning was not heeded. Once the violence started, military and civilian police were equally ineffective in arresting servicemen or in removing them from the Mexican American barrios. The military had, at least for a few nights of organized attacks on civilians, lost control over its enlisted men. Many of Los Angeles's civic leaders joined the *Los Angeles Times* in giving unqualified support to the servicemen, which served to implicitly approve of their further illegal behavior and also to encourage civilians to join with the servicemen against the zoot suiters and other young Mexican American civilians who were not dressed in zoot suits. Hundreds of these young people suffered injuries from assault, some very serious and requiring hospitalization.

The 1940s *Los Angeles Times*'s vilification of zoot suiters, pachucas/os, and, by association, Mexican American working-class youth would have negative implications later for many lowriders—who have since the beginning of lowriding adopted the zoot suit dress style and caló as their own as a form of cultural resistance and a rejection of both mainstream Mexican American and Anglo-American cultural norms.

Chicano youth attacked during the 1943 Zoot Suit Riots. (AP Photo)

In addition to the *Los Angeles Times*, mainstream television and radio would also attempt to denigrate lowriders by falsely associating them with the supposed criminal element of earlier zoot suiters and pachucas/os.

The Sleepy Lagoon Case, the Zoot Suit Riots, and Mexican American and Mexican Attitudes

Along with Los Angeles's established press characterization of pachucas/os and zoot suiters as unpatriotic and criminal, an attitude that was shared by most of the newspapers' Anglo-American readers, there were many Anglo-Americans who rallied to support the Sleepy Lagoon defendants and to protest the physical and media attacks on pachucas/os and zoot suiters. Many Mexican Americans sympathized with the young Mexican Americans who were tried and, later, those who were injured and humiliated during the confrontations with servicemen because they, too, had been victimized and discriminated against for generations by the majority Anglo-American population. At the same time, at least some Mexican Americans Angelenos vocally condemned the defendants and the pachucas/os and zoot suiters for, in their opinion, giving the Mexican American community a bad name; they accused the young people of calling negative attention to the entire Mexican American population. These opposite attitudes of sympathy and antipathy often broke down along class lines, that is, middle-class Mexican Americans who were socioeconomically advantaged generally looked down upon the working-class, poorer, and less-educated barrio dwellers, many of whom were first- and second-generation immigrants from Mexico.

The class differences among Mexican Americans and their different attitudes towards the Sleepy Lagoon case and the Zoot Suit Riots were amply reflected in the Mexican American press in Los Angeles, especially in the pages of *La Opinión* (published in Spanish) and in *El Espectador*, the two highest-circulating Mexican American newspapers in Los Angeles during the World War II era. The first, published by Ignacio E. Lozano, who also owned *La Prensa* newspaper of San Antonio, was directed primarily to an educated Mexican immigrant generation that had come to the United States fleeing the violence and political persecution of the Mexican revolution. The newspaper also counted among its readers many intellectuals and other middle-class Mexicans who had temporarily resided in the United States but who had then returned to Mexico once the revolutionary violence had subsided. Through his two newspapers, Lozano was interested in promoting gradual sociopolitical change in Mexico and the preservation of Mexican values and consciousness among Mexican Americans in the United States. Ignacio L. López, the publisher of *El Espectador*, was more interested in representing and informing the Mexican American middle class whose families had been in the United States for generations (García 1991, 223–24; García 1989, 111–112).

Before the 1943 riots, *La Opinión* generally took a more anti-pachuca/o and zoot suit stance, describing what the newspaper's editor considered to be their culturally deviant and menacing criminal behavior. In the stories carried by the newspaper prior to confrontations between military personnel and Mexican American youth, the publication did not distinguish between the small number of pachucas/os who wore zoot suit attire, those who committed crimes, and the majority of pachucas/os and zoot suiters who did not. Like the *Los Angeles Times* and other Anglo newspapers, *La Opinión* criminalized the entire group, overlooking "the lack of correspondence between drapes and crime, extrapolating a negative picture of zooters in general from the malevo-lence of a relative handful of hoodlums" (García 1985, 202).

Unlike *La Opinión*, *El Espectador* during the pre-riot period generally attributed crime among Los Angeles's Mexican American pachucas/os and zoot suiters to the history of anti-Mexican discrimination on the part of the Anglo population as a whole but also specifically on the part of law enforcement authorities who seemed more interested in applying the full force of the law than in working to reform the young people who had committed crimes. *El Espectador* did not con-demn the larger group of pachucas/os and zoot suiters for the actions of the few. The López weekly defended Mexicans, including zoot suiters, a victimized group; the Lozano daily attacked zooters as a group of victimizers of Mexicans (Gaytán, 1996, 31).

Once the Zoot Suit Riots had begun, *La Opinión* moderated its view somewhat,becoming more sympathetic towards at least the young Mexican Americans who were the victims of violence perpetrated by military personnel and law enforcement officials, whom the news-paper characterized as agents of lawlessness and disorder. In a June 8, 1943, editorial, *La Opinión* drew an implicit parallel between anti-pachuca/o rioters and a lynch mob. After the riots were over, the newspaper returned to pre-riot critical view of pachucas/os and zoot suiters (Gaytán, 1996, 54, 64).

El Espectador continued during the period of the riots and then afterwards to be more positive than *La Opinión* towards pachucas/os and zoot suiters. For example, it opposed as unconstitutional a proposed Los Angeles City Council ordinance to outlaw zoot suits. Consistent with its pre-riot stance, *El Espectador* presented the Zoot Suit Riots "as an outgrowth of long-standing anti-Mexican sentiment," and, as a solution to the riot violence and its causes, it demanded that Anglo-Americans show respect for Americans of Mexican descent, including pachucas/os and zoot suiters. In a series of editorials, López singled out police and media elements for causing the riots (Gaytán 1996, 95).

EVOLVING MEXICAN AND MEXICAN AMERICAN ATTITUDES TOWARD PACHUCAS/OS AND ZOOT SUITERS IN THE POST–WAR WORLD II PERIOD

Almost every significant study of the pachuca/o and zoot suiter life-style mentions Octavio Paz, the internationally known Mexican poet, essayist, diplomat, and winner of the 1990 Nobel Prize for literature.

The first chapter of his 1947 book, *El laberinto de la soledad* (*The Labyrinth of Solitude*), is about pachucos. Paz had become familiar with the lifestyle in the early 1940s when he was living in Los Angeles. In "El pachuco y otros extremos" ("The Pachuco and Other Extremes"), Paz describes pachucos as a group that had lost its Mexican identity: language, religion, customs, and beliefs. He believes that because pachucos had failed to find a new and meaningful identity, they had collectively adopted a disguise or mask consisting of flamboyant dress, caló, and outrageous and aggressive social behavior. Like Ignacio Lozano of *La Opinión*, Paz concluded that they had little to redeem them. Also like the newspaper publisher, he was not interested in examining the historical causes of the conflictive existence of the pachucas/os (Madrid-Barela 1973, 37).

After the end of World War II in 1945, a few years removed from the Sleepy Lagoon episode and the Zoot Suit Riots, the same attitudes towards pachucas/os and zoot suiters continued to persist as during the war period. Most Anglo-Americans who had formed negative opinions about them based on newspaper and other accounts still considered them to be violent and unpatriotic. Poor and working-class Mexican Americans tended to consider them as victims of discrimination, and middle-class Mexican Americans held generally negative views towards them. The last group considered pachucas/os and zoot suiters to be a threat to their desired assimilation into mainstream Anglo-American middle-class society.

Tucson provides a good example of how race, ethnicity, and class dynamics functioned in response to pachucas/os and zoot suiters. The first pachucas/os in Tucson appeared as early as the late 1920s; the heyday of the pachuco era could be defined to be from 1935 to 1945, but it lasted well into the 1950s. Most of the young people who identified themselves through dress, language, and behavior as pachucas/os were Mexican American, but there were also young Native Americans such as Yaquis, Seris, and Yavapai Apache who also had adopted pachuca/o practices. Many young men and women also tattooed a small cross on the hand where the thumb and forefinger come together as well on forehead, chin or below the lower lip. In general, Tucson's local established press as well as the Spanish-speaking press followed the lead of the national press in vilifying pachucas/os. Attitudes among Tucson's Mexican Americans who had either been pachucas/os for a time or had been exposed to them vary from outright scorn to acceptance (Cummings, 2009).

Pachucas/os and zoot suiters were popular in Houston during World War II and a few years afterwards. The behavior, language, and dress associated with them went through a quiet period until the early 1980s when their popularity surged again, probably due to the influence of a growing lowrider community, *Lowrider m*agazine, and the film *Zoot Suit*. Young and old Chicanas/os commonly wore zoot suits to events like *quinceañeras* (coming-of-age celebrations for fifteen-year-olds), high school graduations, weddings, birthdays, and lowrider shows in the Houston area. Coleman's Menswear in North Houston supplied many of the zoot suits and other apparel for these events. The store sold *Lowrider* magazine, in which it regularly advertised its goods. Coleman's was also a vendor at Houston-area lowrider shows. Joe and Virginia Coleman, who owned and operated the store, were involved in the lives of the pachucas/os who became their regular customers. Virginia would design the zoot suits to meet customers' specific requests about color and the kind of material to be used (Bright 1994, 58–63).

Chicana/o writers of the 1940s and the 1950s tended to portray pachucas/os and zoot suiters in a negative light. For example, in his 1947 short story "Kid Zopilote" (Kid Vulture), Mario Suárez, a prominent and popular Tucson writer, paints his protagonist Pepe García as a foolish young man. Pepe spends a summer in Los Angeles with his peers, returning to Tucson wearing a zoot suit and speaking caló. He cuts a ridiculous figure in his long finger-tip coat, plumed hat, thick-soled shoes, and a gold watch chain from which he dangles a knife. His mother is the first to express her displeasure with his new-found pachuco identity. Other adults with whom he comes in contact mock his dress and behavior and give him an unkind name, "Kid Zopilote" (the Buzzard Kid). When the young Chicanas he dates learn that they are acquiring a bad reputation as "Kiddas Zopilotas," they also reject him. Pepe turns to a life of petty crime, joining other Tucson pachucas/os who steal, pimp, and deal marijuana. The young protagonist finally sees the error of his ways and embarks on a path to reform himself (Suárez 2004, 30–36).

José Antonio Villarreal is representative of writers whose fictional characters reflect a range of Mexican American attitudes towards pachuca/o subculture. In his 1959 semi-autobiographical novel *Pocho*, his young protagonist, Richard Rubio, encounters pachucos on the streets of Santa Clara and San José—northern California cities—in 1939. He is a precocious young man who is curious about the pachuco lifestyle and strives to understand why they behave in ways that isolate them from the rest of their community. Richard's father, who had crossed over to the United States from Mexico in the 1920s, reflects the scorn of traditional Mexicans and immigrant Mexican Americans; he describes the zoot suits worn by young people as "clown costumes."

Richard's sister Luz echoes her father's disdain towards the zoot suiters because as the sons of Mexican Indians and mestizos they are darker than she is. Richard and Luz's mother Consuelo, who have darker complexions than Juan and Luz, are more sympathetic towards the pachucos. Although Richard eventually turns away from the pachuca/o lifestyle to explore other alternatives, he has at least given them the benefit of the doubt (Villarreal, 1959).

THE RESURRECTION AND RE-FASHIONING OF
THE PACHUCA/O AND ZOOT SUITERS

The Chicano movement (often referred to as *la causa*), which was at its height from the mid-1960s to the mid-1970s, had a social, political, and cultural agenda. Many of the movement's activists, particularly university professors and students, political leaders, writers, and artists, were intent on reevaluating the historical relationship between Mexican Americans and Anglo-Americans in order to change the dynamics between them for the future. Part of this change involved the elimination of discrimination and racism with a goal of establishing a relationship between the two groups based on social, political, and economic equity and mutual respect.

In their examination of their role in the history of the United States, many Chicana/o scholars gave a lot of attention to historical figures who as early as the 1830s had led insurgencies and resistance efforts against the rapidly encroaching Anglo-American settlement and control of the Southwest. Figures such as Joaquín Murrieta, Tiburcio Vásquez, Gregorio Cortez, and Elfego Baca took on larger-than-life dimensions. This process of identifying and writing about Chicana/o resisters included the exaltation of the role that pachucas/os and zoot suiters had played in the Sleepy Lagoon incident and the Zoot Suit Riots. They were cast as social resisters who refused to conform to the norms of mainstream society, including those of the Mexican American middle class, whose priority it was to assimilate and adopt the goals and behaviors that conformed to mainstream society's norms and expectations.

Tino Villanueva's poem "Pachuco Remembered" provides an excellent example of how writers participated in the creation of legendary social rebels that served the larger agenda of the Chicano movement. "Pachuco Remembered" is a retrospective memorial poem that looks back several decades to the heyday of pachucas/os. The speaker of the poem addresses a fictional pachuco, calling him "a brown anathema of high school principals" who openly rejected the "starched voices of oppression" in helping to establish a 1940s version of *la causa*. In other poems, Villanueva himself and other writers such as José Montoya, J. L. Navarro, Marcos Durán, Raúl Salinas, Tomás Rivera, and Rudy Gallardo present pachucas/os more as antiheroes and tricksters than as heroic social rebels (Grajeda 1980).

J. L. Navarro's 1972 poem "To a Dead Lowrider" is representative of this other view of the pachuco, and it is also one of the earliest Chicana/o literary works to link the pachuco with the lowrider. The poem was published five years before the founding of *Lowrider* magazine, which from the start explicitly and repeatedly linked the two cultural phenomena. Navarro's lowrider, Tito, dies one night when he is stopped and confronted by a traffic policeman who taunts him: "What are you out so late/At night, punk." Tito defiantly answers him with an expletive, they fight, and then the policeman fatally shoots Tito with his .38 service revolver. Navarro does not exonerate the lowrider, but he laments that he had to die violently and tragically (Navarro 1972, 337–339).

PACHUCOS AND ZOOT SUITERS IN *LOWRIDER* MAGAZINE

Founded in 1979, *Lowrider* magazine carried images in the form of photos and ads drawing a close association between pachucas/os, zoot suiters, and lowriders. The magazine's editors and its publisher, A.T.M., had apparently decided that such an association would be a good marketing strategy designed to sell more magazines and to spread the culture of lowriders across the country as the magazine's reach increased beyond California where it was founded. The image of pachucas/os and zoot suiters was already well established in the public's imagination. The "Lowriders Pasados" section, which appeared in the first issues, was apparently designed to further forge the association of present-day lowriders, their counterparts in the past decades, and a mythic and romanticized figure of pachucas/os and zoot suiters. Many of the black-and-white photos included in this section were not even remotely related to pachucas/os, zoot suiters, or lowriders. Many of the cars that appear in the photos are not low and slow cruisers but standard cars, although some are clearly lowrider models from the 1940s and 1950s. Although the attire worn by most of the men and women in the photos reflects standard fashions of past decades, there are occasional photos of both men and women attired in zoot suits as well as photos of early low and slow cruisers. Some examples: The

"Hit up on your hefitos (parents), uncles, brothers, sisters for pictures of the 40's or 50's showing the dress styles, hair do's, and the caruchitas (cars). The pictures will be handled with tender loving care. Send a self-stamped envelope so we can return your pictures. Don't forget to mention the person in the picture and the year it was taken. If a car is included, mention the year and the make. "One picture will become 10,000 pictures." A call for photos in the "Lowriders Pasados" section of the first years of publication of *Lowrider* magazine.

September 1978 issue includes a 1942 photo of Herminio Sánchez Lara decked out in a zoot suit; the 1978 issue pictures four zoot suiters from El Paso; the March 1980 issue carries a 1954 photo of Antonio standing next to his 1950 Mercury lowrider and another photo of Ray García posing proudly next to his 1959 Ford cruiser. That most of the photos did not draw a clear connection between pachucas/os, zoot suiters, and lowriders did not seem to matter to readers who, presumably drawing on positive nostalgic memories of their past, did respond by continuing to submit their photos.

Lowrider magazine discontinued its "Lowriders Pasados" section after a few years, but not before taking advantage of Luis Valdez's 1981 movie *Zoot Suit*, based on the 1978 play. The movie greatly assisted *Lowrider* magazine in firmly establishing the link between pachucas/os, zoot suiters, and lowriders. In fact, the magazine began its aggressive promotion of the zoot-suit-equals-lowrider image shortly after the premier of the play and was given a huge boost two years later when the movie premiered. At the same time, the publication continued to use caló throughout its issues; to carry ads for zoot suit clothing and accessories for both men and women (e.g., El Pachuco Zoot Suits of Fullerton, California and now an online clothing store [www.elpachuco.com]; the Valley Department Store of Ontario, California; Hammer and Lewis of San Jose, specializing in zoot suiter hats; and La Pachuca, a Fullerton-based business that specializes in retro-style women's clothing including the look and fashion of the 1940s-era pachuca [www.lapachuca.com]); and to occasionally do covers (e.g., the December 1980 issue of a zoot suit–clad Santa Claus next to his lowrider; the May 1981 issue of a man and woman zoot suiter with a lowrider in the background; and the September 1981 issue featuring recording artist Jonny Chingas dressed in a long white zoot suit coat standing proudly next to his 1949 Ford lowrider) and features on topics related to pachucas/os and zoot suiters. For example, the

October 2009 issue included a story on Greenspan's, a clothing store that opened in Watts in 1928 and that has supplied zoot attire and accessories to zoot suiters since the late 1930s and, more recently, chola/o dress, such as Pendleton flannel shirts and Dickies pants. Phyllis Estrella and her family founded the business El Pachuco Zoot Suits in the late 1970s, in large part because the popularity of the play *Zoot Suit* made the zoot suit widely popular among young Chicanas/os in the Los Angeles area. The zoot suit also began to take on greater importance at lowrider car shows, whose organizers began holding zoot suit dance contests and contests for the best zoot suit. Vendors also started displaying and selling zoot suits and accessories such as hats and chains.

Luis Valdez has played a central role in contemporary Chicana/o artistic expression since 1965 when, with an undergraduate degree in theater from San Jose State University, he began El Teatro Campesino (The Workers' Theater) as part of César Chávez and Dolores Huerta's efforts to start a union of California farm workers in the state's large agriculturally rich central valleys. Valdez and others, including farm workers themselves, created the *acto*, typically a 10- to 15-minute improvisational one-act play or skit that was meant to educate and to rally the audience to take social action. An essential aspect of El Teatro Campesino's effective dramatizations of the farm workers' plight and other social injustices is the simple device of using stereotypical characters very familiar the theater group's audiences.

Luis Valdez and members of his theater troupe eventually established a permanent home for El Teatro Campesino in San Luis Obispo in central California. He has written and produced many plays, and he has also become a movie director and producer. One of his most successful plays was *Zoot Suit*, which premiered in 1978 in Los Angeles at a very prominent venue, the Mark Taper Forum, as part of its "Theatre for Now" series. The play, which had fourteen performances at the Forum, received much critical acclaim in the Los Angeles, California, and national press. The performances attracted thousands of Chicanas/os from throughout the Los Angeles area, and the play was a great hit with many lowriders who came to the performances dressed in zoot suitsin their low and slow cruisers. El Teatro Campesino later took the play to Broadway's Winter Garden Theater in New York City, where audiences and the press were less enthusiastic about the play.

The play focuses on the 1942 Sleepy Lagoon case. Four young Chicanos represent the pachucos and zoot suiters who were indicted for the murder, found guilty, and later exonerated. The play is the story of their release. Henry (Hank) Reyna, the play's lead defendant, was based on Henry (Hank) Leyvas, one of the twenty defendants in the 1942 case and leader of the 38th Street gang that was falsely accused of murderous violence. Leyvas, who worked on his father's ranch, was handcuffed and beaten by the police, as were others, before being brought before the grand jury. Valdez uses the play to attack the 1940s media coverage of the Sleepy Lagoon defendants and their murder trial.

When the curtain is raised to begin the play, the audience sees a large backdrop of newspaper headlines from the June 7, 1942 *Los Angeles Herald Express* issue announcing the "invasion of pachucos." It is the front page of the War Extra painted on a 24-foot canvas. Under the image of a Japanese air raid, several story titles refer directly to the historical events described above: "Web of Zuit Crime Spreads—Entire L.A. Area Becomes Battleground," "200 Zuit Sooters Held for 'Sleepy Lagoon' Murder," "Jury Finds 12 Guilty in Gang Slaying Trial." The lights dim, a soft jazz melody begins to play, and suddenly and dramatically, the paper is ripped open by a switchblade knife wielded by El Pachuco, who steps through the gaping hole to address the audience. He wears a black zoot suit, a red shirt, a broad brimmed hat, black patent leather *calcos* (shoes), and a long gold watch chain that almost touches the floor. El Pachuco has several theatrical roles: stage manager, advisor to Henry Reyna, and a one-man Greek chorus that comments on the characters, action on stage, and the historical record. As stage manager, he snaps his fingers and the action freezes and restarts on stage, giving him time to address the audience whose full attention is turned to him. El Pachuco addresses the audience in caló at the beginning of the play, but he also uses standard Spanish and standard English. He also struts and maintains a defiant posture towards the audience in the best pachuco or zoot suiter fashion. The actor Edward James Olmos played the role of El Pachuco in the theater productions in Los Angeles and New York City and also starred in the same role in the 1981 movie. Daniel Valdez played Henry Reyna, the other lead role. (The movie based closely on the play will be discussed in greater detail in Chapter 3, "Media.")

Phyllis Estrella, the founder of the business El Pachuco Zoot Suits, remembers driving down a Los Angeles street on a Sunday afternoon in the summer of 1978 and seeing a billboard advertising the play *Zoot Suit* that was opening in a month at the Mark Taper Forum. Phyllis recalls hearing the terms *pachuco* and *zoot suit* in the 1940s and then, in the 1950s, when she was a teenager, seeing young males in her barrio dressed in baggy pants—an adaptation of the full zoot suit—and using caló, which was also known as "pachuco slang." After seeing Edgar James Olmos as El Pachuco prominently displayed on the billboard, Phyllis made reservations for the play. She remembers driving up to the Mark Taper Forum and seeing a huge crowd of well-dressed Latinos. Other people who attended one of the several performances of *Zoot Suit* remember that many in the audience had arrived in low-riders and some were dressed in zoot suits (*Lowrider* May 2010, 14).

Zoot Suit has been performed many times and in many places across the United States and abroad since its premier in 1978. A 30-year anniversary performance of the play took place at Pomona College in Claremont California in early April 2008, not far from the Mark Taper Forum where the play's fame began. Camilo Cuéllar, a young Chicano actor who played the role of El Pachuco in the college production, rivaled Edward James Olmos in portraying the flamboyance, defiance, and dignity of the play's lead character. Similar to the audiences in 1978, people from the local Mexican American communities and throughout Southern California flocked to the several performances of *Zoot Suit* in 2008. One observer recounts that members of the Old Memories lowrider car club of Los Angeles arrived in full zoot suit regalia, parking their lowrider cruisers in front of the theater at each performance (Nayfak, 2009).

CHOLAS/OS AND LOWRIDERS

Concurrent with the prominence of pachucas/os and zoot suiters in *Lowrider* magazine, the publication, from its first issues in the late 1970s, also included images, ads, and some stories on cholas/os, who had become an important part of Chicana/o youth culture and of the lowrider community. Cholas/os form an important segment of the magazine's readership. Chicano rappers such as Frost (see Chapter 5, "Music and Lowrider Culture") frequently refer to cholos—there are no references to cholas—conflating them with pachucos in songs like "La Raza," in which the lyrics suggest that they are "authentic Chicanos" who hark back to the cultural nationalism of the Chicano movement of the 1960s and 1970s.

The term *cholo* is not new to the Southwest, but it has changed over the past 150 years as the group to which the word refers has changed. The term can be traced to early nineteenth-century California (then part of Mexico), when it referred to an offspring of a Spanish father and Indian mother. Its connotation, then, was decidedly negative, synonymous being with lazy, nomadic, vicious, violent, undisciplined, irreligious, generally "good for nothing." In the early part of the twentieth century, the word referred to a recently immigrated person from Mexico, again with negative connotations. The contemporary use of the term *cholo* is applied to a young American male—*chola* refers to a young woman—of Mexican descent who resides in a low-income barrio in the large metropolitan areas of the Southwest.

Just as pachucas/os and zoot suiters in the past have sometimes been associated with gang-related violence, cholas/os are sometimes linked negatively to Chicana/o street gangs. Although it is true that the adolescents and young adults who adopt the street style of dress, speech, gestures, tattoos, and graffiti are sometimes members of gangs who engage in violent behavior, others prefer to copy the style without joining a gang. Even those who belong to gangs reflect a wide difference in degree of commitment to the gang's membership expectations, loyalty, and behaviors (Vigil 1988, 2–3).

Some scholars consider cholas/os to be the modern-day version of pachucas/os and zoot suiters in the sense that they are seen as latter-day social rebels. The stylized dress that seems to be preferred by males consists of Dickies brand chino or khaki baggy pants, or a cheaper off brand; a sleeveless white T-shirt that is often ironed; a bandana worn as a head band or dangling from the back pocket of the pants and sometimes displaying gang colors or affiliation; plaid long-sleeve shirts referred to as "pendletons" (sometimes genuine Pendleton brand shirts but more commonly knockoffs) that are worn buttoned all the way to the top or unbuttoned except for the top button; and traditional athletic shoes or steel-toed work boots. Cholos dress differently in different areas. For example, in northern Mexican cities like Tijuana and Juárez, the above style is mixed with rural ranch dress. Cholos sometimes shave their heads, have their hair neatly trimmed, or wear nets over full heads of hair. Many cholos are copiously tattooed, especially on the arms, and the T-shirt is preferred in order to display the tattoos. Cholas generally wear heavy makeup with thick eyeliner, penciled-on eyebrows, and brown or dark red lip liner. Their hair is permed and shaped straight or arched on top with gel. Eyebrow and nose piercings are common. Like cholos, cholas wear flannel shirts, athletic shoes, and pants that can be tight or very loose. Some cholas/os belong to urban gangs, but others do not. Some are lowriders but are not usually members of long-established lowrider clubs. In fact, many established lowrider club members generally look down on and shun lowrider cholas/os for fear that they will give lowriding and lowrider clubs a bad name. Cholas/os do commonly attend lowrider car shows.

The dilemma that a publication like *Lowrider* magazine faces is how to reconcile the fact that a significant segment of its readers, lowrider club members, do not generally welcome as lowriders another segment of its readership, cholas/os, who are not members of lowrider clubs or who are not lowriders at all. *Lowrider* magazine seems to have adopted a middle road of including both segments of its readership in its issues in the form of images, ads, and articles (Plascencia 1983, 153–155).

FURTHER READING

Acuña, Rodolfo. *Community Under Siege: A Chronicle of Chicanos East of the Los Angeles River, 1945–1975.* Los Angeles: UCLA Chicano Studies Research Center Publications, 1984.

Alvarez, Luis. *The Power of the Zoot: Youth Culture and Resistance during World War II.* Berkeley: University of California Press, 2008.

Bright, Brenda Jo. "Mexican American Low Riders: An Anthropological Approach to Popular Culture." Houston: Rice University Ph.D. dissertation, 1994.

Cummings, Laura L. *Pachucas & Pachucos in Tucson: Situated Border Lives.* Tucson: University of Arizona Press, 2009.

García, Mario T. "Americans All: The Mexican American Generation and the Politics of Wartime Los Angeles, 1941–1945." In *The Mexican American Experience*, edited by Rodolfo O. de la Garza. Austin: University of Texas Press, 1985.

García, Mario T. *Mexican Americans: Leadership, Ideology, and Identity, 1930–1960.* New Haven, CT: Yale University Press, 1989.

García, Richard Amado. *Rise of the Mexican American Middle Class, San Antonio, 1929–1941.* San Antonio: Texas A&M Press, 1991.

Gaytán, David Rojas. *Pachucos in the Wartime Mexican Angeleno Press.* Hayward: California State University–Hayward M.A. thesis, 1996.

Grajeda, Ralph. "The Pachuco in Chicano Poetry: The Process of Legend." *Revista Chicano-Riqueña* 8, no. 4 (1980): 50–62.

Lowrider, May 2010, 14.

Madrid-Barela, Arturo. "In Search of the Authentic Pachuco: An Interpretive Essay." *Aztlán: Chicano Journal of Social Sciences and the Arts* 4, no. 1 (Spring 1973): 31–60.

Martínez, Glenn A. *Mexican Americans and Language: Del dicho al hecho.* Tucson: University of Arizona Press, 2006.

Mazón, Mauricio. *The Zoot-Suit Riots: The Psychology of Symbolic Annihilation.* Austin: University of Texas Press, 1984.

Navarro, J. L. "To a Dead Lowrider." In *Aztlán: An Anthology*, edited by Luis Valdez and Stan Steiner, 337–339. New York: Knopf, 1973.

Nayfak, Shakina. "Que te watcha cabrones: Marking the 30th Anniversary of Luis Valdez's *Zoot Suit.*" *TDR: The Drama Review* 53, no. 3 (Fall 2009). http://muse.jhu.edu/journals/the_drama_review/v053/53.3.nayfack.html.

New York Times, June 11, 1943, 74.

Plascencia, Luis F. B. "Low Riding in the Southwest: Cultural Symbols in the Mexican Community." In *History, Culture and Society: Chicano Studies in the 1980s*, edited by Mario T. García, 141–175. Ypsilanti, Michigan: Bilingual Press/Editorial Bilingue, 1983.

Ramírez, Catherine S. "The Pachuca and Chicana Style Politics." *Meridians: Feminism, Race, Transnationalism* 2, no. 2 (2008), 1–35.

Rosensweig, Jay B. *Caló: Gutter Spanish*. New York: Dutton, 1973.

Sandoval, Denise Michelle. "Cruising through Low Rider Culture: Chicana/o Identity in the Marketing of *Low Rider* Magazine." In *Velvet Barrios: Popular Culture and Chicana/o Sexualities*, edited by Alicia Gaspar de Alba, 179–186. New York: Palgrave Macmillan, 2003.

Suárez, Mario. "El Zopilote Kid." In *Chicano Sketches: Short Stories by Mario Suárez*, edited by Francisco A. Lomelí, Cecilia Cota-Robles Suárez, and Juan José Casillas-Núñez, 30–36. Tucson: University of Arizona Press, 2004.

Vigil, James Diego. *Barrio Gangs: Street Life and Identity in Southern California*. Austin: University of Texas Press, 1988.

Villarreal, José Antonio. *Pocho*. New York: Doubleday and Company, 1959.

3

Media

Various forms of media in the United States have helped to bring public attention to lowrider culture and its related cultural phenomena since the beginning of lowriding itself in the 1940s. Chapter 2, on pachucas/os, zoot suiters, and cholas/os, includes a discussion of how both English- and Spanish-language Los Angeles newspapers covered the Sleepy Lagoon case and the so-called Zoot Suit Riots during the World War II era. This chapter provides a discussion of how different forms of media have covered lowrider culture since the 1970s. Included in this chapter are *Lowrider* magazine and other lowrider publications, newspapers, television, radio, the Internet, and film.

LOWRIDER MAGAZINE

Lowrider magazine—it is currently known as one word, *Lowrider*, the form that will be used in this and other chapters, sometimes followed by "magazine" for clarification—was the brainchild of a group of San José State University students who had produced several low-budget political and cultural magazines during their college years. The core group, consisting of Sonny Madrid, "El Larry" González, and David Núñez, founded and published magazines such as *El Machete*, *Bronze*, *La Palabra* (*The Word*), and *Trucha* (*Alert*) in the late 1960s and early 1970s. In keeping with the heightened political consciousness of Chicana/o students of their generation, the three young men gave their earliest publications a decidedly pro–Chicano movement slant amply reflected in the content of the stories and the editorials. Drawing on the journalistic and business experience they had garnered from running these publications, the three formed a partnership called Low Rider Associates that among other activities organized and promoted cultural events such as dances and concerts on campus. Madrid, González, and Núñez started a free, independent publication called the *San José Community News* that was distributed on campus and in the Chicano barrios to help advertise the dances and concerts. But the success of these events depended heavily on the very hard work of going to small student events as well as to barrio events such as Cinco de Mayo celebrations, community dances, and other venues to distribute the free publication. This is a strategy that they would later use very effectively to increase the readership of *Lowrider* magazine in California and then later in Arizona, Colorado, New Mexico, and Texas. Another related strategy used later within the magazine itself was to include photographs of people and their lowriders in the *Community News* as a way to generate interest and reach an increasingly wider audience.

Although lowriding had become increasingly popular in Northern California throughout the 1960s and 1970s, its epicenter was located in the Los Angeles barrios (see Chapter 1, "The History and Evolution of Lowrider Culture"). It was logical that *Lowrider* magazine be founded in the Los Angeles area, but in recalling the decision not to do so, Sonny Madrid has alluded to his perception that the "scene was too violent" in barrios such as East Los Angeles where rival car clubs would wage battles over club plaques and colors. Another factor was that the law enforcement authorities, particularly the Los Angeles County Sheriff's Department, were openly hostile towards lowriders (Penland 2003, 74).

On July 3, 1976, over 8,000 lowriders appeared from throughout Northern California at the San Jose Chicano Bicentennial. Taking advantage of this large cruising "happening" and the help of some seed money generated from a dance that Low Rider Associates had organized at the Santa Clara Fairgrounds, they began planning for the first issue of *Lowrider*. Low Rider Associates then added other members to round out the talent and skill pool they would need to launch a new and profitable publication. Madrid, González, Núñez, and others began networking with car clubs to include photos of some of their signature lowrider cruisers. At the same time they began promoting a large lowrider show at Christmas Hill Park in Gilroy, California that was attended by a large number of men and women in their cars as well as thousands of spectators.

The Gilroy Low Rider Happening provided some of the photos that Low Rider Associates included in the January 1977 inaugural issue of *Lowrider* magazine. For example, the first cover was of a woman from Soledad, California, who had attended the Gilroy event representing the New Image car club. She is pictured getting into a car wearing a long raincoat with the club name on its back.

Included in the first issue is an editorial by Sonny Madrid titled "Low Riders vs. Chico and the Man." *Chico and the Man* was a popular television sitcom that ran on NBC from September 1974 to July 1978. It starred Jack Albertson as Ed Brown (The Man), a bad-tempered and hard-drinking widower, who according to the show's script owns a run-down garage in East Los Angeles. Chico (Rodríguez) is played by Freddy Prinze, a young actor of Puerto Rican and Hungarian parents who grew up in New York City. He is portrayed as an upbeat and energetic barrio Chicano with street smarts who convinces Brown to hire him to clean up the garage. Brown, who is Anglo-American, is given a lot of latitude by the show's producers to spew forth ethnic slurs directed at his Chicano neighbors and at Chico.

The show was popular among Anglo-American viewers but much less so among Latinas/os, who viewed Chico as a kind of clownish stereotype of a young barrio Chicano. The steady stream of ethnic slurs was particularly objectionable despite the producers' attempt to depict them as part of The Man's irascible character. Gypsy Rose, a classic lowrider car, was part of the barrio backdrop in many of the show's episodes. The car served as a prop designed by the producers to try to give the show an authentic Chicano barrio feeling. The car they used as a prop had already become a highly recognized icon among young Chicanos, but the use of the cruiser was not sufficient to reflect in a meaningful way the 1970s lowrider culture of East Los Angeles. The show was abruptly cancelled in 1977 when Prinze, who suffered from drug abuse, committed suicide.

Madrid's editorial was meant to characterize and depict Chicanas/os in *Lowrider* as an alternative to the negative stereotypes of the television show. He tries to build a case that the magazine would include images and stories about authentic Chicanas/os as opposed to non-Chicanas/os or even Chicanas/os who acted on the show but who portrayed the barrio and its inhabitants in a superficial and sometimes damaging way. Madrid also emphasizes that lowriders are central to the essential and authentic character of Chicana/o culture.

Low Rider Associates printed only 1,000 copies of the first issue, which they and their friends hand delivered to small businesses and individuals in barrios across Northern California. Convincing store owners to display the magazine was not always easy at the beginning. As staff photographer Salvador Casillas recalls: "They would open up the magazine and say, 'This is in English. I have mostly Mexican customers.' " Gradually the argument that the magazine was directed at a young audience of Chicanas/os who spoke and read mainly English won out as more businesses began to accept *Lowrider,* which they would display on their shelves along with other popular magazines such as *Alarma* and *Hot Rod* (www.paigerpenland.com).

Low Rider Associates had learned from their journalistic background and experience in college that in order to develop a loyal readership for a new magazine, it was essential to include photos and stories about local lowrider events and the people that participated in them. In keeping with this strategy, included in the first issue of *Lowrider* are many photos and stories with a local emphasis. Among the black-and-white photos in this issue are the following photos: (1) a 1963 Chevy lowrider with three unidentified young women and a young man leaning or sitting on the car. The photo draws the connection between lowriding and Chicana/o youth who dressed in styles popular at the time such as gaucho pants and high-waisted elephant bells. In the background are a stand of trees suggesting a park where young lowriders might spend a leisurely weekend afternoon socializing with each other. (2) several lowrider cars cruising in caravan style down a road that leads to the Gilroy Low Rider Happening, an emphasis on a local car show as a popular activity in an era when local law enforcement authorities did not perceive it as threat to public safety. (3) a group of young Chicanas posing in tight "Charley's Angels" shirts. It is probable that the name is associated with a local figure or car club and not with the popular television show by the same name; (4) two lowrider cars that are clearly identified with two lowrider clubs: Three Individuals and Las Carruchitas (cars); and (5) two young Chicanos dressed in shirts identifying their affiliation with a Northern California car club, the Nationals.

Low Rider Associates had also learned that including local advertising in the magazine would provide a steady and sustainable income to cover production costs, particularly at the beginning when the publication struggled to create a readership base. Among the advertisements included in the first issue is an ad sponsored by Tire and Wheel Specialties of San Jose, a business that carried a wide variety of items for low-rider cars: hydraulics, electric trunk kits, tires, wheels, custom grilles, tailpipes, alarms, custom steering wheels, teardrop lights, and hood ornaments. One the retailer's two locations is identified as the San Jose Flea Market, indicating the store's easy access and competitive prices for lowrider buyers. Another ad was placed by Stereo City that lists a number of items that lowriders might acquire to build or enhance their sound systems, including 8-track and cassette units and powerful speakers. Another ad was placed by a San Jose shop that specialized in custom chrome plating, custom polishing, and bumpers.

By the end of 1977 and its first year of publication, the ad base in *Lowrider* had expanded to include more Northern California businesses: Rabin's Fashions, specializing in wedding gowns; Ernie's Auto Sales; San Jose Men's Wear & Soccer Shop; The Hair Affair, specializing in men's hair styles; California Designs, specializing in furniture; Paul's Custom Auto Upholstery; LowRiders Hydraulics; and Stadium Liquors. Significantly, a few lowrider-related businesses from the Los Angeles area were also included: Newhouse Speed Shop in East Los Angeles and Tire and Wheel Specialties in San Bernardino. The magazine started including a list of California businesses where *Lowrider* could be purchased, and although the majority of these sites were in and around San Jose and East (San Francisco) Bay the expansion into Southern California is impressive.

Apparently to cover all readership bases, a couple of images included in the first issue of *Lowrider* are directed at Chicanos who were currently or had been incarcerated. In one ad, readers are encouraged to buy gift subscriptions of the magazine for "All your friends in the joint." The editors have also included a pencil drawing of a muscle-bound "homeboy" with his arms grasped behind his back defiantly staring out at the reader from behind dark glasses. He wears a headband with the initials "C/S" (Con Safos) prominently displayed on the front. This phrase, which was popular among politically active and hip Chicanas/os during the 1960s and 1970s, is at once an expression of cultural pride and a warning not to mess with the proud person who wears the initials as a of badge of strength and courage. The image of the homeboy and the narrative that accompanies the image portray a Chicano lowrider who has survived the mean barrio streets and done time at Soledad State Prison (close to the city of Salinas and in easy driving distance from San Jose). Having survived in a facility that was at the time one of the most violent prisons in the California state system, he has returned to the streets to take his rightful place among Northern California's lowriding community.

In order to significantly increase its readership, *Lowrider* had greatly increased the placement of the magazine in businesses beyond Northern California. Madrid and other members of the Low Rider Associates sales team continued negotiating with small store owners in some of the most gang-ridden barrios in Southern California employing a strategy that had been successful in Northern California. Occasionally, they would succeed in placing the magazine in businesses such as Major Liquors in San Fernando, which in late 1970s sold more than 600 copies of the magazine, but more frequently they would place only a few issues at a time in much smaller businesses whose owners were not eager to have the homeboys whom *Lowrider* seemed to be targeting coming into their stores.

Another successful sales strategy was to form alliances with Los Angeles–area lowrider clubs such as the Dukes car club, allowing Low Rider Associates to establish their credibility ("street cred") and gain the trust of the wider lowriding community. Madrid was particularly interested in featuring clubs in *Lowrider* that had put a major emphasis on converting older cars from the 1940s into lowriders. These cars are still referred to as "bombs," probably because of their elliptical shape and the fact that they were designed in an era before tail fins and other embellishments were added in order to make cars look faster and more aerodynamic.

In its November 1979 issue, Low Rider Associates launched a new sales strategy by featuring an attractive and scantily clad young model on the magazine's cover and within its pages. As reflected in some of the letters that *Lowrider* published in subsequent issues, this decision was controversial both with female readers as well as with more traditional and probably older male readers who considered such an open display of women's bodies as a betrayal of the lowriding tradition. According to Salvador Casillas, the magazine's photographer, "Even the guys in the car clubs got upset. They took it personally, saying, 'This a nice homegirl and you're trying to make her look real trashy. You're making a cheese magazine, not a car magazine' " (www.paigerpenland.com).

Despite criticism such as this, Low Riders Associates discovered that the new covers increased sales by 15 to 20 percent. This sales strategy has remained constant for over 30 years even as the magazine's editors and publishers have changed. Building on the increased readership that resulted from the new covers, Sonny Madrid implemented an apparent promotional plan in states other than California, particularly in places such as Phoenix, Las Vegas, Albuquerque, El Paso and

San Antonio. Although neither Madrid nor other Low Rider associates have ever clearly articulated this plan, it seems to have had a few essential components: the establishment of branch offices and the hiring of distribution representatives in key cities; the extensive travels of Madrid over a three-year period to different sites in the Southwest (but particularly Texas), sometimes in a fully customized lowrider from California designed to serve as an example to lowriders he encountered; and the magazine's sponsorship of large lowrider shows in cities that had been identified as promising in terms of its growth in readership (Plascencia 1983, 163–164).

Alberto López, who would become the publisher of *Lowrider* in 1978, met Madrid at the Chicano Film Festival in San Antonio. He agreed to join the magazine's staff as an account executive but also as a writer, photographer, and local representative. López was primarily responsible for finding venues in the San Antonio area that would sell *Lowrider*. Johnny Lozoya, who had experience as a large event promoter, took on the task of popularizing the magazine in Arizona. Roberto Rodríguez, the magazine's chief photographer who was severely injured in 1979 by police on Whittier Avenue, distributed *Lowrider* outside of California, believing that he would be safer out of California after he filed a civil suit against authorities for assault.

In the late 1970s and early 1980s, *Lowrider* began sponsoring large lowrider shows in California as well as in places such as San Antonio, Albuquerque, and Phoenix. The shows served to create positive and widespread publicity for the magazine, which could market its products and services at the shows themselves. The shows afforded the magazine the opportunity to greatly increase the number of ads it carried, for example, to advertise future shows. *Lowrider* ran stories with accompanying photos on the sponsored events as a means of increasing a loyal city-specific and regional readership.

The first large sponsored show in California was the 1979 Supershow in the Los Angeles Convention Center, attended by more than 20,000 spectators. One of the first large sponsored shows outside of California was held in the same year on the Gila River Indian Reservation close to Phoenix. Jimmy Borunda, a long-time lowrider from Tucson, had helped the magazine fine a venue for the Arizona show (www .paigerpenland.com).

Lowrider's readership continued to grow at a rapid rate in the late early 1980s, and at the same time it increased its ad revenues and income from other ventures such as the sponsorship of shows. The magazine began including ads from national companies such as beer companies (Schlitz and Budweiser) and cigarette manufacturers

(Winston). Despite increased revenues, its rapid expansion led to financial difficulties and staff discontent. Its distribution network had rapidly expanded, but the core staff still handled the magazine's distribution responsibilities. Alberto López explains: "That really put some constraints on the growth of the publication. At least one week out of the month we'd all be distributing the magazine, which killed 25% production." Salvador Casillas recalls that even as the readership increased, the production methods lagged behind what competing publications such as *Firme* and *Q-Vo* were doing. Some of the original staff quit due to the lack of a steady paycheck. Sonny Madrid went into debt and was forced to forfeit the entire operation to the magazine's printer, TechnoWeb. Despite a change in editorship and the addition of lifestyle features such as an advice column, TechnoWeb went bankrupt and *Lowrider* ceased publication for three years, from December 1985 to June 1988 (www.paigerpenland.com).

Alberto López and Dina Loya formed a new publishing company, Park Avenue Publishing, that acquired the rights to the magazine in 1987. They published their first issue in June 1988 as *Lowrider* (one word) with a run of 20,000 copies. López was listed on the masthead as the publisher, Loya as managing editor, and Lorenzo Gonzales as senior editor. Also listed were several field representatives in Arizona, New Mexico, Texas, and Michigan. Compared to the staff listed on the masthead in the last year under Sonny Madrid as editor and publisher, the resurrected version in 1988 was much leaner.

The first issues continued to feature the best cars from lowrider shows but gave a new emphasis to the lowrider mini-trucks, high-tech sports cars, and designer motorcycles that were becoming more popular among younger lowriders, who exhibited these new kinds of lowrider vehicles at lowrider shows. The magazine's new leadership continued the strategy of featuring several local and regional shows in each issue in order to attract a new readership and to maintain the readership that had remained loyal to the magazine during its hiatus from 1985 to 1988. A greater emphasis was placed on the quality of the photography and the printing even while keeping the newsstand and subscription prices reasonable.

As *Lowrider* increased its readership and its revenues from ads, the staff grew as well over the next 10 years to reflect the increasing importance of distribution, financial stability, and enhanced professionalism in the production elements of the magazine, including writing, photography and ad quality. The January 1997 issue celebrated the 20th anniversary of the magazine. Included in this issue is a history of the magazine from its founding by Sonny Madrid and his associates in

1977 to its financial difficulties that led to three years of nonpublication and then its rebirth under new editorial and publishing leadership. This issue is filled with iconic images of lowriding. Notably, its cover features the famous 1963 Chevy Impala "Gypsy Rose," owned by Jesse Valadez, past president of the Imperials Car Club of East Los Angeles. The car was eventually acquired by the Petersen Car Museum of Los Angeles for its permanent collection (See Chapter 4, "Art").

The editor and publisher of *Lowrider* would change again at the beginning of the new century. By 2002, Primedia, a very large and prosperous distributor of popular guides and magazines, bought the magazine and installed yet another editor, Ralph Fuentes, former president of the Imperials Car Club and a hydraulics specialist. In 2007, Primedia then sold the vast majority of its magazines, including *Lowrider*, to Source Interlink Media. Joe Ray was installed as the new editor. Reflecting the new corporate ownership as well as the rapid growth and spread of lowriding in the first decade of the twenty-first century, the national sales offices for the magazine are listed as New York, Los Angeles, Detroit, and Chicago. During the period of Primedia's ownership, the magazine had swelled to almost 250 pages, most of its length reflecting much more advertising than in the period before it acquired *Lowrider*. The average length of an issue under Source Link Media's ownership has shrunk to between 100 and 120 pages. Lowrider clubs from across the United States and abroad have continued to be featured in the magazine, as have stories on individuals who have played important roles in the evolution of lowriders, for example event promoter Johnny Lozoya and car restorer John Kennedy in the April 2010 issue and hydraulics specialist Anthony Fuentes in the May 2010 issue.

OTHER LOWRIDER PUBLICATIONS

Even before the first issue of *Lowrider* was published in January 1977, two other magazines, *Firme: Chicano Life* and *Q-Vo*, had already been launched in 1976. Although neither magazine focused as narrowly on lowrider culture as *Lowrider*, they did feature lowrider cars and clubs in almost every one of their early issues. *Firme*, more than *Q-Vo*, also adopted the sales strategy of featuring bikini-clad models on its covers. The two magazines were part of the same publishing enterprise for a time, went their separate ways, and then, in 1980, *Firme* reacquired *Q-Vo*. Today, each magazine has its own website (http://firmemagazine.com and http://q-vomagazine.com/chusma.html).

The *Q-Vo* website includes links to national and international news such as the pedophile scandal in the Catholic Church, the nuclear threat posed by North Korea, and health care legislation and related issues. Both magazines include ads for many of the same lowrider, apparel, music, and other businesses that advertise in *Lowrider*, and like *Lowrider*, the magazines also run features on prominent lowriders, musical groups, individual entertainers, and prominent Chicana/o political figures from the past and the present.

During the 1990s, *Lowrider* magazine and a new business entity, The Lowrider Group, spun off several other magazines: *Lowrider Euro, Lowrider Japan, Lowrider Bicycle, Lowrider Arte, Lowrider Classics, Lowrider Best Of, LowRider Girls,* and *Readers' Rides.* With the exception of *Lowrider Bicycle,* all of these magazines, which were very similar to the parent magazine at the time they were created, focused on specific segments of the lowriding community in the United States and in foreign countries. As the name implies, *Lowrider Euro,* which is published every three months, carries features on European automobile imports that had become popular in the 1980s and 1990s as modified lowrider cars. *Lowrider Japan* was begun due to the burgeoning popularity of lowrider culture in Japan. The magazine features and ads are in both English and Japanese.

Lowrider Bicycle is directed mainly at a younger readership who, due to limited financial resources, invests in customizing bicycles rather than far more expensive vehicles. Lowrider bicycles have become more prominent at lowrider shows, where they are able to compete for prizes in a different category from cars and trucks. Taking into consideration their younger readership, the editors of *Lowrider Bicycle* avoid the use of seminude women on the covers and within the magazine itself. In recognition of a new trend among its readership, the magazine began doing features on lowrider model cars whose owners were entering them into competition at model car shows. In order to continue to appeal to changes like the model car hobbyists, *Lowrider Bicycle*'s editor, Nathan Trujillo, wrote in the Summer 1994 issue, the magazine's second issue: "This magazine is young, like the sport it covers, and we greatly value our reader response from both the young and the old. It's going to be a fun ride, and the *LRB* staff is poised to deliver an even better magazine than the last" (*Lowrider Bicycle,* Summer 1994, 4).

Lowrider Arte, the main magazine outlet for art, including tattoo art, submitted by readers, is discussed in Chapter 4. *Lowrider Best Of,* which heavily emphasizes visual elements, carries quality color photos and short features on some of the classic lowrider cars and trucks such as Gangster of Love, Art Moreno's 1939 Chevy Deluxe (see Chapter 4); The Penthouse, Armando Montes' 1978 Buick Regal; and Dress to Kill, Joe Ray's 1973 Buick Riviera. Each issue also includes many photos of seminude models posed seductively on, around, or in the featured cars.

Two more recent spinoffs of *Lowrider* as a part of Source Interlink Media are *LowRider Girls* and *Readers' Rides*. Both began publishing in 2008. The first publication, like its parent *Lowrider*, features models, and the emphasis seems to be on them rather than on cars. The website (www.lowridermagazine.com/index.html) explicitly states that the magazine includes photos and stories about "the exotic and girls-next-door whom this niche audience loves to read about. *LowRider Girls Magazine* is here to provide you with some of the realest and, most importantly, sexiest 'eye candy' out there." *Readers' Rides* is targeted at a different segment of the lowrider community: families. As reflected on its covers, which are collages of photos of children and families with their favorite lowrider rides, including bicycles, tricycles, wagons, and even baby strollers, this publication seems designed to appeal to a general audience of readers and viewers of all ages. Many of the features focus on how the lowrider tradition has been passed down not only from father to son but from father to daughter, mother to daughter, and so on. Unlike most other lowrider magazines, stories on girls and young women are common in *Readers' Rides*. The underlying theme of the magazine seems to be that lowrider families make happy families because all the members can participate at some level of lowriding.

In addition to *Lowrider* magazine and its spinoffs, there were several other independent lowrider magazines that began publishing from as early as the mid-1990s: *Street Customs*, 1994; *Orlie's Lowriding*, mid-1990s; *Vajito*, 1996; *Street Low Magazine*, late 1990s; *Scrape: The Lowrider and Euro Magazine*, late 1990s; *Lowridaz*, early 2000s; *Low Company*, early 2000s; *Wheels 2000*, early 2000s; and *Impalas*, 2008. While the majority of these publications were located in California, the epicenter of lowrider culture, several were not. This reflected the spread of the popularity of lowriding across the country outward from California, where it had prospered from the 1960s forward. These magazines emphasized local and regional lowrider culture, but at the same time their publishers seemed to be aware that it was important not to neglect a wider readership. For example, *Orlie's Lowriding* was published in Corrales, New Mexico, close to Albuquerque. It featured many New Mexico–based club events, individuals, shows, and local lowrider businesses while at the same time occasionally including photos, stories, and ads from California and elsewhere. *Scrape*, whose executive offices were located in New York and its editorial offices in New Jersey, emphasized lowrider culture on the East Coast and in the upper Midwest but included features and ads from California and other states. *Vajito* was published in San Antonio, but its editor, Alexis G. Velázquez, seemed intent on broadening the magazine's focus to appeal to a national Latina/o readership.

Street Low Magazine (*SLM*) is today perhaps *Lowrider* magazine's most competitive rival. It was founded in the late 1990s by Gilbert Chávez and George Arteaga in San Jose, California, where its publishing operation and editorial office are still located. Most of the stories and photos in the first few issues focused almost exclusively on lowriding events in the San Jose area, and the ads carried in its pages also had a local emphasis. As its readership base grew, *SLM*, much as *Lowrider* had done in the early 1980s, broadened its focus beyond San Jose to include features and ads from throughout the San Francisco Bay area and Central and Southern California. Similar to most other lowrider publications, *SLM* has pursued from its very beginning the strategy of displaying seminude models on its covers and within its pages. Its website has numerous photos of models as well as art work of nude women in provocative poses (www.streetlowmagazine.com). Unlike other publications, the magazine carries occasional stories of a cultural nature such as the one in issue 42 on the Mexican artist and muralist Diego Rivera.

NEWSPAPER COVERAGE

Since the 1970s, coverage by large, established urban newspapers in cities such as Los Angeles, San Jose, Denver, Phoenix, Tucson, Albuquerque, and San Antonio has tended to become increasingly more positive as lowrider culture has evolved through its various phases. In the 1970s, when cruising was popular on city streets—Whittier Avenue in East Los Angeles, Central Avenue in Phoenix, Central Avenue in Albuquerque, West San Antonio, and Federal Avenue in Denver—newspaper coverage tended to be negative in its portrayal of lowriders as members of gangs who invited violent confrontation with law enforcement authorities. Cruising was seen as a threat to public safety. But as lowriding left the streets, due mainly to crackdowns by law enforcement, and lowrider shows became more prominent in the latter part of the twentieth century and first decade of the twenty-first century, newspaper coverage has become increasingly more positive. As lowriding has become more mainstream, popular, and acceptable among a non-Latina/o public, newspapers have increasingly emphasized its artistic, cultural, and family aspects. The readership of large urban newspapers in California and the rest of the Southwest has remained largely Anglo-American, although the Latina/o readership has continued to increase in several states.

The *Los Angeles Times*, one of the California's largest and most important newspapers, offers an example of how print media coverage of lowriding has become more favorable. The October 16, 1995 issue carried a feature on the huge financial success of Park Avenue Publishing, the parent company of *Lowrider* magazine and its spinoffs. A February 3, 2000 story, titled "High Times for Lowriders," features the Petersen Museum's exhibit "Arte y Estilo: The Lowriding Tradition" in a very favorable light. A followup article in the April 19, 2000 issue calls the exhibit attendance "stunning." The story quotes Ricardo González, the publisher of *Lowrider* magazine, who states that the attendance should not have been a surprise given the success of the publication, the principal promoter of the lowrider lifestyles, in being the best-selling newsstand automotive periodical in the country. The November 26, 2006 issue includes a story about lowriding's transformation from it presence on the streets of Los Angeles to local exhibit halls and museums. The story features Alejandro "Chino" Vega, a Mexican immigrant, whose candy-green 1979 Monte Carlo, "Orgullo Mexicano" (Mexican Pride), had won many awards on the lowrider show tour. In its March 6, 2008 issue, the *Los Angeles Times* reported the announcement by television executives of the launching of the "Livin' the Low Life" series on the Speed cable channel starring the show's host Vida Guerra. The newspaper's February 16, 2010 issue carried a story with many photos on the spread of lowriding in Southern California.

Like the *Los Angeles Times*, the *Arizona Republic*, Arizona's most important newspaper, became more favorably disposed towards lowrider culture in Phoenix once cruising on the public streets declined. For example, this newspaper carried several stories from 2000 to 2010 emphasizing the evolution of lowriding into the mainstream of local, middle-class culture and therefore into a cultural practice that was more acceptable to its largely Anglo-American readership. An August 18, 2001 story recounts how Richard Ochoa's family has been involved in local lowriding for two generations, handing down the requisite mechanical skills and artistic talent from father to son. Richard, who describes lowriding "as such a family thing," works on cars with his own sons and grandchildren. The story's author describes Ochoa, a manager for the city of Mesa, "as settled as a man can be" with a new house, a wife, four children, and three grandchildren. He is characterized as typical of comfortable baby boomers who go to work in massive SUVs, the newspaper's code language for middle class, just like most of the newspaper's readership. The story goes on to describe the substantial investment that other latter-day car owners in Phoenix make in their lowrider vehicles as a source of cultural pride that can be displayed publicly at car shows, which are characterized as social gatherings where individuals and families can reconnect with familiar faces. The *Arizona Republic* continued to give lowriding a patina of respectability during the next few years in (1) stories that described how lowriding as part of officially sanctioned public events, such as the 2010 "Cruise on Central at Park Central Mall," could be a benign activity for all to enjoy; and (2) stories that celebrated lowriding's artistic achievements as, for example, a special exhibit, "Low and Slow: Art of the Lowrider," at the Phoenix Art Museum in August 2009.

The *San Antonio Express News* has generally portrayed lowriding in a positive light in the first decade of the twenty-first century, especially the large lowrider festivals held annually at the Mateo Camargo Park and sponsored by the Centro Cultural Aztlán. In a series of the newspaper's web postings in its "My San Antonio" section in 2007 and 2008, the festival is celebrated as a respectable and inviting event attended by Latina/o and non-Latina/o car enthusiasts and families from San Antonio and its surrounding communities. Quoting representatives of the Centro and other prominent Latina/o community representatives, the artistic aspects of lowrider cars are emphasized. The cars are portrayed as a form of cultural pride and self-expression that is community oriented and supportive of family values.

The *Denver Post* has been more ambivalent towards the lowriding community than Los Angeles, Phoenix, and San Antonio newspapers, perhaps reflecting the tension that has persisted between municipal and state officials and the lowriding segment of the city's Latina/o population. In 1998, Frana Araujo Mace, a state representative from Denver, sponsored a bill in the state legislature to outlaw cruising on Federal Avenue on weekend nights and Mexican holidays—Federal Avenue had long been a favorite cruising route in north Denver, a largely Latina/o section of the city. She cited as one of the reasons for the bill the public safety and crime prevention concern of some her Latina/o constituents, reflecting the historical antipathy within the Latina/o community itself towards lowriding. Denver-area lowrider clubs and advocacy groups such as the American Civil Liberties Union opposed the bill as discriminatory and unconstitutional. The bill did not pass, but local law enforcement authorities did strictly limit cruising on Federal Avenue during, for example, the annual Cinco de Mayo celebration in north and northwest Denver. The newspaper seemed to be supportive of such measures in a series of stories from 2000 to 2010 by negatively associating the annual cruising event with gang violence. The newspaper also seemed to oppose lowriding during the annual celebration, apparently implying that many of the revelers would come in from out of town to celebrate in inappropriate ways. In an April 13, 2010 story, the *Denver Post* portrayed Cinco de Mayo cruisers in the following way: "The low, rhythmic boom vibrating from the car stereo created the perfect ambiance for a Saturday morning mating dance of metal along Broadway in Denver." The story goes on to describe the lowrider part of the Latina/o's annual celebration as mixing machismo, style, and attitude.

In general, urban newspapers in regions of the country other than the Southwest have not given continuous nor extensive coverage to lowrider culture, but when lowriders are associated with an established mainstream institution such as museums there has been some coverage. For example, the *New York Times*, perhaps the United States's most respected newspapers, ran a story on the 2007 lowrider exhibit at the Petersen Automotive Museum in Los Angeles. In its November 18, 2007 issue and web posting, Phil Patton, the story's author, emphasizes the evolution of lowrider cars over the decades from what he describes as "teenage toys, swaggering, snarling, sulking symbols of youth" to a level of being worthy of having a prestigious museum sponsor not one but two exhibits featuring lowriders. The *New York Times* has therefore bestowed upon lowrider cars, if not lowriding culture itself, a high level of respectability. The story quotes from Professor Denise M. Sandoval, the curator of both shows, who has written extensively and authoritatively on lowriding for many years. Sandoval describes lowriding as an expression of neighborhood and family pride that cuts across ethnic communities.

RADIO

Radio has been a part of lowriding culture from the very beginning. This electronic medium has played a major role in providing lowriders—whether they were cruising down urban streets on a Saturday night, hanging out at the park on a lazy Sunday afternoon, or working on their cars—the music popular at the time. Local radio stations in cities across the Southwest broadcast at one time or another música tejana, conjunto, swing, blues, jazz, rhythm and blues, the Eastside sound, rock and roll, punk, and rap. (See Chapter 5, "Music," for a discussion of the kinds of music that lowriders listened to from the mid-1940s on.) Even when lowriders installed 8-track tape decks, regular tape decks, and CD players with louder and more sophisticated sound systems, local radio stations have continued to keep drivers and their passengers in touch with the latest musical currents. It has been a practice of lowrider show organizers to have a local radio station—sometimes more than one in large radio markets like Los Angeles, Phoenix, and Las Vegas—broadcast live from the show grounds. Local radio stations have also broadcast from lowrider exhibits, as Edge Radio did at the 2009 Mesa (Arizona) Contemporary Arts museum exhibit, "Low and Slow: The 'Art' of the Lowrider."

There are currently commercial radio stations and networks that are dedicated to lowriding culture. For example, Q-VO Radio, whose home is Sunnyvale, California, is associated with the lowrider magazine by the same name and is part of a radio group that includes Low Rider Radio, Vato Talk Radio, Firme Radio, and Q-VO Angeles radio. These radio outlets that broadcast over a wide spectrum of radio channels also have a live streaming option so that they can be accessed over the Internet. They carry current lowrider news and interviews and play lowrider music and other "oldies" such as the Beatles. Like many radio stations, these radio outlets also provide downloads of their programming.

National commercial radio has given scant coverage to lowrider culture, but an exception is a story, "Low Riders Grow Up," carried by *The Osgood File* on the CBS Radio Network on October 3, 2002. As the title implies, this story is about some older lowriders, "middle-aged, middle-class men," who have continued to be active in their lowrider community but who also have integrated this activity into the family structure. The story also mentions that lowriding at the beginning of the twenty-first century is multicultural, that is, African Americans and Anglo-Americans have increasingly been attracted to lowriding by what the story identifies as "a uniquely American tradition where cultural interchange and style are constantly evolving" (ACF News Source).

Publicly supported radio stations have been also had an important role in bringing lowrider culture to an audience that would not normally be included among lowrider aficionados. For example, KPFA radio station of Berkeley, California has had a long-running lowrider cruising show, "La Onda Bajita," that features mainly music as well as news about the lowriding scene in the San Francisco Bay area. Other public radio stations occasionally carry news about local lowriding events. For example, Minnesota Public Radio gave coverage in 2009 to the 10th annual lowrider show in St. Paul that included an interview with Enrique Alcocer, a fan and owner of a lowrider, who gave a brief overview of the evolution of lowrider cars. The station also interviewed his friend, Sergio Maldonado, also a proud lowrider car owner, who emphasized the family involvement in lowriding in an attempt to counter the negative perception that lowriders were gang members. Finally, National Public Radio devoted a part of its June 9, 2009 "All Things Considered" national broadcast to the lowrider phenomenon. It featured an interview with Joe Ray, editor of *Lowrider* magazine, who commented on the San Bernardino, California lowrider show that was part of the Lowrider 2009 Tour.

TELEVISION

Except for occasional news stories on local television channels, television has paid lowrider culture scant attention. Usually, lowrider vehicles have served as props on television shows, such as a lowrider bike, a converted Schwinn Stingray, that appeared on some episodes of the 1960s version of *The Munsters.* Another example is the 1963 Impala lowrider that was shown in the opening credits of the 1970s comic series *Chico and the Man.* More recently, African American and Latina/o "gangsta" rappers have used lowriders as props in some of their videos on MTV and elsewhere, serving to give lowriding culture a very negative image that reinforces what some consider to be the connection between gangs and lowriders.

The HBO series *Americanos* did an entire segment of its October 11, 2006 program on lowriders in the Midwest, focusing on a lowrider show in Dixon, Illinois. The segment opens with an image of lowrider cars and trucks cruising down a rural country road to the show site, which seems to have been held in an open field surrounded by crops. Organizers and participants emphasize the cultural pride of owning, maintaining, and showing their vehicles, especially those that display traditional images of Aztec symbols, warriors, and maidens. One person interviewed makes the point that lowriders are anti-gang and family oriented, a point of view echoed by an on-duty policeman who stresses the civility of those attending the show. Another person interviewed is a young Chicana who has been involved in lowriding for years, and now not only drives her own car but also judges hopping contests at lowrider shows.

In early March, 2008, Speed cable channel launched a weekly lowrider reality show, "Livin' the Low Life," featuring Cuban-born model and actress Vida Guerra as the show's host. Correctly assessing the market, Speed programming vice president Robert Ecker was quoted as saying that the lowrider lifestyle had been underserved and that the series "will provide the community with the spotlight and the platform it so richly deserves, in a format that respects and reflects the vibrant history it has had on the American automotive landscape." The first episode was devoted to the Ruelas family, founders of the historically important Dukes car club in the Los Angeles area. Segments of the future episodes included auto body and paint shops. Speed's plan was to make the episodes available on the Internet through www.SPEEDtv.com, iTunes video podcasts, mobile phones, cable broadband, and viral distribution (Hispanic PR Wire).

The PBS (Public Broadcasting Service) has covered an aspect of lowriding in its children's programming: episode 125, "The Lowriders (East Los Angeles, California)," of *Postcards from Buster*. In this episode, the loveable bunny Buster sets out to buy a bicycle directly from a factory in Los Angeles. His younger cousins, Brian and Anthony, who live in East Los Angeles, introduce him to lowrider bikes, which fascinate Buster. The episode's underlying lesson is that sometimes children can themselves build some really exciting and satisfying toys rather than buy them from the store or the factory (Alabama Public Television).

THE INTERNET

All of the media discussed above have easily accessible websites, although some of the sites are more useful than others. The better ones have attractive and well-organized home pages and links that provide much useful information. In addition to these sites, other media that can be found on the Internet are professionally produced videos of many of lowrider shows and other events, as well as YouTube and MySpace videos that are not carefully edited yet provide a sense of the immediacy and authenticity of fan participation and enthusiasm. There are also websites that carry photos of lowrider material such as cars, models, and CDs of music. One can access these websites by entering words and phrases associated with lowrider culture—"lowriding," "lowrider," "lowrider clubs," "lowrider shows," "lowrider art," "lowrider paint," "modifying lowriders," "lowrider events," "cruising"—in a search engine such as Google. The most useful websites are www.lowridermagazine.com, www.lowriderarte.com, www.lowriderbike.com/index.html, and www.brownpride.com.

FILM

Lowrider culture has been represented on the silver screen since at least 1979, when the feature-length film *Boulevard Nights* premiered in Los Angeles. Other feature-length films in which aspects of the lowrider lifestyle have played an important role are *Zoot Suit* (1981), *Heartbreaker* (1983), and *Lowrider Weekend* (2004). Some feature-length films in which lowriders and their vehicles appear as props but not as elements essential to the plot are *Up in Smoke* (1978), *Born in East L.A.* (1987), *Boyz N the Hood* (1991), *American Me* (1992), *Mi vida loca* (*My Crazy Life*, 1993), *Mi Familia* (*My Family*, 1995), *Training Day* (2001), *La Mission* (2010), and *Machete* (2010). Documentary films that deal exclusively with lowrider culture are *The Ups and Downs of Lowriding* (1981), *Low N' Slow: The Art of Lowriding* (1984), *Rag Top Ralph* (1984), *Low and Slow: San Antonio Lowriders* (1991), *Lowriding in Aztlán* (2005), and *Sunday Driver: A Look at the Guys Behind the Chrome* (2005). In addition, there are dozens of documentary-like videos and DVDs of lowrider shows and videos based on *Lowrider* magazine content, including *Ventura Best of Lowrider, Lowrider Magazine's '98 Caliente Tour* (1999), *Cherry Rides,* and *Lowriding in Aztlán: The Truth about Lowriding!* (2005), *Cruizin' TV Vol. 2: Cars, Girls, Music* (2006), *Wild about Lowriders* (2007), *Lowrider Magazine's "The Video" (2007), Lowrider Magazine's Video X Los Angeles Super Show* (2007), *Lowrider Magazine's Cruise Down Memory Lane* (2007) and *Best of the Las Vegas Supershow* (2009).

Feature-Length Films

Boulevard Nights is the first feature-length film in which lowriding plays a prominent role. The movie premiered on June 18, 1979 at a theater on Whittier Boulevard in the midst of an atmosphere of tension between the East Los Angeles lowriding community and law enforcement authorities. Whittier Boulevard had been for a decade the most popular route for cruisers in the Los Angeles area, but the local police and sheriff's office had repeatedly tried to discourage cruising by either shutting down parts of the Boulevard or severely restricting access to it, especially at night (see Chapter 1). According to several accounts, the opening of the film at a local theater served to escalate tensions, particularly because of the negative portrayal of young Chicanas/os, whom the film stereotyped as violent gang members, a portrayal that could have been offensive to many residents in East Los Angeles where the movie was set.

The plot revolves around two Chicano brothers, Raymond Avila and his younger brother Chuco Avila, who live with their mother in a residential section of East Los Angeles. Raymond is characterized as a loyal and loving son. He owns a lowrider car and works in a local chop shop that specializes in modifying lowriders. He is depicted as an older, wiser, and more mature individual who has a steady girlfriend, Shady Londeros, a beautiful young Chicana whom he marries later in the film. Shady, who holds a steady middle-class job outside of the barrio, is critical of Raymond's gang membership and his love of lowriding. She believes he lacks ambition by working in a chop shop and is therefore not a good marriage prospect. At the same time, he is the leader of the VGV gang, but he is portrayed as being much less prone to violence than some of the other members of the gang, including his younger brother, Chuco, an immature and brash 16-year-old who sniffs glue and gets into trouble by challenging members of the rival Eleventh Street gang.

A scene early in the movie is of young lowrider men and women—including Raymond, Shady, and Chuco—cruising one evening on what is presumably Whittier Boulevard. Raymond challenges another cruiser owner to a hopping contest which Raymond wins. The contest is characterized as competitive, with money riding on the outcome, but it is carried out peacefully. At the same time, a clash between the VGV and Eleventh Street gangs occurs on the boulevard that results in the stabbing death of a member of the latter gang. The police intervene, and Chuco is arrested under suspicion of being the assailant. Despite Raymond's repeated attempts to deter his younger brother from criminality, Chuco continues to get in trouble: he and his friends trash an Eleventh Street gang's lowrider; he gets fired from his job in the chop shop for repeated absenteeism; he becomes a full-fledged cholo, dressing in a fedora, Pendleton shirt, ironed T-shirt, and khaki pants, and he stays away from home at night, hanging out with his like-minded gang friends.

Raymond wins over Shady when he convinces her that he has begun to reassess his goals and values to correspond to her expectations. They soon marry at a typical barrio wedding at the local Catholic church, followed by a parade of decorated lowriders through the barrio streets to the reception at Raymond's house. Chuco, who has not attended the wedding, shows up late and remorseful at the reception. In what seems to be a happy ending, Raymond hugs him and invites him in to the reception. Suddenly, members of the Eleventh Street gang drive by the house, riddling it with bullets. Raymond and Chuco's mother is fatally shot. Chuco avenges her death by killing the gang member who had fired the shots. He in turn is shot and dies in Raymond's arms on the way to the hospital. In the film's last scene, Raymond and his new bride Shady are pictured gazing into each other's eyes with a mixture of sadness and hope.

Film critics and social scientists have been very critical of *Boulevard Nights*, accusing its creators of stereotyping barrio youth as violent and criminal and for associating lowriding with these behaviors. The film's message is that in order to redeem himself, Raymond must abandon the lowrider life in order to pursue a more acceptable, middle-class future that corresponds more closely to the values of his new wife. Chuco is representative of a lowrider and gang member who suffers the ultimate price, death, for not heeding Raymond's advice and following his example. Given the film's association of low-riding with gangbanger life, it is not surprising that the premier on Whittier Boulevard drew crowds of protestors.

Heartbreaker focuses much more on the lowriding scene than *Boulevard Nights*. In this feature-length film, the primary and secondary plot lines revolve around Beto, the main male character, who is played by Fernando Allende, a young handsome Chicano actor. The primary plot line follows Beto's transition towards a more mature character as he develops a love interest in Kim, played by the actor Dawn Dunlap, a young, attractive, blond woman who he has met at a barrio beauty salon where she cuts his hair. Early in the film, Beto has announced to the lowrider club members that very soon he intends to pass on his position as president of the club to Angel, a younger member, in whom he sees leadership potential. He gives Angel a Golden Knight statuette, thereby symbolically passing on the leadership of the club. The secondary plot line revolves around Angel's struggle over whether to maintain his loyalty to his car club companions or to strike out as an independent lowrider who pursues financial gain.

Kim is characterized as a young adult in the midst of a struggle to establish her independence from her parents, a caring but rigid middle-class couple who oppose their daughter's desire to move out of the family home into her own apartment. Kim is at once attracted to Beto but also reluctant to encourage their relationship. Like Shady in *Boulevard Nights*, she is critical of the lowriding scene, especially the flirtatious and highly sexualized young women who throw themselves at the young men. She is described as having higher expectations of wanting a more meaningful relationship with Beto and not acting merely as an object of his sexual fantasies. Much of their interaction revolves around Beto trying to persuade Kim that his feelings are deeper than sexual attraction.

Angel faces a crisis when his lowrider, in which he has invested many hours and much money, is torched by a mysterious arsonist right before an important car show in which he was going to compete. The arsonist has also stolen the Golden Knight statuette from his car. Rather than accept the help of the car club members to prepare a new car for competition, he agrees to have Héctor, a selfish and sleazy

Chicano promoter, sponsor a new lowrider in the show. The promoter drives a Corvette, the antithesis of a lowrider car and therefore symbolic of his exclusion from the lowrider community.

Beto eventually succeeds in convincing Kim that he loves her, and she reciprocates by becoming more open in showing her feelings towards him. The final scenes of the movie take place at the lowrider car show, where it becomes clear to the Golden Knights Car Club members that Angel has betrayed them. They also learn that Héctor is the arsonist and thief who had stolen the statuette, which is recovered at the car show. Angel realizes that he has been duped by Héctor, and he is redeemed when he expresses his regret to Beto and other club members for betraying their trust. In a magnanimous gesture, Beto forgives him, welcomes him back to the club, and gives him the statuette, an expression of Beto's continuing confidence in Angel to be the club's future president. Order is restored: Beto and Kim are now a couple with a promising future and the Golden Knights Car Club is once again returned to its prior state of mutual trust and stability.

The film is interesting for a couple of reasons. The emotional maturation of Beto develops along with his decreasing investment in the car club, suggesting that it is both natural and healthy for an individual's involvement with lowriding to change over time as other priorities such as marriage, career, and family become more important. Another interesting aspect of the film is the role that African Americans males play in the fictional lowriding community. Although they are stereotypically and superficially characterized as fun loving and jive talking, they are also depicted as trustworthy and loyal friends of Chicano lowriders. It is one of Beto's African American friends who discovers and then informs Beto who had burned Angel's car and stolen the statuette.

Lowrider Weekend (2004) is a comedy directed by the respected San Antonio Chicano filmmaker Efraín Gutiérrez, who is best known for the 1976 bilingual film, *¡No me entierren vivo!* (*Don't Bury Me Alive!*), one of the first Chicano feature-length films, about a Chicano whose brother is killed in Vietnam. Gutiérrez then went on to produce, direct, and self-distribute two other feature films in the late 1970s: *Amor Chicano, Es Para Siempre* (Chicano Love is Forever, 1978) and *Run Tecato Run* (1979). *Lowrider Weekend* was Gutiérrez's first film in more than 25 years.

None of Gutiérrez's prior feature films had been comedies, so it is surprising that *Lowrider Weekend* is decidedly comical. It is a film that can be categorized within the genres of slapstick and comedy-of-errors films. Sonny is a small-time Chicano entertainment promoter who, confronted by a mafia figure to whom he is in serious debt, improvises to try to create a profitable lowrider show in his hometown of San Quilmas (San Antonio as it is popularly known in the Chicana/ o community). Sonny, played by Jesse Borrego, an experienced Chicano actor, knows that the key to the show's financial success is an appearance by his brother, Danny de La Paz, a very popular actor who played Chuco in *Boulevard Nights*. Sonny must first convince Danny to make an appearance. Danny, who plays himself in the film, is reluctant to commit to his brother because he is already under contract to appear at a lowrider show in Japan. Danny finally agrees to come to San Quilmas provided Sonny sends him a contract. Part of the film's humor is based on the depiction of Sonny as a barely competent promoter who, because of numerous distractions—most of them women—never gets around to issuing the contract.

The tension builds throughout the film as the day of the show approaches, the mafia figure intensifies pressure on Sonny, and it seems increasingly unlikely that Danny will make an appearance at the show. Baby Marin, a rotund, free-spirited friend of Sonny's, hatches a plot to kidnap Danny before he leaves for Japan and bring him to the show. He and his sidekick, a mysterious and anonymous Pachuco figure who seems to be a kind shaman endowed with special powers, carry through with the plot but not before fending off the attempts of two Japanese ninja warriors to rescue Danny and fly him to Japan (see Chapter 2 for a detailed discussion on the Pachuco figure).

The show is a resounding success. Lowriders come to the weekend show from as far away as California, Arizona, and New Mexico, but Sonny is still faced with the dilemma of announcing to the crowd that Danny will not be there. In one of the film's final scenes, Sonny is on the verge of making a disappointing announcement to the show's audience when—just in time—a stretch limousine adorned with Japanese flags and bearing Danny, a ninja warrior, a Japanese car club promoter, Baby Marin, and the mysterious Pachuco figure appears. The show is a financial success, the crowd is pleased with Danny's appearance, Sonny extricates himself from his financial difficulties, and, thanks to the intercession of his precocious teenage daughter, he discovers that his secretary, Irma—hidden for most of the film behind her large glasses, modest clothing, and timid behavior—is an attractive young woman in whom he takes an immediate interest.

A secondary plot line involves Armando, a young lowrider from Laredo, Texas, who is building a Chevrolet Impala lowrider in order to enter it in the San Antonio show competition. His motivation is to win the prize money in order to allow his wheelchair-bound younger sister to have a crucial operation so that she can walk again. He finishes in time, but his car is stolen by a renowned car thief at the show. Friends help him recover the car and capture the thief. The reward money is given to Armando for his sister's operation. He is also rewarded when he meets a young attractive Chicana at the show.

Lowriders as Props in Feature Films

Just as in the television series *Chico and the Man*, lowrider vehicles have been used as props in several feature movies presumably to communicate to their audience a sense of authenticity and street credibility. For example, Cheech Marín drives a lightly modified and beat-up lowrider in the Cheech and Chong movie *Up in Smoke* (1978), a parody of the 1970s drug culture and of law enforcement's failed attempts to stem the flow of marijuana from Mexico. In *Born in East L.A.*, Cheech stars as a hapless Chicano, born a U.S. citizen in East Los Angeles, who gets swept up in a Border Patrol raid and deported to Mexico. Unable to prove his citizenship, he is stranded in Mexico for a time. Before his deportation, Cheech is shown driving a champagne-colored VW Bug; although the car is not lowered it has some of the characteristics of a lowrider cruiser such as a small steering wheel, interior decorations, and a low driver's seat. Another, more traditional cruiser, a lowered Chevy Impala with hydraulics, also appears in the film. Its passengers are three *vatos locos* (crazy dudes) who sit so low in the car that they can barely be seen.

In *Boyz N the Hood*, the African American rapper Ice Cube often appears with a lowrider, indicating the cross-ethnic nature of lowriding scene in Los Angeles. In *Training Day*, starring Denzel Washington as a veteran Los Angeles Police Department detective, lowriders appear in street scenes of South Central Los Angeles where the drug trade is portrayed as being open and rampant. The lowriders are apparently included in the film as one of props to make the street scenes credible. The film *American Me* is largely about the life of crime of Santana, played in the movie by Edward James Olmos. Lowriders appear in just one scene, a barrio wedding in which the cruisers are parked outside a church ready to take the bride and groom and their party on a traditional lowrider parade to the wedding reception.

Lowriders also appear briefly in the following films: *Mi Vida Loca*, about young Chicanas growing up in a Los Angeles barrio where drugs and gang violence are prevalent; *Mi Familia*, about the travails and successes of several generations of a Chicano family in Los Angeles; and *La Mission*, about a gay Chicano whose traditional family lives in San Francisco's Mission District. The aesthetically pleasing lowrider

The 2010 movie, *Machete*: Robert Rodriguez, director and Danny Trejo and Jessica Alba, actors. (AP Photo/Andrew Medichini)

cruisers in this film are linked in a positive way to their owners' cultural pride. In *Machete*, a 2010 film co-directed by Robert Rodríguez and Ethan Maniquis, lowrider vehicles make brief appearances in passing shots of the barrio. Towards the end of the film, Machete, the hero and main character, an illegal immigrant and former member of the Mexican federal police force, rallies a lowrider club to confront a border vigilante group that has been assassinating Mexican border crossers. In a dramatic and violent scene that last several minutes, the lowrider club lays siege to the vigilantes' compound, systematically overcoming their armed resistance and forcing the vigilantes to flee.

Documentaries

Some early documentaries about lowrider culture are *The Ups and Downs of Lowriding* (1981), which presents a balanced view of lowriding by lowriders, the public, and the police; *Low 'N Slow: The Art of Lowriding*, which views lowriding as an important form of industrial folk art; *Rag Top Ralph* (1984), about Ralph Carrillo, a well-known lowrider who was very competitive in hopping contests; and *Low and Slow— San Antonio Lowriders* (1981), about car clubs and the public perception of lowriders (Keller 1994, 203).

A more recent video, *Lowriding in Aztlan: The Truth about Lowriding!*, is representative of several documentaries about the lowriding scene. As indicated in the subtitle and blurb on video's back cover, the stated purpose of this documentary is to give the viewer an overview: "From cruising the boulevard and street battles to police harassment caught on tape, *Lowriding in Aztlan* will take you up close and personal into the dangers of lowriding while showcasing some of the hottest lowrider cars, murals, and artwork that lowriding has to offer." The video revolves around several interviews with individuals who are representative of the lowriding scene. In general, the tone of the interviews is defensive in addressing the issue of police harassment—footage of some incidents is included—and a double standard in law enforcement's treatment of hot rodders and lowriders. Some of the interviewees also address what they consider to be the mistaken perception among the general public that lowriders are members of gangs and therefore are involved in violence and criminal behavior. At the same time, some of those interviewed do acknowledge that there is some validity to the accusation that a few lowriders have gotten on the wrong side of the law. As a counter to this accusation, several of the individuals who appear in the video emphasize that lowriding is inherently family friendly and that it promotes camaraderie and mutual respect among those engaged in it.

There are many images of wives and children involved in activities such as picnics and community-oriented events such as working with the police to improve communication with the lowrider community, volunteer work with charities and schools, and graffiti removal. Part of the video deals with the high level of skill and artistry required to bring a lowrider car up to the standards required to exhibit it at a car show. Several in the documentary express their obvious pride in their work and welcome the admiration that their efforts garner. One of the car clubs featured has a religious focus. Its members, many of them former gangbangers and drug addicts, come together to pray and provide support for each other and their families.

Another documentary, *Sunday Drivers: A Look at the Guys behind the Chrome*, is unique in its focus on the first African American lowrider car club, founded in Compton, California, in 1978 and later expanded to include a club in Watts; both Los Angeles locations have a largely African American population. The documentary features interviews with several prominent members of the club: cofounders Craig Parker and Kevin Smith; Dee Dee Girl, the only woman in the car club at the time of the documentary; Wally Dog, a Los Angeles commodities trader; a prominent member known only as Gangster; Dr. Get Low, also known as "Doc," who is a lowrider design and paint expert; and Twin, a younger member of the club. Several of those interviewed have been involved in lowriding since the 1970s and as members of the club from the earliest days. Some are explicit in admitting that they were formerly members of gangs involved in criminal behavior but express loyalty to the car club members who have provided them with an alternative to such activity. One individual remembers being involved in a gang shoot-out over a disputed drug deal and doing time in a state penitentiary. The attraction of being part of a group that initially attracted some to gangs is now a reason for being a member of the car club. The documentary shows members participating in several activities that reinforce a sense of group cohesiveness, friendship, and mutual support: playing dominoes together at a weekly meeting; a car wash organized to help a member repair his damaged car; and being part of a march in support of "Parents Against Violence." Similar to the documentary *Lowriding in Aztlan*, club members view the police with a mixture of irritation and anger stemming from what some identify as harassment of club cruises on Crenshaw Boulevard. Included in the documentary is footage of the police shutting down the Boulevard in the late 1990s, an act that caused resentment among club members. Unlike *Lowriding in Aztlan*, *Sunday Driver* includes an interview with a high-ranking member of the local police force, an

African American, who presents a different take on why it is necessary to have a police presence when lowriders cruise public streets. His view is that clashes between lowriders can quickly escalate into violent confrontations that can result in the use of weapons. The officer also mentions that the police are concerned about a resurgence of gang activity among lowriders (Palm Pictures).

Lowrider Event Videos

In addition to the documentaries about different aspects of lowriding culture, there are dozens of videos that focus on lowrider car shows and material derived from *Lowrider* magazine content. *The Lowrider Experience* provides an excellent example of this kind of video; it is about the 2002 lowrider show at the Los Angeles Sports Arena, a significant achievement because the show had not been held in this large and impressive a venue for several years. The video about the show is hosted by Dean Karns and Ulises "Truucha" Ríos, two prominent figures in the lowrider community. A well-known *Boulevard Magazine* model, Kitana Baker, known as "Cat Fight Girl," appears in many scenes commenting on the show's various events. This video focuses on the hydraulic competition in which car owners in various categories vie for recognition and prize money. Some of the competitions included in the video are the single pump class, in which cars outfitted with one hydraulic pump participate; the double pump, in which owners regularly lift their cars vertically over 120 inches with the hood end in the air and the back bumper resting on the ground; heavier cars that compete in the double hop category; the single pump truck competition; and the dancing competition, in which all of a car's four wheels are lifted off the ground at the same time. The video is interspersed with rapid shots of lowriders in the arena's main exhibit area and of women in very revealing bikinis who seductively dance and briefly reveal their breast and buttocks. The video's soundtrack features rap, hip hop, and contemporary rock music. (Image Entertainment).

FURTHER READING

ACF News Source, www.acfnewsource.org.
Alabama Public Television, www.aptv.org.
Hispanic PR Wire, http://hispanicprwire.com/.
Image Entertainment, www.image-entertainment.com.
Palm Pictures, www.palmpictures.com.
Penland, Paige R. *Lowrider: History, Pride, Culture.* St. Paul, Minnesota: Motorbooks International. 2003.

4

Art

Lowrider cars have been called "cathedrals on wheels," which is an apt description because they, along with trucks, motorcycles, bicycles, and other vehicles, offer artisans and artists many opportunities to exhibit their various talents, just as cathedrals afforded many skilled individuals multiple and varied opportunities to display their talents. Customizers, upholsterers, car body painters, pinstripers, glass etchers, and mural artists who have varying degrees of formal training have used lowrider vehicles since the late 1930s as concrete objects to express their pride, skill, and cultural and artistic values. This chapter provides an overview of lowrider vehicles, first as customized, painted sculptures and then as flat and curved surfaces on which abstract and representational figures are painted. The chapter also provides a discussion of the role of various elements of lowrider art in the artistic works of nonlowrider artists and the inclusion of lowrider vehicles as art in mainstream museum collections and exhibitions.

METAL SCULPTURES

Harry Westergard

Although Southern California became the center after World War II for the customizing of cars (see Chapter 1), it was Harry Westergard from the Sacramento area in Northern California who is generally acknowledged to be the leading early prewar figure in altering standard assembly line cars to become vehicles with distinctive features. The lowrider artist Teen Angel pays homage to Westergard in his column "Cruising Into the Past" in the March 1980 issue of *Lowrider* magazine. Referring to a photograph of a 1936 Ford Roadster included with his article, Teen Angel draws the connection between Westergard and the beginning of the craze among Chicanos in the late 1930s and 1940s to convert cars into works of popular art. Teen Angel "gives credit where credit is due" to this Northern Californian who set an early standard for customizing cars (*Lowrider* March 1980, 11–12).

Born in 1916, Westergard moved with his family from Michigan to Sacramento, the capital of California, in the late 1920s or early 1930s. In the late 1930s, he began customizing cars in a converted chicken coop next to his family home. One of his first modified cars was a Ford Model A roadster that was known locally more for its speed than its appearance. His car customizing efforts were temporarily put on hold during the war years from about 1941 to 1945, but then, soon after the war ended, he formed a car club, aptly named the Capitol Auto Club, that eventually changed its name to the Thunderbolt Car Club. It is thought that this car club became the first lowrider club anywhere. Teen Angel, who claims to have conducted extensive research on Westergard for his article, quotes a friend who describes Westergard as a very inventive but humble and selfless person who was "the first to do a lot of things, but he never worried about getting credit for his ideas. He was a good man" (*Lowrider* March 1980, 12).

Teen Angel also discovered in his research that Westergard was a generous mentor who cared about young people. He would welcome them to hang out with him in his backyard shop, where he would teach them about the finer points of auto mechanics and especially customizing cars. An essential part of his customizing was to remove all the accessories, including the hood ornaments and factory chrome, from a car in order to give it a "smooth" look, which he then enhanced by filling in the seams on the car with lead or metal from melted clothes hangers. Teen Angel credits Westergard with inventing a special custom door, making smooth hood sides and grille panels by hand, and installing commercially manufactured fender skirts over

The interior of a lowrider car exhibited at a lowrider show. (Courtesy Anne Tatum)

the rear wheels. He would also remove the running boards and install frame rail covers in order to give a car a desired low, wide look. Jumping ahead a few years, Teen Angel describes how many of these modifications became the basis for the 1950s lowrider cruiser look, but he differentiates between Westergard's inventiveness in creating these changes and accessories from scratch and what lowriders could later purchase in auto supply stores, including smooth hood side panels and custom grilles (*Lowrider* March 1980, 12).

One of Westergard's best-known cars was a brand new 1950 Mercury that he customized for a celebrity who had brought the factory version of the car to the customizer's shop. Over the next couple of years, Westergard converted the Mercury into a classy chrome-stripped custom car painted cherry red with a lowered body, a modified white convertible top, large white-wall tires, teardrop custom fenders, a fancy grille, and twin spotlights mounted on each side of the car. He lowered or "chopped" the windshield about 3 inches and modified the hood to look like the prow of a ship. The car was shown at the first Autorama show in Sacramento in 1950 (*How Stuff Works*).

Westergard died tragically in an automobile accident in 1956 when he was driving his new "souped up" 1955 Ford Thunderbird, already equipped for speed, at over 100 miles an hour on a narrow road outside of Sacramento. A car pulled out in front of him; he swerved but was unable to avoid hitting a tree. His car came apart and he died instantly. Thousands of mourners attended his funeral, and most of them in their own customized cars formed part of the funeral caravan to his final resting place in a Sacramento cemetery.

George Barris

Westergard's fame as a pioneering customizer continued, and many of his innovations spread to Southern California and from there to other parts of the Southwest in the 1950s and 1960s. Teen Angel credits George and Sam Barris, two of the many high school–age youngsters who learned from Westergard in Sacramento, with carrying on with some of their mentor's custom ideas and then building on and popularizing them in the Los Angeles area. Teen Angel recalls in his March 1980 *Lowrider* magazine article that when he was in high school in the 1950s, George especially was highly revered among his teenage peers who were beginning to get into the lowrider scene. "He was the king of customizers in Southern California . . . the one who spread the popularity of his chopped down '49 Merc creations in the magazines and car shows. He was the one everybody copied back in the fifties" (*Lowrider* March 1980, 12).

The Barris brothers were born in Chicago in the 1920s, George in 1928. They moved to the Sacramento area as children to live with relatives after both of their parents died. The brothers were good at school subjects and George excelled in drawing class. George won awards when he was only a high school student for building aircraft model planes from scratch and then won competitions for construction and design. Their relatives gave them an old family 1925 Buick to which they devoted many hours of mechanical repair and of changes to the body; this was the first of many custom cars that they would build together before each brother went his own way after the Second World War. George, who excelled as a budding artist, painted the car in orange with blue stripes. His first fully built custom car was a 1936 Ford convertible, which he sold to an eager customer. He soon formed the Kustoms Car Club; the "K" was to become associated with George for the rest of his life (www.barris.com).

Barris moved to Los Angeles in 1944, where he soon opened his first shop in one of many of the city's growing suburbs. After serving in the military during the war, Sam joined him in Los Angeles, and they opened an expanded business, Barris Brothers Custom Shop, in Compton. Sam excelled at metal craftsmanship and George at design and paint. They exhibited their first custom car at a hot rod show sponsored by *Hot Rod Magazine*'s founder Robert "Pete" Petersen, who later established the Petersen Automotive Museum in Los Angeles. The reaction to the Barris brothers' entry in the show was very positive.

The establishment of several new automotive magazines, including *Hot Rod Magazine*, allowed George to write about and publish his photos on customized cars. Particularly popular were his articles that demonstrated clear and easy-to-understand techniques for customizing cars. He also spread his influence among lowriders when he bought and customized a new two-door Mercury, a model that lowriders held in high esteem. According to Gil Ayala, a Chicano lowrider customizer, Barris's customized Mercury "would spawn a whole generation of 'bathtub' Mercury customs. Gil and his brother Al began customizing this car model in their own body shop in East Los Angeles" (Penland 2003, 14).

The Barris brothers moved their business to Lynwood, another Los Angeles suburb, in the early 1950s, and George, perhaps the more enterprising and savvy of the two brothers, formed Kustoms of Los Angeles, a club that later became and is still known as Kustoms of America. Movie studios around Los Angeles soon began commissioning custom-built Barris cars for their movies, and, seizing on the exposure that this gave the business, George began customizing cars for the stars in Hollywood. He continued his practice of designing custom cars, and others, including some of custom cars' most skilled fabricators and craftsmen, were commissioned by him to turn the designs into finished products.

George designed many signature cars used in movies and television series, including the Batmobile for the *Batman* television series, the Munster Coach for the series *The Munsters*, the truck seen on *The Beverly Hillbillies* series, a modified roadster for the *Mannix* series, and a car for the 1965 movie comedy *My Mother the Car*. He has also designed vehicles for Hollywood stars including Bob Hope, Bing Crosby, Ann-Margaret, John Wayne, Dean Martin, Glen Campbell, Sonny and Cher, Elton John, and Elvis Presley.

CUSTOM PAINTING

Early customizers such as Westergard, the Barris brothers, and Ayala all became extremely knowledgeable about painting the surfaces of hot rods, lowriders, or cars customized for celebrities. Since the 1960s, car painting has become more sophisticated and more complex. Car owners have had the option to commission professionals to paint

An elaborately designed side panel on a lowrider car. (Courtesy Anne Tatum)

their cars in body shops, or they themselves have learned about various techniques to achieve different results. In any case, the steps followed to prepare a car body for painting, the selection of custom paints, and the techniques of applying the paint to the car's surfaces demand great skill and patience.

Basic to custom painting any car, including a lowrider car, is the preparation of the vehicle's various surfaces. The custom painter must first decide whether to strip down the existing paint in order to expose the car's bare metal, fiberglass, or plastic surface. This decision depends on the number and condition of the layers of paint (topcoat, undercoat, primer, sealer, and filler) that cover the surface and on the condition of the metal itself. Many custom painters prefer to strip down all layers just to be satisfied that the basic surface has no rust or dents that have gone undetected. However, if the factory-applied paint and other layers are in good shape or stable without bubbling, cracking, or peeling, it may be a waste of time and even counterproductive to do a more thorough paint stripping.

It is difficult for a custom painter to replicate techniques such as baking or chemical bonding that factories use to apply sealers, undercoats, and topcoats. However, because it is much more common for a lowrider to customize an older vehicle—an older model increases the incidence of aging paint, dents, and even rust—the customizer may not have the option to forgo a more thorough stripping away of various layers. In order to improve the car's overall painted surface, dents must be eliminated, rust spots must be sanded out, and filler material must be applied where necessary. One expert sets forth the basics of custom car painting as follows: (1) prepare, align, and sand the car's surface so that it is completely straight and smooth; (2) paint all surfaces better than the factory did; (3) once the custom paint has been applied, sand the surface perfectly smooth and then buff it to a high luster and gloss (Ganahl 2008, 31).

Originally, custom painters in the 1940s and 1950s preferred lacquer paint over enamel paint, the only two kinds of paint available as car paints at that time. Paint and body repair shops preferred enamel because it dried faster and was more durable than lacquer, which dried harder. Customizers chose lacquer because, even though it was more labor intensive, they could sand the hard dried surface to a glass-like finish. Lacquer paint continued to be preferred particularly when other paint enhancements and effects began to be used, because clearcoats could be sprayed over base coats such as metallics and pearls, giving a deeper look to the paint job and allowing the lacquer clearcoat to be sanded and rubbed without disturbing the coats below it. A disadvantage of the lacquer-based paint used first by customizers was that it was chemically unstable and could eat through and cause lifting and wrinkling of the layers below it. Lacquer was eventually replaced by urethanes, epoxies, and other surfaces that produce a broad spectrum of color choices and special effects. They are stronger and adhere better than lacquer clearcoats and do not yellow over time. Also available to custom painters today are what are described as "catalyzed, chemically linking" primers, sealers, and paints, which prevent a topcoat from eating through layers below it and vice versa.

Today's custom painters need to be more technically sophisticated that their counterparts of even the 1970s. Today's paints, which produce better-adhering, more durable finishes, are also chemically complex and require the user to have precise knowledge about things like mixing ratios, temperature control, and set times before and after more layers of paint can be applied. In general, today's paints are significantly trickier to apply. Lowrider owners today can select from a variety of car painting options to improve on the factory-applied paint chosen by the car company during the manufacturing of the vehicle. These options include the following applications: straight painting, pearl painting, candy apple painting, and metal-flake and micro-sequin applications. Straight painting starts with selecting a color from a wide palette available from different paint companies that specialize in custom paints, that is, paints that are generally different from those applied by manufacturers. This process is similar to selecting exterior and interior colors for a house and its various rooms. Prior to spray painting a vehicle, its surfaces have to be prepared following the afore-mentioned steps.

Car owners often work with color matchers who can match as closely as possible a preferred color with the color that will eventually cover the surface of a car. Color matching is sometimes done visually by an experienced matcher but can also be done by a spectrometer machine that is found in better-stocked paint and body shops. The opaque colors black and blue are often chosen because they require fewer coats than those colors that are less opaque, such as white, yellow, orange, and red. Requiring less paint, opaque colors are often chosen because they make a paint job less expensive. Lowrider cars that have received straight painting applications come in all shades of custom colors including white, green, black, red, blue, yellow and orange. In addition to these solid colors, lowrider owners often select what are described as metallic paints, or simply "metallics," which are a variation on the solid custom colors mentioned in that they are solid colors to which a certain amount of small metallic particles have been added. A clearcoat paint is often applied over the metallic paint in order to rub or sand the exterior coat to a high gloss without damaging the metallic coat below it. Metallics give the surface of the car a slightly silvery sparkle, especially when outside on a sunny day or inside a lowrider show lit by bright lights.

Pearl painting gives a lowrider car a certain hue or elegance. Originally, a pearl paint was prepared by mixing of precise amount of thick paste, often composed of ground fish scales, into a gallon of clear paint. This produced a classic white pearl color, but later pastel shades imitating fruit colors such peach, tangerine, lime, lemon, and grape were produced by mixing in different pastes. Today, a wide variety of pearl shades are available in premixed form available at car paint stores. In terms of application, because pearl paints are transparent, care must be taken to apply various layers of them over a solid color layer that has been previously applied without flaws. Clearcoat layers are then sprayed over the pearl paint layers so that, once dry, the car's surface can be sanded and buffed to a high luster.

Candy apple paint was in the 1950s only available in red when its similarity to one shade of the red fruit gave it its name. Joe Bailon is usually credited with inventing and perfecting the red paint in 1956. He experimented with different paints and powders to come up with a red that had the same color as a car's taillight. He finally achieved his desired color when one day when he mixed some maroon dye with gold paint. Today, candy paint is available in greens, blues, reds, oranges, and yellows. Like pearl paint, candy paint is semitransparent, and it is normally painted over a light, bright, sparkly base color such as silver or gold. It has both a sparkle and rich depth when properly applied. Its color spectrum, which has the full range of candy colors, has been described as "pretty, fun, fanciful, and even somewhat magical" (Ganahl 2008, 46).

Despite its unique qualities, candy paint is difficult to apply because it requires a base color underneath it and a clearcoat paint on top of it, thus requiring more materials, time, steps, and expertise. It is more transparent than pearl paint, so the base color surface below it has to be flawless; any sanding scratches, filler pits, blotches, streaks, or mottling in the base color coat will show through. Spraying candy paint also requires a high degree of experience and skill, mainly because its uneven application will result in some areas being darker than others. Unlike pearl paint, candy paints require several layers that have to be gradually built up, a process that increases the chances of making an error. Despite the difficulty in working with candy paints, it is common to see them on higher-end lowrider vehicles, including cars, trucks, and motorcycles, at lowrider shows.

The addition of dry metal flakes and micro-sequins to clear paint is an embellishment that became popular in the early 1960s among the custom car crowd and eventually among lowriders. "Metalflake," which was invented and patented as a product by Dow Chemical Company, is made in different colors from aluminum foil that is cut into tiny squares or from plastic-like Mylar film. Metal flakes are all very small but they can be as big as 1/8 inch. They also come in various shapes such as round flakes, stars, and hearts. Generally, painters try to match the color of the selected flakes to a usually metallic basecoat, but there are other application methods as well. "MicroSequins," also a patented product, are Mylar or plastic-based particles that are usually clearer and smaller than metal flakes. They can be applied as part of a clearcoat sprayed over a metallic or pearl-colored base coat (Ganahl 2008, 62).

A lowrider's knowledge of primers, topcoats, and clearcoat paints, as well as of the various applications described briefly, is essential to the creation of a smooth, lush, and distinctive external surface of a lowrider vehicle. The time-consuming work of spraying on different coats designed to produce a desired look requires the patience and talent of any respected artist, regardless of the medium. The result of painting a lowrider vehicle can be an artistic end in itself, just as a

> "Modern automobiles need some human element on them. Without it they look like they've been grounded out by a mechanical monster—which they have! I treat striping brushes like a musical instrument and whatever I stripe becomes a melody." (Von Dutch)

sculptor produces a marble, iron, or fiberglass work that stands out for its distinctive artistic and aesthetic qualities. The painted car can also function as a surface like a canvas or a wall that is only the first phase in creating the work of art on which others who are more skilled at drawing can paint designs and lettering as well as abstract and representational figures.

DESIGNS AND ABSTRACT FIGURES

The painting of designs on vehicles dates back as far as Romans, who painted stripes on their chariots; in the modern era designs were often painted on smooth, painted surfaces such as sewing machines, safes, and appliances such as refrigerators, stoves, and washing machines. On these surfaces, the painted lines followed the contours of the object being decorated, but freestyle designs on cars became hugely popular in the United States in the 1950s (Stecyk 1993, 20).

Von Dutch

Two of the most popular figures to be painted on lowrider cars were pinstripes and flames, both commonly associated with Von Dutch (born Kenneth Howard in 1929), who grew up in the Maywood area of southeast Los Angeles. Von Dutch acquired many of his early skills in his father's sign painting shop, where he began painting designs at a professional level by the time he was 10 years old. He was a talented musician and track and field star in high school who began as a teenager devoting more and more of his time to pinstriping and "flaming" the hot rods and other custom vehicles that had become so popular in Los Angeles in the late 1940s and early 1950s.

Early on, Von Dutch worked in the Barris brothers' Barris Kustoms shop, where car owners would bring their vehicles to be customized. Von Dutch became known for painting pinstripes (fine lines painted by hand using a "dagger" brush) on cars with sloppy body work in order to cover over the blemishes with original decorative designs.

He also began painting flames not only on cars but also on other vehicles like fire trucks that he had been commissioned to customize. After he became better known, if an owner wanted a car custom striped, it was common to ask for it to be "Dutched." Von Dutch also became known as an artist in his own right; several of his surrealistic paintings were exhibited in local galleries. Von Dutch and others who learned from him perfected pinstripes, flames, and other lettering by adding them freehand over a car's topcoat. Whether he was adding pinstripes, flames, or other designs to a car or painting on canvas, he strictly adhered to his own high artistic values and standards. His unique style of lettering would become a popular standard among customizers and lowriders of the 1970s.

Larry Watson

Larry Watson was one of the young Los Angeles car painters that Von Dutch inspired. Not only did he perfect the preparation and painting of custom car surfaces but he also became accomplished at painting designs, including his signature "Seaweed Flames," which were typically more sinewy, serpentine, and undulating than normal flames. He was born in 1939 in Los Angeles, and by the time he was 17 he had opened his first shop, Watson's House of Style, in north Long Beach. He is generally thought to be the first custom painter to paint designs along the full length of a car, a touch that made the car look sleeker and more elegant. Such a design, known as "scallops," is very popular today among lowriders. Watson painted or striped many luxury or sports cars for actors, directors, producers, and others involved in the Hollywood film industry. He soon left behind his custom painting business to become a budding television and film actor, appearing in over 141 different shows such as "Columbo" and "Mission Impossible" between 1967 and 1985 (Kustomrama).

Chicano Painters

Watson mentored several Chicano custom car painters who painted lowriders in the Los Angeles area from the 1960s through the 1980s. Other Chicano painters, such as Rubén "Buggs" Ochoa, got their start working alongside Chicano car upholsterers and body shop owners such as Gil Ayala. Still others, including Mario López, "Big Ed" Madrigal, Gary Baca and Benny Flores, established their own reputations early on and mentored a second generation of Chicano lowrider painters in the 1970s, some of whom are still practicing their craft in the Los Angeles area. Later, in the 1980s, two of the most respected Chicano lowrider painters were Bob Mercado, of Bob and Son's, and Mario Martínez (Penland 2003, 27–28, 107–108).

Lowrider magazine has recognized Rubén "Buggs" Ochoa as a member of "The Official Low Rider Hall of Fame." The magazine called him one of the best custom painters to emerge from East Los Angeles. He received a Craftsmanship Honor for more than three decades of creating his unique painting style on lowrider and other custom cars. Ochoa became interested in customized cars as a boy, and as a teenager in the late 1960s he began picking up work in body and custom shops, developing his skills in high school shop classes. His first paint job was a Volkswagen "Bug," which explains how he acquired the nickname, "Buggs," for which he is best known. He remembers hanging around the Klique lowrider club, two of whose members were future state senator Gil Cedillo and future Los Angeles mayor Antonio Villaraigosa, who owned a 1965 Chevy Malibu. Los Angeles–area lowrider clubs such Groupe Car Club began commissioning Ochoa to paint their cars in preparation for showing them at car shows. One of the cars he painted, a 1966 Pontiac LeMans, appeared on a cover of *Lowrider* magazine and was also part of a 2000 exhibition at the Petersen Automotive

A lowrider on display at the Petersen Automotive Museum in Los Angeles. (AP Photo/Ric Francis)

Museum in Los Angeles. Always the meticulous and perfectionist craftsman, Ochoa told the magazine that prepping a car is essential for any painter who wishes to produce quality paint jobs. Most recently, Ochoa has developed a video series in English and Spanish on automotive painting, particularly custom paint schemes. He also showcases some of the lowrider and other custom cars that have been awarded prizes at car shows since the mid-1990s.

Design Application Techniques

While pinstripes are generally painted freehand on lowrider vehicles, scallops, panels, and other designs are almost always applied using a spray gun and a technique called tape masking. The painter or designer typically lays out a design on a car's side, fender, or hood panel by using tape to make a custom pattern over a painted surface. More experienced and professional designers can either sketch a design on a car with a layout sketching utensil called a Stabilo pencil or using an expensive masking tape that comes in different widths. The shape of designs is dictated by the shape and lines of a vehicle's body. Once the design is sketched out, all the other areas of the vehicle

A fully customized 1957 Chevy Bel Air with beautifully painted side panel murals. (PRNewsFoto/Primedia)

must be masked off before applying spray paint over the sketched-out areas. The artful application of paint with a spray gun requires a great deal of experience, knowledge, and touch similar to, for example, a painter creating a landscape with nuanced colors. Once the paint has been sprayed and allowed to dry, the tape is peeled off, revealing the design below. A clearcoat paint is then usually applied over the entire surface of the car to protect the custom design as well as the topcoat paint that was previously applied.

Some lowriders cars exhibited at car shows commonly have other designs, including cobwebs, marbling, and old lace. These designs require different applications. For example, an old lace pattern is applied by spraying over a pattern of thin lace material such as a lace used for bridal veils. The material, which is readily available at a fabric store, is cut out to fit the size of the area of the car that the designer wishes to cover with an old lace pattern. Other designs are applied using a variety of templates, cutouts, waxes, cloths, or other design materials that paint can be sprayed through (Ganahl 2008, 104–105).

UPHOLSTERERS

Already in the late 1950s and the 1960s, custom painters began to concentrate on the interiors of cars, especially the upholstery. Initially, customizers would send the car owners to Tijuana, across the U.S.-Mexico border from San Diego, where a very good *tapcicero* (upholsterer) could do a good "nip and tuck" for $100 or less or other, more elegant options for more. Soon, Chicano upholsterers began to open up shops in the Los Angeles area and gradually began to do most of the upholstery work for the higher-end customizers. One, Eddie Martínez, became famous for his interiors such as the installation of swiveling bucket seats accented with chrome and silver piping. He installed an upholstered television and telephone in one custom car, which was innovative at the time but would become common on high-end lowriders in the coming decades. Watson worked with Martínez on many custom car projects and later with Joe Pérez. Upholsterers such as Martínez and Pérez did high-level, detailed interior developing styles that would soon become standard for lowrider owners who could afford their work (Penland 2003, 14).

REPRESENTATIONAL FIGURES

Most of the designs painted on lowrider vehicles are abstract, that is, they are not intended to depict objects such as people, landscapes, or

An interesting upholstery design for the interior of a lowrider vehicle. (Courtesy Anne Tatum)

recognizable symbols that the viewer would relate to the physical world. These designs are created completely independent of such visual representations; instead, the designs are combinations of color and shape. On the other hand, many lowrider owners have chosen to paint or have painted on their cars representational figures that need not be literal representations of these objects. These figures may symbolize or suggest ideas and concepts such as cultural pride, religious beliefs, death, and evil.

Mexican and Chicana/o Wall Muralists

Although abstract designs were common on lowrider cars as early as the 1950s, representational figures did not become popular until the mid-1960s. These figures are often referred to as car murals, and they began appearing about the same time as Chicana/o artists were painting murals on walls and other flat surfaces in East Los Angeles and in other urban barrios in public locations such as housing projects and Chicano arts centers. Chicano mural art eventually spread across California, the Southwest, and wherever there were significant concentrations of Americans of Mexican descent.

Chicana/o muralists were directly inspired by the Mexican muralist movement that flourished in Mexico after the end of the Mexican

Revolution about 1920. Many Mexican painters who had been trained in the finest art schools in Mexico and Europe turned away from so-called studio art that emphasized the mastery of traditional painting on canvas destined to be sold to private collectors and museums. The vast majority of the Mexican population had up to this point been kept from viewing these works of art because museums and galleries were not made accessible to them. Painters like Diego Rivera, who returned from a prolonged period of formal study to offer his services to the new revolutionary government that enthusiastically supported him and his counterparts, carried out plans to paint large murals with social and political messages on the walls of public buildings open to the masses of Mexican people, especially those from the poor sectors of society.

Encouraged by José Vasconcelos, the new minister of education, who was intent on encouraging renaissance in Mexico and promoting a strong sense of nationalism, Rivera and other prominent artists such as David Alfaro Siqueiros and José Clemente Orozco set about the task of covering the exterior walls of buildings such as the Secretariat of Public Education and the National Preparatory School in Mexico City's central district. Rivera's murals are best displayed in the National Palace, which is located on the Zócalo, Mexico City's central plaza, where the National Cathedral is also located. His murals, which cover the walls of the massive central staircase, depict the liberation of the poor Mexican Indian and mestizo population from successive colonialist Spanish governments as well as from the recent political dictatorship of Porfirio Díaz, who had welcomed foreign influence. Significantly,*Street Low Magazine*, a popular lowrider publication, carried a short but very informative overview of Rivera's artistic career, including his sojourn in the United States, where he painted murals in San Francisco, Detroit, and New York. Tlecu Omitl, the article's author, states that Rivera "is seen as one of the most influenced [sic] person in Mexican history" (*Street Low Magazine*).

The Mexican mural movement influenced the development of public art in the United States. Some of these artists received financial support from the Works Progress Administration, a government agency created during the presidency of Franklin D. Roosevelt. During the political upheaval in this country in the 1960s and the 1970s, the heyday of the Chicano movement, Chicana/o artists turned to Mexican muralism to inspire their commitment to giving artistic expression to their political and ideological beliefs. Rivera, Orozco, and Siqueiros had all come to the United States in 1920s, 1930s, and 1940s to paint commissioned murals and to lecture at museums and universities, but Chicana/o muralists were attracted to their art as a part of a general

A mural painted on the inside of the hood of a lowrider car. (Courtesy Anne Tatum)

renewed interest in Mexico, especially indigenous Mexico, that occurred among Chicano movement activists. Unlike Mexican muralism, which was supported by a revolutionary government that gave muralists access to public buildings, Chicana/o murals were painted in predominantly Chicano barrios and working-class neighborhoods in outdoor public spaces such as parks, housing projects, and community centers (Jackson 2009, 75).

Chicana/o artists used the mural to bypass the mainstream cultural "gatekeepers" who dictated what aesthetic and artistic currents and themes were acceptable for consideration to be included in gallery and museum exhibits and collections. Murals created by Chicana/o artists not only reclaimed public places and encouraged community participation on the part of individuals who perhaps had received no formal artistic training; they also provided the visual imagery for the wider community's civil rights struggles while reclaiming their people's cultural heritage and identity (Barnet-Sánchez & Sperling 1990).

Lowrider Muralists

The recovery of and renewed pride in Mexican Indian, indigenous, and mestizo cultural heritage was often expressed through the incorporation of Aztec and Mayan historical figures and religious icons and symbols such the Virgin of Guadalupe, Mexico's most important religious figure. Mexico's revolutionary past of the early twentieth century was often invoked through images of revolutionary heroes such as Emiliano Zapata and Pancho Villa and, from the nineteenth century, Father Miguel Hidalgo and Benito Juárez, who had led their own earlier revolutions. These indigenous, religious, and historical images have been commonly represented on lowrider cars. The Chicana/o muralist movement has clearly inspired lowrider murals, and the images painted on cars reflect the social concerns represented by the images and symbols painted on walls, perhaps because some lowriders of especially the 1960s and 1970s were as politically and culturally aware as the Chicana/o wall muralists. Although less so today, some lowrider murals continue to portray social, political, and cultural themes. The owners and the artists who paint the murals also have in common with the Mexican muralists and their Chicana/o counterparts the "idea that the ultimate destination of a material object of artistic creativity should be the public domain and not some secluded gallery or private collection" (Gradante 1985, 74).

Lowrider mural painters use an airbrush to paint figures on exterior and interior faces of hoods and trunks, front and rear door panels, the thick panel that separates the exterior and interior part of a door, roof panels, front and rear fender panels, fender skirts, and instrument panels. Figures also appear within the motor compartment itself, usually on the smooth firewall that has a paintable surface. Airbrushing is different from spray painting, and airbrushes differ from spray guns. The former uses much less pressure, and the paint emitted is controlled by a trigger on the top of the gun that is manipulated with tip of the painter's forefinger. The air brush gun is a sensitive instrument that requires great skill to manipulate correctly to achieve the desired result of painting a recognizable figure on different parts of a car's surface.

Lowrider Mural Themes

Most lowrider mural art includes images that depict Mexican Indian themes; Mexican revolutionary themes; Mexican and Chicana/o religious themes; gangsters, crime, and violence; cinematic, nightmarish themes; and women. Some other murals subjects are not common enough to merit a separate category, yet they are interesting thematically and artistically.

An essential aspect of the Chicano movement was the recuperation of a culture and historical memory that was thought to have been lost beginning in 1848 when Mexico ceded to the United States a large part of its northern territory as a consequence of losing the mid–nineteenth century Mexican-American War. The erasure of this history and culture accelerated over the next 100 years as more Americans of Mexican descent became assimilated into mainstream Anglo-American society. To revive this historical and cultural heritage, Chicano movement activists, writers, and artists strove to renew interest, knowledge, and pride in their indigenous Mexican Indian roots, especially Aztec culture and civilization. Figures of Aztec princes, warriors, and maidens as well as pyramids and smoldering volcanoes were common in Chicana/o wall murals of the 1960s and 1970s, and they very soon began appearing as murals on lowrider cars, where they still continue to appear.

A stunning example of an indigenous figure is found on Jorge and Rosa Salazar's 1978 Ford Thunderbird lowrider, aptly named "Azteca." The mural, which stretches over the entire area of both sides of the car, is painted in vibrant yellows, reds, and oranges against a dark green topcoat. The mural depicts a young, muscular Aztec warrior dressed in a decorated, plumed helmet and a beautifully adorned cape reaching out to seize an enraged, fanged rattlesnake off of a cactus. The serpent and the cactus are standard Mexican icons found on the Mexican flag, and they symbolize the national legend of the founding of ancient Mexico. According to this legend, the Aztec nation would be founded where wandering tribes from the north would come across a serpent perched on a cactus. This place was Tenochtitlán, the ancient Aztec capital—today's Mexico City—which would become Mexico's most important city and capital. The helmet worn by the warrior has long, unfurled feathers suggesting Quetzalcoatl ("feathered serpent" in the Nahua indigenous language), a key Aztec deity associated with life, earth, and fertility.

Although not quite as elaborate as this mural, it is common to see lowriders at car shows today adorned with Aztec figures and gods. For example, at the October 2009 Las Vegas Lowrider Supershow, Quetzalcoatl and other Aztec gods were painted along the side of a curved hood on a Chevrolet truck. At the September 2009 lowrider show in Phoenix, a menacing Aztec warrior in full headdress was painted on a narrow door panel and an Aztec maiden with a helmet was depicted on another door panel. Other Aztec figures seen on lowrider cars in the Dallas area are of an Aztec princess and an Aztec warrior with a maiden in his arms.

All of the Aztec figures discussed here are well drawn and are similar to the figures found on Mexican calendars made famous by the Mexican artist Jesús Helguera, who was most productive in the 1940s and 1950s. It is common to see these calendars hung in traditional Mexican restaurants. Restaurants and other Chicana/o-owned businesses such as barrio grocery stores, liquor stores, and bakeries often give the calendars as gifts to their best customers, who might typically hang them in their kitchens. Many Chicanas/os grew up viewing these prototypical Aztec figures of legendary warrior kings and warriors with muscular physiques, often rescuing young, scantily dressed, and sultry Aztec maidens from some danger. *Low Rider Arte* magazine carries an article on its website on Helguera in which the writer, Benjamín Francisco Hernández, pays tribute to the artist and invokes his fond memories of growing up with Helguera's images, including rural scenes inhabited by Mexican *campesinos* (peasants) and images of erupting volcanoes. Also on the magazine's website is a hood panel mural by Chicano artist David "Bigg Shadow" Ibarra in which a stylized Aztec warrior looks stoically at a dying or dead Aztec maiden with exposed breasts who lies in his arms. This is definitely a more risqué version of the calendar art depictions, an image not likely to be found hanging on the walls of most Chicana/o family homes (*Lowrider Arte*).

Different manifestations of Mexican revolutionary scenes have been popular lowrider mural subjects since the mid-1960s. As with the reassessment of Mexican indigenous culture, the Chicano movement's political agenda included a reevaluation and reappropriation of Mexico's revolutionary past that resulted in an idealization of some of Mexico's revolutionary heroes, including Father Miguel Hidalgo, who is associated with the first attempts to liberate Mexico from Spain in the early nineteenth century; Benito Juárez, Mexico's first indigenous president, who drove the French out and introduced a liberal democracy in the 1860s; Emiliano Zapata, a revolutionary leader from the state of Madero who is credited with agrarian and land reform; and Pancho Villa, the fearless leader from Chihuahua who led a band of mounted soldiers on guerrilla raids against opposing armies and defied a U.S. Army expeditionary force sent to Mexico to capture him after his raid on Columbus, New Mexico in 1916.

Zapata and Villa appear as lowrider murals more often than Hidalgo and Juárez. For example, at the 2009 Las Vegas show, a classic photograph of Zapata and Villa seated together at a meeting of revolutionary leaders in Mexico City's National Palace dominates an entire side window of a lowrider van. At the same show, a mural of Zapata appears on a hood panel with "Revolucionario" (Revolutionary) lettering above him and a Mexican flag with the emblem of the serpent and the cactus integrated into the background. At the 2009 Phoenix show, a sexy and seductively dressed *revolucionaria* (a female revolutionary) is depicted on a hood panel holding a Mexican flag and peering out defiantly at the viewer with her hands on her hips. Women known as *soldaderas* did participate as combatants in the revolutionary armies, and some rose to prominence for their bravery and leadership. At the same show, a *revolucionaria* appears as a mural on a hood panel. She wears gun belts crossed over her bosom showing her ferocity as an armed soldier. She wears a hat with the lettering *Phoenix* across its front, indicating that the lowrider car represents a Phoenix lowrider club. On either side of the woman soldier is a stylized face, one crying and one laughing, symbolizing the triumphs and sorrows of the Mexican Revolution of 1910.

Another mural by David "Bigg Shadow" Ibarra that adorns the underside hood panel shows a male revolutionary in a bar accompanied by a seductive young woman with a bow in her hair. The man, who has a Zapata-like drooping moustache, bears the prototypical crossed gun belts and large *charro* hat. He holds a smoking rifle in his right hand as though he is taking a break from battle in the company of a young woman in a bar. Another of Ibarra's murals, also on the underside hood panel, pictures a *soldadera* with a large *charro* hat and crossed gun belts covering her breasts. She is holding a cocked pistol in her right hand. Her facial expression is one of narrowed eyes and pursed lips, probably meant to convey a battle-hardened demeanor (*Lowrider Arte*).

Religious themes and images were not common in Mexican muralism, but they are popular in Chicana/o muralism and in lowrider mural art. Two Catholic religious figures predominate: Jesus in various incarnations, such as the *corazón sangrante* (Sacred Heart of Jesus), the suffering Christ who according to Christian belief sacrificed himself so that humans could be saved; and the Virgin of Guadalupe, who plays a central role in Mexican and Chicana/o religious culture. Usually when a Christ figure is depicted on a vehicle, other religious items or symbols are found elsewhere on the vehicle.

A variation on the suffering Christ theme was captured in a 1990s photograph taken in Los Angeles by Brenda Jo Bright in which a beautifully painted lowrider is parked in a liquor store parking lot where what are presumably ghetto gangbangers and other criminals are standing around the car. A mural of the Sacred Heart is painted on the liquor store wall looking down sympathetically on the scene in the parking lot. The presence of a beneficent Jesus figure serves to invoke a silent prayer for deliverance from worldly evil and salvation (Bright 1994, 104).

In a series of photographs taken by Bright in Chimayó, a village just a few miles from Española, the small northern New Mexico city that has a heavy concentration of lowriders, Bright notes that there is a prevalence of lowrider cars with religious-themed murals with images of Jesus and the Virgin of Guadalupe, in part because Chimayó is the site of the Santuario, the sanctuary church that is visited each year by thousands of Catholic pilgrims hoping to have their prayers and petitions answered. It is thought that the dirt from this sacred spot has curative powers. In one photograph, Bright captures a white 1975 Cadillac called "Low Rider Heaven" that has the head of Jesus painted on its trunk panel. When asked about the name of the car and the image, the owner Arthur Medina explained that "I put on it what I feel." He simply felt better about painting the religious mural on the car rather than a random secular image like a knight because within the popular religious tradition of Chimayó the image was more compelling (Bright 1994, 126–127).

The figure of the Virgin of Guadalupe is much more common than the Christ figure in lowrider mural art. She is said to have appeared to a poor Mexican Indian, Juan Pablo, in 1531 on a hill close to Mexican city of Cholula, which is located south of Mexico City in the state of Puebla. Part of the religious legend surrounding the multiple appearances of the Virgin to Juan Pablo is that she directed him to go gather roses in a place where roses did not grow and to deliver the roses to a skeptical Catholic bishop as proof that the appearances were real. Roses are frequently included in religious images of the Virgin. Mexican and Chicana/o Catholics often pray to the Virgin, asking her to intercede on their behalf with her son, Jesus. The figure of the Virgin was prominent in the iconography associated with the César Chávez and Dolores Huerta–led United Farm Workers (UFW), which played an important role in the Chicano movement of the 1960s and 1970s. Banners with the figures of the Virgin were prominent at the front of UFW's rallies, demonstrations, parades, and marches.

A good example of a lowrider mural of the Virgin of Guadalupe was found at the 2009 Las Vegas show. The mural of the hood panel of the car depicts Juan Pablo praying to the Virgin, and roses are displayed on another panel. On the same car there is a mural of two scantily clad women in seductive poses. Bright has photographed the image of the Virgin of Guadalupe on a lowrider car in Chimayó. The mural adorns the hood panel of a 1959 Ford El Camino, which is now part of the Smithsonian Museum's permanent collection in Washington, D.C. (Bright 1994, 128).

In addition to individual religious murals found on lowrider cars, there are entire car clubs whose main purpose it is to form a tight religious community of like-minded lowriders who are expected to adhere

A Virgin of Guadalupe mural painted on the hood of a lowrider vehicle.
(Courtesy Anne Tatum)

to certain moral and religious standards. The Redeemed Christian Car
Club of Phoenix is an example. At the September 2009 Phoenix Show,
they proudly displayed their banner with the name of the club and
references to Scripture (Hebrews 4:12, Psalms 34:22, and Ephesians
6:16). Several of the cars clustered around the banner bore quotations
from Scripture on different panels.

In stark contrast to the lowrider murals with religious themes are
murals depicting different aspects of gangsterism and the implied violent world in which gangsters live. In Los Angeles, a 1939 four-door
Chevrolet with a windshield shade, fender skirts, impeccable grille
and chrome work, an elegant hood decoration, and elegant gold- and
silver-chromed hubcaps, named "Gangster of Love," corresponds to
the several car murals painted in the late 1970s by Jesús Mata. The
trunk and hood panels, the rear fender panels, the front side panels,
and the under-hood panel each have a distinct mural that portrays a
gangster theme with 1920s and 1930s gangsters, such as Al Capone's
bank and David Dillinger's saloon, on one side of the car and on the

other side a mural of a caravan of gangster cars cruising down an urban avenue, presumably Whittier Boulevard in East Los Angeles, under a sign reading "Aztlán." The cars are driving past a movie theater featuring *East Side Story,* a late 1970s film that focused on the violent gang activities of lowriders in East Los Angeles. The small mural on a rear wheel skirt is of the car's owner and his friends dressed in suits, nice hats, and shiny shoes that are implied to be gangster dress because of the overall theme of gangsterism portrayed by the year, model, and other more explicit gangster murals. The owner and a beautiful woman standing together next to his car are depicted on the hood panel. The combination of murals depicting historical gangsters and contemporary Chicanas/os who live *la vida loca* (the crazy, reckless, and sometimes violent life of the barrio) seems to convey an overall defiant message that contemporary American gangsterism is now located in the barrio, where money, sex, drugs, and violence predominate. *La vida loca* is not so much glorified as given legitimacy (Bright 1994, 107).

At least one of the murals on the "Gangster of Love" lowrider refers to a movie, *East Side Story,* that was popular in Los Angeles's barrio theaters when it first came out. This mural suggests a theme seen in the murals of other lowrider cars in Central Los Angeles in the 1990s: the references to current films and film characters that have a nightmarish quality. For example, Freddy Martínez's "Freddy's 3" lowrider, a beautiful red 1963 Chevy convertible, features Freddy Kruger from the horror film series *Nightmare on Elm Street.* Freddy Kruger is a janitor and alleged child murderer who is killed by a group of vigilante parents. Kruger then returns in successive films to haunt the dreams of the parents' children. The mural on the lowrider depicts a sexual nightmare of three scantily clad women. A pair of dark hands—Freddy Kruger's—caresses and constrains the women as a raised razor-fingered glove threatens violence and death (Bright 1997, 23–25).

Scantily clad and seminude women in seductive poses are the most common theme of lowrider murals. Images of buxom and curvaceous women seem to appear on every available panel on cars: hoods, trunks, side panels, doors, fenders, and door jambs. The more provocative images are sometimes painted discretely on the inside hood and trunk panels, but at the car shows it is common to raise the hood and panels or even detach them for better viewing. Women are usually depicted seductively, inviting a gaze from predominantly male viewers. For example, five nude and seminude women appeared on the inside of an open hood panel of a car at the 2009 Phoenix car show. The mural, "Ace of Spades," depicts one woman smoking a cigar, with one her hands holding a fistful of money and the other pulling down her bra strap. An ace of spades card barely covers one of her breasts. Smaller images of money bills and the words "Score" and "Strip Bar" appear in the mural. Even the murals of women in revolutionary garb discussed previously are almost as provocative.

It is also common to have women in tight, revealing two-piece outfits walk the floor of car shows, usually followed by a professional photographer who takes their pictures for future inclusion in *Lowrider* magazine issues, for the magazine's website, or for publicity. (The subject of women in lowrider culture, including their depictions in magazines and roles at car shows and in car clubs will be discussed separate chapters on women, lowrider clubs, and lowrider shows—Chapters 6, 7, and 8 respectively).

LOWRIDER ART TODAY

With the proliferation of lowrider car clubs and car shows in the first decades of the twenty-first century, lowrider artists are in great demand. *Lowrider Arte* magazine and its website are as reliable a way as any to document who some of the outstanding artist are. The magazine, which currently publishes biweekly, encourages readers to submit art for prizes, contests, and inclusion in its pages. Every issue is filled with both black-and-white and color drawings and paintings. The magazine also features emerging and established artists who are known for their car airbrushed mural paintings, window etchings, and in some cases also for their canvas art, "flesh" or tattoo art, T-shirt art ,and art painted on surfaces such as surf boards and tennis shoes. Not all of the artists included in *Lowrider Arte* are versatile in producing drawings in several of these forms. Artists who are primarily or even exclusively tattooists include Mister Cartoon (Mark Machado), Kiki Platas, "Pint," "Krazy Kay," Adrian "Spider" Castrejón, Alan Padilla, and Pedro Alvarez.

David Ibarra is one of the most versatile of the recently featured artists. Best known as "Bigg Shadow," he is accomplished at airbrushing mural art, window etching, and tattooing. He was born in Dallas in 1967 but spent his childhood and adolescence in Sacramento, where he was exposed to, in his words, "the whole Chicano scene." He was inspired by the active lowrider cruising activity in the Sacramento area, which led to his first serious artistic efforts. Growing up in a large family, it was difficult to afford art supplies, so he ended up drawing on paper on an ironing board that could be adjusted to his height. He moved back to Dallas with his family in 1982, where he now lives. Ibarra painted his first car panel mural in 1990, a collage of Aztec figures and scenes.

"The inspiration of my arte is a reflection of my life. Whether family, love, pain, death, religion or my political views, I try and stay true to my arte by using experiences." (David "Bigg Shadow" Ibarra)

He soon began receiving commissions to adorn whole cars with Aztec and other themes, all of it freehand. Today, he continues to be a popular car mural artist, and he also creates designs for tattoos, shoes, and T-shirts (*Lowrider Arte*).

MUSEUM EXHIBITIONS

Lowrider vehicles have been exhibited at a number of museums across the United States, including the Smithsonian Institution's National Museum of American History (NMAH) in Washington, D.C., the Petersen Automotive Museum in Los Angeles, and the UCLA Fowler Museum of Cultural History. The NMAH has a lowrider car, "Dave's Dream," on permanent display in the museum's former Road Transportation hall, and the Petersen Automotive Museum has several lowrider cars in its permanent collection.

"Dave's Dream" is a 1969 Ford LED that Dave Jaramillo of Chimayó, New Mexico, bought from his uncle in 1978. He had hoped to covert the car into a classy lowrider that would compete well at car shows, but he died in a tragic automobile accident the same year. His widow, Irene, and members of his family decided to keep working on the car as a tribute and memorial to Jaramillo. Between 1979 and 1982, it won a number of awards at lowrider regional shows. The Smithsonian Institution acquired the lowrider in 1990, but it was not sent to Washington, D.C. until 1992 and only after Irene, family, and friends had secured the museum's agreement to let skilled artisans and technicians from Albuquerque, Santa Fe, Esapañola, and Chimayó further change the car, including the addition of several layers of acrylic paint to produce the car's iridescent appearance, the installation of a powerful hydraulic system powered by electric pumps in the trunk, the addition of red velour upholstery, and several airbrushed murals of the Jaramillo family. A photomural of the Sanctuary of Chimayó and the assembly of trophies that the car won are displayed with the lowrider (National Museum of American History).

The Petersen Automotive Museum has hosted lowrider vehicle exhibits in 2000 and 2007. The 2000 exhibition, "Arte y estilo: The Lowriding Tradition," is described by *Low Rider Magazine* as "one of the

The famous "Gypsy Road" 1964 Chevrolet Impala on display at the Petersen Automobile Museum in Los Angeles. (AP Photos/Ric Francis)

most comprehensive lowrider exhibitions ever." It attracted many thousands of visitors from across southern California and beyond setting a record on the opening day for museum attendees. The 2007 exhibit, titled "La Vida Lowrider: Cruising the City of Los Angeles," traces the evolution of lowrider culture and draws the connection between the history of lowrider culture and the city of Los Angeles. More than 20 cars were represented in the exhibit including Jesse Valadez's legendary 1964 Chevy Impala, "Gypsy Rose" and musician Ry Cooder's mural-covered 1953 Chevy ice cream truck, "El Chávez Ravine." Also represented were lowrider "euros," such as a 1988 Volkswagen Jetta. There were also several lowrider bicycles and motorcycles. The exhibit's narrative guide emphasized the multi-ethnic nature of lowriding in the twenty-first century and its geographical spread to countries such as Japan and Germany. Photographs documented the history of lowrider culture and style and how lowriding has affected music, fashion and art (Peterson Automotive Museum).

IMAGES OF LOWRIDER CULTURE IN ART

Representations of lowrider culture are found in the works of non-lowrider artists whose work is often exhibited in cultural centers, public and private art museums, and galleries. These representations are also reproduced in published collections of Chicana/o and Latina/o art. These works are not of lesser artistic value, nor do they make a more authentic or profound statement than lowrider art. The art is painted on canvas or surfaces other than cars, trucks, bicycles, or motorcycles. Most of these artists have received at least some formal academic training or have apprenticed with art mentors. Perhaps the best way to differentiate between these artists and the hundreds of lowrider artists is that lowrider art is usually viewed at car shows, at public parks, or on the street, while the work of Chicana/o artists is commonly exhibited at local and regional exhibitions at cultural centers, universities, libraries, and other public venues and to a lesser extent at art museum exhibitions and at private galleries. The Chicana/o wall muralists discussed earlier are an exception; much of their art is displayed in very public places, usually locations in the barrio in full view of interested viewers.

The "Chicano Art: Resistance and Affirmation" (CARA) interpretive exhibition of the Chicano art movement from 1965 to 1985 contained several works with lowrider images and themes. The exhibition, which opened at the UCLA Wright Art Gallery in late 1990, toured for two years through Denver, Albuquerque, San Francisco, Fresno, Tucson, El Paso, Washington, D.C., New York City, and San Antonio. It was by far the largest traveling exhibition of art by Chicana/o artists, and it was generally praised by critics for its comprehensiveness, variety, and quality. Given lowriders' importance as a cultural icon, they were a prominent part of a car show outside the Albuquerque Museum of Art the day the CARA exhibit opened in that city, and a lowrider parade initiated CARA's opening at the El Paso Museum of Art (Gaspar de Alba 1998, footnote 7).

Among the many exhibited works are several images that directly reference lowrider culture: Joe B. Ramos's *Lowrider Couple* dressed in formal pachuco dress; an altar installation by four artists that includes a bumper from a 1957 Chevy, one of the most popular lowrider models; Daniel Gálvez's *Home Girl*, a painting depicting a young Chicana wearing a T-shirt with an image of a blue 1940s Chevy lowrider with the slogan "Do it low and slow"; Judith Baca's untitled photograph of two large charro hats and three young women dressed as beauty queens arrayed on a lowrider car hood; Ricardo Valverde's *Boulevard Night*, a photograph of a young chicana with a rose tattooed on her back standing next to a lowrider; David Avalos's *Hubcap Milagro*, a metal sculpture of a saint mounted on a hubcap; Carlos Santistevan's *Santo Niño de Atocha*, a sculpture of the patron saint of travelers made from welded-together car parts; Gilbert "Magu" Luján's mixed-media installation of a *carrucha* (old car) with lowrider designs and murals; and Carlos Almaraz's painting of a car crash, *West Coast* (Griswold del Castillo, McKenna and Yarbro-Bejarano 1991).

"Chicano Visions: American Painters on the Verge" is another travelling exhibition of Chicana/o art. Although it is not as comprehensive and has not exhibited in as many cities, it presents an impressive array of contemporary works, most of them from the art collection of Cheech Marín, the well-known Chicano actor, performer, philanthropist, and art collector. The exhibition debuted at the San Antonio Museum of Art in 2001 and has since continued to appear at other museums, including the Smithsonian Museum in Washington, D.C., and the Young Museum in San Francisco. The exhibition guide, published as a book in 2002, contains several images of lowrider culture. Carmen Loma Garza's *Quinceañera* (fifteenth birthday) depicts a typical celebration scene of several young couples—the young women in pink dresses and their male companions in black suits—who are celebrating the female coming-out ritual. A blue lowrider cruiser appears at the bottom right of the painting with another couple in the back seat. Frank Romero's *Cruising, #1* depicts a rust-colored lowrider convertible being driven down a palm-lined street. John Valadez has two images in the exhibition. One, *Getting Them Out of the Car*, two distinct tableaux set side by side and connected by a purple lowrider convertible, is a scene of violence on a beach. Included in the painting are several distressed, wounded, or dead young Chicanas and Chicanos; they have evidently been the targets of violence. A second painting, *Car Show*, shows several young Chicanas and Chicanos around partially shown lowrider vehicles. They are apparently enjoying a lowrider car show in the open on a bright, sunny day. This image stands out in stark contrast to the first one (Marin 2002).

Only one lowrider image, Carlos Santistevan's *Red and Gold Lowrider*, is included in the May 1–September 19, 2002 exhibition, "Chicano Art for Our Millenium," held at the Mesa Southwest Museum in Mesa, Arizona. The artist transforms a red, high-heeled shoe into a red Chevrolet lowrider with flames, pinstriping, and a mural on a back panel. The miniature lowrider, titled *Red and Gold Lowrider*, is raked forward with huge rear wheels and smaller front wheels, which is somewhat characteristic of a drag strip vehicle. This lowrider in miniature is one of series of lowrider shoes that Santistevan has produced during his career(Keller, Erickson, & Villeneuve 2002).

Images of lowrider culture are also included in various recently published books on Chicana/o art. The 2002 publications *Contemporary Chicana and Chicano Art: Volume I* and *Volume II* contain a number of images of lowrider culture. The first volume includes two images by Carlos Frésquez. In the first, *The Obsidian Ranfla Series #1*, the artist links the concept of sacrifice in contemporary Chicana/o society with the practice of ritual human sacrifice in Aztec culture. The black *ranfla* (lowrider cruiser) is constructed of obsidian, the material used for the Aztec sacrificial knife. A red heart is superimposed on the image of the car. In the second, *Por vida* (For life), the artist has a foregrounded image of Batman descending over a lowrider car, a Chicana/o version of the Batmobile. The second volume includes the following images: Gilbert "Magu" Luján's *Family Car* is a color photo of an orange 1949 Chevrolet that is elaborately painted with flames and an image of a Chicano "Superman" portrayed on a rear wheel panel; Rodolfo O. Cuéllar Jr.'s *Mercado de las flores* (flowermarket) *Lowrider Show, 1976–1977* is a poster depicting a red lowrider with rear wheel skirts, a fancy grille, and custom striped upholstery; a second poster, *Lowrider Carucha Show, 1978*, depicts a lowrider with hydraulics with the front end elevated several feet in a "hopping" position; Carlos Frésquez's *A Westside Wedding* has a lowrider covered with painted and real roses parked in front of a church waiting for the newlyweds to emerge from the church; Luis Eligio Tapia's *Chima Altar II: Bertram's Cruise* depicts a lowrider created from chairs and folk art typical of northern New Mexico ("Chima" refers to the sacred Santuario de Chimayó); Gilbert "Magu" Luján's *Fifty Nifty Chevy* shows a miniature bright red, stripped-down 1950s Chevrolet with rear wheel skirts over double rear wheels; and another of Santistevan's lowrider shoes, *Lowrider*, is made from a black shoe that sports hood and side panel flames (Keller 2002, 158–163).

FURTHER READING

Barnet-Sánchez, Holly, and Eva Sperling, eds. *Signs from the Heart: California Chicano Murals*. Venice, CA: Social Public Art Resource Center, 1990.

Bright, Brenda Jo. "Nightmares in the New Metropolis: The Cinematic Poetics of Low Riders." *Studies in Latin American Popular Culture* 16 (1997): 13–29.

Ganahl, Pat. *Custom Painting*. North Branch, MN: CarTech, 2008.

Gaspar de Alba, Alicia. *Chicano Art: Inside Outside the Master's House.* Austin: University of Texas Press, 1998.

Gradante, William. "Art among the Low Riders." In *Folk Art in Texas*, edited by Francis Edward Abernethy, 75–77. Dallas: SMU Press and the Texas Folklore Society. 1985.

Griswold del Castillo, Richard, Teresa McKenna, and Yvonne Yarbro-Bejarano, eds. *Chicano Art: Resistance and Affirmation, 1965–1985.* Los Angeles: UCLA Wright Gallery, 1991.

How Stuff Works, http://howstuffworks.com/westergard-mercury -custom-car.thm.

Jackson, Carlos Francisco. *Chicana and Chicano Art.* Tucson: University of Arizona Press, 2009.

Keller, Gary D, ed. *Contemporary Chicana and Chicano Art, Volumes I and II.* Tempe, AZ: Bilingual Press/Editorial Bilingue, 2002.

Keller, Gary, Mary Erickson, and Pat Villeneuve, et al. *Chicano Art for the New Millennium.* Tempe, AZ: Bilingual Press/Editorial Bilingue, 2002.

Kustomrama, www.kustomrama.com/index.php?title_Watson.

Lowrider Arte, http://lowriderarte.com.

Lowrider magazine www.lowridermagazine.com/editorial/0808 _lrmp_low_rider_hall_of_fame/index.html.

Marín, Cheech, ed. *Chicano Visions: American Painters on the Verge.* Boston: Little, Brown and Company, 2002.

National Museum of American History, http://americanhistory.si.edu.

Penland, Paige R. *Lowrider: History, Pride, Culture.* St. Paul, MN: MBI Publishing, 2003.

Petersen Automotive Museum, www.petersen.org.

Stecyk, C. R., guest curator with Bolton Colburn. *KustomKulture: Von Dutch, Ed "Big Daddy" Roth, Robert Williams and Others.* San Francisco: Laguna Art Museum and Last Gasp of San Francisco, 1993.

Street Low Magazine, http://streetlowmagazine.com.

5

Music

The music that lowriders have listened and danced to over the past several decades has changed as popular musical currents and tastes among young and old Mexican Americans alike have come and gone. Beginning in the post–World War II period, the primary currents and tastes have included *música tejana* (Texas-style music), including *conjuntos* (small musical groups) and *orquestas* (large dance bands); African American swing, blues, and jazz; rhythm and blues; the remakes of ballads and dance tunes which became known in California as the "Eastside Sound"; rock and roll; punk; and rap. At the beginning, lowriders, whether they were cruising or parked at popular gathering locations such as drive-ins and outside of barrio dance halls, listened to music on their radios tuned in to popular disc jockeys. Later, when music became available on audio tapes, they installed players in their cars, and then, more recently, they outfitted their cars with expensive and sophisticated CD players and sound systems to play the latest sounds.

EARLY FORMS OF MEXICAN AMERICAN MUSIC

The myriad kinds of music popular that lowriders listened to after World War II grew out of a long tradition stretching back to the sixteenth century, when Spanish colonists moved north from the Spanish viceroyalty established in what is today's Mexico City and began settling in what is now the American Southwest. They had brought with them from Spain living and ever-changing cultural forms that were adapting to new social conditions and musical currents. At first, folk music and other popular traditions prospered in the Spanish mountain communities of New Mexico and southern Colorado and along the Rio Grande River. Later these traditions became rooted in growing Hispanic population centers such as San Antonio and Los Angeles. Some musical forms survived into the twentieth century but disappeared due to neglect or were changed and altered as inventive and innovative musicians modernized the music and adapted it to their circumstances (Robb 1980, 5).

The most popular forms of Hispanic folk music found in the Southwest are the *canción*, the *decima*, and the *romance*. The canción is a song form that was originally a favorite of lovers expressing their deep-felt sentiments for each other. Then, after about the 1920s, the original form evolved into the *canción ranchera*, which addressed social issues and was popular on both sides of the U.S.-Mexico border as well as in the Los Angeles area. The decima is a ten-line song form that flourished in the late nineteenth and early twentieth century especially in New Mexico and in the Lower Rio Grande Valley of Texas, where *decimeros* (composers and singers) performed them at public events and at weddings and birthdays. The romance, or ballad, is a short narrative song form that usually deals with an event or set of events that occurred or that are supposed to have occurred. Typically, a *romancero* (balladeer) would sing praises to a hero or express religious sentiments.

Corridos

A ballad form closely related to the romance is the *corrido*. The so-called *romances corridos* were composed to celebrate the Spanish colonization of Florida in 1745 and the independence of Mexico from Spain in 1821. The corrido went into a period of decline in Mexico after the end of the U.S.-Mexican War in 1848, but it enjoyed renewed popularity between about 1875 and the 1930s. After about 1930, the corrido in Mexico became highly commercialized with the advent of radio, the increasing popularity of the movies, and the establishment of a thriving recording industry.

Along the U.S.-Mexico border, especially along the Lower Rio Grande Valley border with Mexico, the corrido had a different history from that in the interior of Mexico. It became very popular among the Spanish-speaking population with the increase of immigration into Texas after 1848. *Corridistas* (corrido composers) used the song form to record the sharp increase in incidents of social conflict arising from Anglo-American social and racial oppression of the Mexican American population. The corrido became a form of cultural resistance composed and sung in Spanish at a wide variety of public and private events. The use of the corrido to express intercultural conflict along the U.S.-Mexico border continued throughout the twentieth century, and even today such songs can be heard on Spanish-language radio stations in border cities. Chicano historian Ricardo Romo recalls his days as a tejano low-rider who, as a high school student growing up in San Antonio, would listen to corridos on the radio while he and his friends tinkered with their cruisers.

Along with Latin *cumbia* and *salsa* music, corrido music was a traditional Mexican and Mexican American song form that many East Los Angeles bands would play at clubs, weddings, birthdays, high school dances, and band contests ("battles of the bands") during much of the 1970s. Joe Sandoval, a prominent contest producer, would distribute leaflets among lowriders who were cruising on Whittier Avenue to encourage them to attend the events. Corridos were included in the repertory of music they played on their cars radios.

Several corridos about lowriders have been composed and performed since the 1970s. For example, the contemporary tejano musical group Da Krazy Pimpz regularly plays "El corrido del Lowrider Blanco," which is a car version of the famous "Corrido del caballo blanco" ("The Corrido of the White Horse"), popularized by the modern Mexican singer and actor José Alfredo Jiménez. In this corrido, a white horse is set free in Guadalajara to undertake a courageous and dangerous trek to the U.S.-Mexico border where, exhausted and battered from the long trip, it dies. The musical group Da Krazy Pimpz mocks the original song; their version is about a lowrider cruiser that gives out after serving its proud owner. Another example is the "Corrido de los dos carnales" ("Corrido of the Two Buddies"), performed by the legendary tejano musician Esteban "Steve" Jordan. The ballad is about a couple of good friends who in their lowrider vehicles—a truck and a DeSoto—plan to rob a supermarket. One of the would-be robbers is arrested and then escapes. (The author is grateful to Celestino Fernández and Laura Cummings for bringing these corridos to his attention.)

Conjunto and Orquesta Music

Texas can be described as a kind of Chicano musical epicenter from which the influence of musical styles, instrumentation, and performers radiates outward to the Southwest. In Texas, it has been noted that Mexican American music as a form of expressive culture grew out of a complex combination of historical circumstances surrounding the conflict between Anglo-American Texans and Texas Mexicans before and after the U.S.-Mexican War. After 1848, Texas Mexicans, now American citizens, found themselves subordinated within a new social order dominated by Anglo-American Texans. Because armed resistance was rarely viable, Texas Mexicans and Mexican immigrants who followed created a rich expressive culture that included music. The tejanos, among all Mexican American groups in the Southwest, have stood out as having a strongly innovative musical spirit (Peña 1985, 14).

Conjunto Music

Like the corrido, the Texas-Mexican conjunto became a powerful oppositional form of resistance against Anglo-American values and oppressive conditions as well as a way for working-class Tejanos to distinguish themselves from those tejanos they considered more Americanized in their dress, speech, values, customs, and ultimately musical preferences. Conjunto is an accordion ensemble that originally also included a guitar or *bajo sexto* (a basslike, 12-string instrument), and a *tambora de rancho* (an improvised drum made from materials such as goatskin heads and wire rims). The accordion has always been the preferred instrument of rural and working-class tejanos, who even today play for family functions such as weddings and birthdays and other festive occasions. Conjunto steadily moved west from Texas as Texas Mexican Americans resettled in Southern California, especially in the Los Angeles area, a phenomenon that accelerated during the World War II years. After World War II, radio stations throughout the Southwest continued to play conjunto music in response to popular demand. It became part of the music that the early lowriders in the late 1940s and 1950s across the Southwest listened to on their cruiser radios. Although conjunto music has remained popular for the past several decades, especially in Texas, it is no longer preferred by lowriders, who have supplanted it with other kinds of music.

Orquesta Tejana

In addition to conjunto music, *orquesta tejana* is another distinct musical style that became popular in the years before after World War II and whose growth and prominence are heavily associated with Texas. The development of orquesta music roughly parallels that of conjunto but differs in an important way: rather than being built "from the ground up" with meager resources associate with the working class, it had ready-made models to imitate: the orchestral ensembles, ranging from symphonic units to brass bands, that were already well established by the beginning of the twentieth century in Texas and in Mexico. Also, orquesta music was preferred over conjunto music by middle-class Mexican Americans and those who aspired to become middle class. It was considered to be a more Anglo-American type of music, and therefore its preference by some Mexican Americans was associated with a desire to become more assimilated into the dominant society. However, Mexican American youth in Texas, including the first lowriders in cities like San Antonio and El Paso, became attracted to this type of music as it changed in the late 1940s and early 1950s in order to appeal to a wider audience. As large Anglo-American swing bands became popular in the United States, orquesta groups in Texas began modeling themselves on this new and exciting music (Peña 1999, 118–119).

THE MUSIC SCENE IN LOS ANGELES IN THE POST–WORLD WAR II ERA

Los Angeles became, after World War II, a second center for the development and popularization of a variety of Mexican American musical forms and tastes. It had been a vibrant place in the pre-war years, but became even more so as the Mexican American and Mexican immigrant population grew substantially after 1945. An overview of Mexican American music in Los Angeles serves also as a glimpse of the music that was popular among lowriders.

Lalo Guerrero

Lalo Guerrero—perhaps the best-known and the most versatile and prolific Mexican American musician ever—had moved in 1937 from Tucson, Arizona, to Los Angeles to develop his career. Due to his long and active career—he died in 2005—he has served as an invaluable source for historians and musicologists who have written about the Mexican American musical landscape of Los Angeles during the 1940s and 1950s. Guerrero, whose parents were born in Mexico, grew up in a Tucson barrio where he began learning about the music of Mexico from his mother, who played the guitar and sang popular

Lalo Guerrero in 2004. (AP Photo/Damian Dovarganes)

Mexican romantic ballads and traditional folk songs. Once Guerrero began elementary school and learned English, he began listening to Anglo-American popular music on the radio and at the movies. Although he knew Spanish well, he began performing English-language songs in order to join the American musical mainstream. Nonetheless, as a Mexican American with decided Mexican Indian physical features, he had difficulty scheduling performances in Tucson. He went to Mexico City for about a year where he enjoyed more success singing in Spanish by himself or with small groups in night clubs, bars, and dance halls.

Guerrero returned to the United States at the beginning of the war, first to San Diego and then to Los Angeles when the war ended. He landed record contracts with several prominent record companies that produced Spanish-language music and was in great demand in Latin nightclubs that attracted a large Mexican American patronage. He was particularly adept at composing music that encompassed different musical styles such as mambo, boogie woogie (piano-based blues music composed for dancing), Cuban rhythms, and swing, but what drove his popularity among his Spanish-speaking fans was his use of themes that reflected the cultural and social realities of Mexican Americans. Of particular interest for the first generation of lowriders in Los Angeles area was his incorporation of caló, the dialect used by pachucos and zoot suiters (see Chapter 2), who were some of the first lowriders. His song "Marijuana Boogie" was centered on the wide practice among Mexican American working class youth of smoking marijuana (Loza 1993, 161).

In the early 1960s, Guerrero bought a nightclub, "Tony's Inn," in East Los Angeles that he renamed "Lalo's," where he performed frequently and hosted numerous Mexican American musicians and groups. During the same period, he had his own conjunto, which toured extensively throughout the Southwest performing the most popular Latin music of the day. For several decades, Guerrero traveled and performed across the United States, Latin America, and Europe. He had a lasting influence on countless young Mexican American musicians, including his own son Mark, who has become a well-known rock and roll songwriter. Although he retired to Palm Springs, California, in 1974, Guerrero continued to be productive long after.

Guerrero's connection with lowrider culture began after he moved to Los Angeles and particularly during the 14-year time span that his nightclub existed in East Los Angeles. It was a popular venue frequented by young Mexican Americans from the barrio and from throughout the Los Angeles area. Shortly before his retirement, Guerrero reengaged with the lowrider community in the early 1970s with the music he had composed for the play (and later movie) *Zoot Suit*, by the well-known Chicano playwright Luis Valdez. Due in large part to the popularity of the zoot suit style among lowriders, the music was very appealing. A representative example of the music was "Chucos suaves" ("chuco" is an abbreviate form of *pachuco*).

Continuing a practice he had initiated in the 1940s, Guerrero incorporates caló (the Spanish slang spoken by pachucos) into the Spanish lyrics, and the sound is based on an Afro-Cuban *son* form, a sensuous dance rhythm that was popular from the mid-1940s, and one that pachucos and lowriders certainly swayed to at East Los Angeles nightclubs and dance halls that were established as the barrio itself increased in population. The lyrics use a first-person narrator, a pachuco, who recounts that on Saturday night he would go dancing with his girlfriend, who would become transformed on the dance floor as she effortlessly moved with the music. The lyrics also urge the listener to take up the then-new music and to leave behind swing, boogie woogie, and jitterbug.

Swing was probably the most popular music and dance style among the zoot suiters in the era of the 1940s, but competing with it was an assortment of Latin styles, including mambo and rumba, that arrived from Cuba via Mexico. These so-called tropical rhythms were played at venues that attracted the fully outfitted zoot suit crowd, who later turned away from swing and Latin rhythms to embrace "jump blues," a hybrid form described as a pre–rock and roll swing style derived from the blues that had arrived in South Central Los Angeles with the rapidly growing post–World War II African American population. The popularity of swing blues among both Mexican Americans and African Americans was spread primarily by disc jockeys on radio stations such as KFVD. For example, in 1952 a disc jockey named Hunter Hancock aired a lowrider favorite, "Pachuco Hop," an instrumental by African American saxophonist Chuck Higgins (Loza 1993, 81).

As the Mexican American and Mexican immigrant population began leaving the downtown Los Angeles area for more affordable housing east of downtown, the center of gravity for their music also shifted. Numerous clubs and record shops opened up to accommodate the Mexican American clientele. Guerrero, who had later been a part of this new entrepreneurial spirit with the opening of Lalo's, recalled nightclubs and dance clubs such as La Noche (The Night), El Club Ballón, Agnes's Place, La Casita (The Little House), Beto's, and The Latin Lover. He also fondly remembered performers such as Eddie Cano, promoters such as Chico Sesma and Richard Seja, and bandleaders such as Manny López, all of whom contributed to creating an exciting musical environment in East Los Angeles where Mexican American young people and older adults were exposed to musicians from the East Coast like the Cuban Tito Puente, bands and performers from Mexico and other Latin American countries, and the successful and up-and-coming Mexican American talent (Loza 1993, 73–74).

During the late 1950s and early 1960s, the El Monte Legion Stadium in East Los Angeles was a popular performance and dance venue attended mainly by Mexican American young adults who would come decked out in carefully pressed and creased khaki pants, well-tailored shirts, and meticulously shined French-toed shoes. The young women would stack their hair and wear white shoes called "bunnies"; black, tight, short skirts; and feathered earrings. The dancers' favorite musical pieces were the Pachuco Hop, the Hully Gully, and the Corrido Rock, the last attracting from 150 to 250 dancers on the floor to perform a dance similar to slam dancing. After the evening ended with slow dancing, the crowd would spill outside to the parking lot to meet friends and continue the party elsewhere. The Jesters Low Rider Car Club from Boyle Heights as well as all-female lowrider clubs such as the Chevelles would often parade around the parking lot in their carefully painted cars; sometimes the police would show up to break up the crowd (Guevara 1994, 118).

THE EASTSIDE SOUND

The mid-1960s was the beginning of the era when most young Mexican Americans across the Southwest began to prefer to identify themselves as Chicanos to convey pride in their Mexican Indian origins, a heightened political awareness of the world around them, and a commitment to strive for social, economic, and cultural change in their schools and barrios. East Los Angeles, which was a center of this ferment for change, was also the home to many Chicano bands that began to dominate the musical life of Chicanos throughout Los Angeles. This new musical trend, which came to be known as the Eastside Sound, or the Chicano style, sprung from, grew, borrowed, and adapted genres such as the more African American sounds of rhythm and blues, soul, rock and roll, and funk; the Latin salsa; and established Mexican traditional styles (Loza 1993, 95).

Luis J. Rodríguez, a young journalist, wrote about the popular eastside Chicano bands such as Thee Midniters, The Village Callers, Cannibal and the Headhunters, The Ambertones, El Chicano, and Tierra, calling them "heroes and heroines of lowrider clubs, street gangs and high school teens." All of these groups are included in the 2002 book *The Barrio Guide to Low Rider Music, 1950–1975*. These groups' records were sold as soon as they came out, and whenever they made appearances they crowded dance halls and concerts. In most cases, they were well known within the East Los Angeles barrio and in cities where there were large concentrations of Americans of Mexican descent, but it was difficult to garner the kind of record and performance contracts that would expose their music to a much wider non–Mexican American audience.

Ritchie Valens (born Richard Valenzuela) was of the earliest entertainment artist to be associated with the Eastside Sound, and, notably, he was one of a handful of Mexican American performers who were highly successful among a crossover audience of Anglo-Americans and African Americans. He achieved national recognition with rock and roll hits such as "Donna," "That's My Little Susie," "Come On, Lets Go," and "La Bamba" before he was tragically killed in a 1959 airplane accident along with teen idols Buddy Holly and J. R. "Big Bopper" Richardson. His young life and premature death were later portrayed in the 1987 Movie *La Bamba*, in which the actor Lou Diamond Phillips portrays Valens during his adolescence and then after he is discovered and signed to a recording contract with Del-Fi Records.

Valens was a significant loss for Chicano popular music, but there were up-and-coming bands and individual performers who would soon fill the gap left by his death. Key to the emergence and success of some of them was the promotional and entrepreneurial savvy of Eddie Davis, an Anglo-American who negotiated record productions for many eastside groups on three record labels he founded: Faro, Linda, and Ramparts. These were by far the most important of the three for East Los Angeles musicians and singers. In partnership with Billy Cárdenas, a Chicano entrepreneur, Davis bought the Rhythm Room, a nightclub in Fullerton. There and at the Rainbow Gardens nightclub in Pomona, Davis featured, in the mid-1960s, East Los Angeles musical talent such as Cannibal and the Headhunters, the Premiers, and Ray Jiménez (Lil' Ray). Cárdenas was often referred to as "the Godfather of the Eastside Sound." As the proprietor of the Faro/Ramparts label, he "was becoming part of a whole record buying public on the Eastside of Los Angeles that other companies were ignoring" (Rodríguez 1980, 29).

Cannibal and the Headhunters

Cannibal and the Headhunters was a quintessentially East Los Angeles band that consisted of four young Chicano musicians raised in the tough Ramona Gardens housing project in the middle of the barrio: Richard "Scar" López, Bobby "Rabbit" Jaramillo, Joe "Jo Jo" Jaramillo, and Frankie "Cannibal" García. Unlike most of the other Chicano groups who recorded with the Faro/Ramparts label, the Headhunters were strictly a harmony group. At the time, African American groups in East Los Angles excelled in harmony mainly because this style had been popularized nationwide by the so-called Motown sound out of Detroit (and later Los Angeles), which was dominated by outstanding African American groups. The Showcases, an African American group from the same Ramona Gardens project, generously helped the Headhunters perfect their harmony. The Headhunters toured nationally and opened for the Beatles at the Hollywood Bowl in 1965. The Headhunters' greatest success by far was their version of a popular song, "Land of a Thousand Dances," written by the African American rock and roll great Fats Domino and Chris Kenner. The Headhunters' version of the song, which was in great demand at early lowrider shows from the late 1960s to the early 1980s, was recorded by several Chicano and non-Chicano bands and individual singers, but none attained the national popularity that the Headhunters' version did, peaking at number 30 on the Billboard music charts. It has been noted that the Headhunters' version of "Land of a Thousand Dances" became "an anthem for East L.A., a song that manages to sound fresh but also brings back memories of a particular place and time" (Reyes & Waldman 1998, 70).

Thee Midniters

Another key Chicano group for lowrider music is Thee Midniters. Like the Headhunters, many of the band's members grew up in the Estrada Courts Housing Project in Boyle Heights in East Los Angeles and received much of their musical training in local public high school music programs. Several were members of the Stockers Car Club, a close association with lowrider culture that guaranteed them wide acceptance among cruisers; this was particularly important at the beginning as they began to build their reputation. Another essential part of their fan base consisted of high school students who regularly attended the band's performances at Salesian and other East Los Angeles high schools and Battle of the Bands performances. Unlike the harmony music for which the Headhunters became known, Thee Midniters played several string, horn, and percussive instruments and featured a lead singer or two. Their music consisted of popular rock and roll and R&B tunes such as "Love Special Delivery," "The Town I Live In," and "Giving Up on Love." They also produced a version of "Land of a Thousand Dances," and they competed with the Headhunters in the mid-1960s as both versions raced up the Billboard charts. Thee Midniters' version peaked at number 67, which was not quite as high as the Headhunters' version, which peaked at number 30. Thee Midniters' release of "Whittier Boulevard" in 1965 was a loud and raucous rock and roll tribute to lowriders' favorite cruising route. Although not as popular, the song "Sad Girl" has been called "one the most popular songs to ever be associate with the low rider culture." Although the band remained extremely popular among Chicano audiences throughout California and neighboring states, they never reached a national audience. However, there was never any doubt about their excellent musicianship. It has been noted that "their professionalism and stage presence was unequaled" (Molina 2002, 151–152).

El Chicano

Aptly named for the period in Chicano history from the mid-1960s to the early 1970s, when cultural nationalism and political activism were at their peak, the East Los Angeles musical group El Chicano recorded "Sabor a mí" (recorded later in English as "Be True to Me"), a popular tune among lowriders. The group evolved out two bands that had broken up when their members were either drafted or volunteered for military service during the Vietnam War. The group consisted of a mixture of instrumentalists (bass, trumpet player, percussionist, guitarist) but stood out from many other East Los Angeles groups because of their vocalist, Ersi Arvizu, whose rendition of "Sabor a mí" (on the group's second album) rivaled that of other, better-known vocalists such as Edye Gorme and Vickie Carr. The song is highly romantic, sensual, and rhythmic and follows a beat that made it a favorite at high school dances and dance halls all over Los Angeles for a decade. During the height of their popularity, El Chicano recorded seven albums, and they were one of the eastside groups to enjoy the greatest success beyond their local audience, playing at venues such as the Apollo Theater in New York City. Another of their hits, a Latin rock version of "Viva Tirado," about a legendary Mexican bullfighter who refused to kill his bull, climbed to number one in Los Angeles and number 28 on the national pop charts (Molina 2002, 44).

El Chicano continued to perform throughout the 1970s, adapting to new musical trends such as disco music. In one of the first issues of *Lowrider* (December 1977), Larry Gonzales, one of the publication's writers, describes going to an El Chicano performance at Disco Odyssey, a dance club that specialized in what he calls Latin Disco Sounds. He urges lowriders in his column, "Night Life," to call in to their local radio stations to request the latest El Chicano disco music: "Like these dudes once said, music is the universal language and sabes que [you know] that these vatos have made the words El Chicano hear throughout the Universe and paid their dues" (*Lowrider* December 1977, 36).

Tierra

Like El Chicano, Tierra was another East Los Angles band that successfully combined an impressive variety of instrument (piano, trumpet, reeds, drums and Latin percussion, bass, and keyboards) with outstanding vocals. Rudy and Steve Salas were child prodigies as popular singers from East Los Angeles in the 1960s. In the early to mid-1970s, they performed with Tierra to produce a wide spectrum of sounds such as R&B, rock, salsa, and romantic ballads. They were stylistically and thematically one of the most innovative groups to be associated with the Eastside Sound. On one of the group's first albums, the single "Barrio Suite" specifically refers to the Chicano experience of the early 1970s. It is noted that "social statement, idealism, and musical experimentation weaved an interesting combination of sound, thought and sentiment" (Loza 1993, 104).

Tierra continued to record albums and play to increasingly large audiences throughout the 1970s, and in the early 1980s the group achieved great popularity across the United States, boosted in part by appearances on popular television shows such as *American Bandstand,*

Soul Train, and *The American Music Awards*. During their tour of the East Coast they played at Carnegie Hall in New York City, a singular accomplishment for a group whose roots were deep in the East Los Angeles barrio.

Tierra has been a favorite of lowriders, appearing frequently in the pages of *Lowrider* magazine. For example, in the July 1982 issue, their new album, "Bad City Boys," is announced and fans are encouraged to join their fan club. The band has made many appearances at lowrider shows, such as the September 11, 1988 super show at the Los Angeles Arena. The January 2010 issue of *Lowrider* magazine includes a retrospective article that traces the musical trajectory and success of Tierra from their inception in 1973 through 2009, with an emphasis on how loyal they have remained to their East Los Angeles origins while at the same time continuing to tour nationally and internationally. This issue also includes a short obituary of Isaac Campos Ávila, the group's lead singer until his death in 2009.

OTHER LOWRIDER FAVORITES

Although not as popular as Thee Midniters, Cannibal and the Head-hunters,

El Chicano, and Tierra, Rudy and the Cruisers were a favorite of the lowrider crowd and appeared frequently with other, better-known groups at lowrider shows. For example, the group appeared in the August 1981 Tulare, California, Lowrider Happening along with the Headhunters. Their hit single, "Cruisin Baby," was representative of the kind of tunes that made them popular among lowriders. In the July 1981 issue of *Lowrider*, Sonny Madrid, the publisher and editor, encourages readers to support Chicano musical groups by requesting that the radio stations they listen to give greater air time to groups like Rudy and the Cruisers. Madrid observes that it is difficult for Latino-Chicano groups to obtain contracts with the major record companies such as CBS, Warner, Electra, and Polydor; to be heard on most large radio stations; and to get listed in Billboard and other national ranking publications (*Lowrider* July 1981, 6).

NEW WAVE AND PUNK ROCK

Underground music from England, often referred to as New Wave music, swept across the Atlantic to the United States in the mid to late 1970s. It incorporated several features of electronic, experimental, disco, and 1960s pop music as well as a mod style that was associated with young British rock groups of the time. Although New Wave is sometimes confused with punk rock and was initially a part of the same musical scene, its music and lyrics tend to be more complex. Punk rock is often characterized as more exuberant and energetic than New Wave. Punk rock is considered to be more overtly political and angry than New Wave, with an emphasis on punching out short songs with strong and explicit lyrics directed at a young, restless audience. Although East Los Angeles bands such as Cannibal and the Head-hunters released a few singles that could be associated with this latest music trend, most of the bands discussed here did not. Tierra and El Chicano did not shy away from political messages in their music, but their style was tame when compared with that of most emerging Chicano punk bands such as Los Illegales, the Brat, and the Plugz.

In the July 1982 issue of *Lowrider*, Sonny Madrid highlights the Plugz, a local band founded in 1978 that was performing widely throughout the Los Angeles area, not only to Chicano but also European American and African American audiences. Madrid describes their sound as "power music" with a heavy rhythm pro-duced by a bass and a lead guitarist and keyboardist, a sound that appealed to those who wanted to dance (*Lowrider* July 1982, 31).

In the same issue, Madrid writes about other Chicano New Wave groups in a short article entitled "The Odd Squad: Boyle Height's Progressive Musicians." Although most of the members of the Odd Squad band were born and raised in East Los Angeles and grew up lis-tening to the 1960s and 1970s Eastside Sound, their music also reflects the influence of New York punk groups such as the Ramones. In an accompanying article, Madrid writes about a Texas-based band, Joe King Carrasco and the Crowns, whose music reflects various tastes such as traditional Tex-Mex and New Wave/punk rock (*Lowrider* July 1982, 34).

Among other New Wave bands featured by *Lowrider* was the Brat, founded in the late 1970s by Rudy Medina and featuring Teresa Covar-rubias, the group's lead singer. Many East Los Angeles music fans did not accept their music in the beginning because it was too much of a departure from the Eastside Sound of the 1960s and 1970s, so coverage by *Lowrider* was somewhat risky. After one performance, the group walked into a liquor store, where they were immediately harassed and threatened by a group of Chicano toughs ("gangbangers"). Finally, one of them recognized the Brats from a story that the maga-zine had recently done on them; the musicians were then left alone (Reyes & Waldman 1998, 140).

Los Lobos

Los Lobos, arguably the most popular Chicano band since the 1970s with the possible exception of Santana, was known originally as Los Lobos del Este de Los Angeles (The East Los Angeles Wolves), a name the band members chose to identify themselves with their barrio roots. Since their founding in 1973, they have undergone various stages of transformation, adapting their music and the language of their lyrics to different audiences at different times and venues. Steeped in rock and roll, funk music, and soul, they nonetheless began performing at weddings, parties, and small halls with a repertoire of traditional Mexican songs in Spanish. By the end of the 1970s, they began playing a New Wave repertoire especially before larger audiences outside of East Los Angeles at places like the Whiskey, one of Hollywood's most popular nightclubs, and on California college campuses. Unlike many other musical groups, the four members of Los Lobos have remained a tight-knit group, mutually supportive and totally committed to improving and varying their music. They now tour extensively in the United States and internationally even as they continue to record albums at a steady pace.

Lowrider featured Los Lobos in its July 1982 issue, approximately a decade after they came together as a band and at a time when they were not nearly as famous as they are today. The article noted that

Los Lobos in 1997. (AP Photo/Reed Saxon)

their music could be best described as "fusion of Chicano roots—
Chicano music and the pop sound of today's Nu Music rhythms." Their
arrangement of the single "Farmer John," a song recorded by earlier
Chicano groups in the 1960s and 1970s, sets them apart as "New Wave
hop-folk." Readers are urged to check to "check out these homeboys"
(*Lowrider* July 1982, 33).

RAP MUSIC

Rap music, which has been an important aspect of lowrider culture
since the early 1990s, is just one manifestation of a larger cultural phenomenon widely known as hip-hop. Hip-hop probably has its origins
in the 1980s in the street culture of African American and Puerto Rican
youth of New York City, and it is often associated with 1980s break
dancing; graffiti; the technologies that disc jockeys developed for
dances, weddings, birthdays, and other events; and rap music. Rap
music, in turn, "is a form of rhymed storytelling accompanied by
highly rhythmic, electronically based music" (Rose 1994, 2).

Hip-hop culture moved west from New York City in the 1980s to establish itself first among young African Americans in large Midwestern and
Southwestern cities such as Chicago, St. Louis, and Los Angeles. It then
became increasingly popular among urban Chicano youth and young
adults, who began to participate actively in hip-hop's various expressive
forms, including rap. At least in the early years, African American hip
hop influenced Chicano hip-hop, and occasionally the reverse was true.
African American performers such as rapper and actor Ice-T and Easy-
E willingly shared their music and market insights with young Chicano
rappers in the late 1980s. Kid Frost, who is often referred to as the
godfather of Chicano rap, is said to have been a protégé of Ice-T. It was
also common to see Chicano lowrider cruisers in the background shots
of the some of the established Los Angeles African American rappers'
videos. Since the 1990s Chicano rappers have addressed in their music
themes running from gangbanging to peace and love in the barrio. They
have developed different lyrical and musical styles in English, Spanish, a
combination of the two, and caló. Chicano rappers are an extremely
varied and complex group (McFarland 2008, 35).

An Overview of Chicano Rap

Many rappers have performed at lowrider shows and other lowrider
events across the Southwest since the 1990s. The most popular
performers who have been featured are Kid Frost, Lighter Shade of

Brown (LSOB), Rappin 4-Tay, JV, Zapp and Roger, Slow Pain, Johnny Z, Delinquent Habits, L'il Bob, and L'il Rob. Typically, lesser-known local rappers will often perform with these featured musicians, and occasionally other kinds of music such as rock and roll, mariachi music, and tejano music will share stage time at lowrider shows.

There is a lowrider style of Chicano rap that has the longest history and that has been associated with rappers such as Frost and A Lighter Shade of Brown since the very early 1990s and with L'il Rob more recently. References to and images of lowriders and cruising are common in song repertoires. When performing at lowrider shows and events, some rappers typically dress like cholos (young barrio Chicanos) in jeans, bandanas, T-shirts or Pendleton shirts, and tennis shoes, work boots, or walking shoes. Dressing in this distinct style enhances their ability to connect with their audience. Rappers invariably wear sunglasses, even while performing in semidark auditoriums, and assume a defiant attitude befitting the most combative cholo on the streets of his barrio. Although not associated exclusively with the lowrider rapper style, the language that is heard from performers such as Frost, LSOB, and L'il Rob is caló, code-switching (an alternating use of Spanish, English, anglicized Spanish words, and hispanicized English words, often in the same sentence or song verse), hip-hop slang, and new words currently in use among urban working-class Chicanos (McFarland 2008, 54).

As in much of rap music, violence is a common theme in Chicano rap. Many songs seem to promote violence against gang members, women, and the police and other figures of authority. At the same time, Chicano rappers such as Frost, Delinquent Habits, Slow Pain, and SPM (South Park Mexican) have songs that focus on peace and love among barrio dwellers. Other songs depict lowriders and their families gathering in parks and at celebrations to enjoy leisure time together. This emphasis on community and collective cohesion and support is almost as prevalent as songs about violence (McFarland 2008, 114).

Frost

Frost—up to 1995, he was known as Kid Frost—was born Arturo Molina Jr. in 1964 in Los Angeles. Because his father was in the military, he was raised on different military bases in the United States and abroad. Frost began his career in 1982 in East Los Angeles as a member of several musical groups. Although he had released records as a solo performer early in his career, his first major rap song was

"La Raza," which was included on his first album, *Hispanic Causing Panic*, released in 1990. The single and the album are considered by some to represent one of the founding moments of Chicano rap music and an important milestone in a shift away from rap and hip-hop as solely African American cultural productions. The song was an instant hit among Chicanos as "radio stations, booming sound systems in many cars and trucks, and music video programs frequently played the song and video in 1990" (Rodríguez 2003, 112–115).

"La Raza" was so instantly popular perhaps because Kid Frost expresses in song a deep pride in his ethnicity, his extended brown family, and its cultural traditions in a way that has been compared with the 1967 epic poem "I Am Joaquín" by Chicano activist Rodolfo "Corky" Gonzales. The poem, which is considered highly representative of the cultural nationalism of the Chicano movement of the 1960s and early 1970s, traces the roots of Mexican Americans back to their Aztec culture. Just as Gonzales urged his people to come together in a spirit of self-determination and solidarity to oppose racism and exploitation, Frost invokes a call to defiant opposition of oppressive forces like the police who harass young Chicanos on the streets of their own barrios. At the same time, Frost is critical of those Chicanos—*vavosos* (slobbering idiots)—who are, in his view, not worthy of respect because they are not masculine enough, especially in their heterosexuality and in their macho behavior toward women, who are considered to be mere sexual objects. This strong misogynist message in "La Raza" is found in much of Chicano rap music.

Frost has gone on to record more than a dozen albums and has remained a favorite performer at lowrider shows, especially those sponsored by *Lowrider* magazine, which also frequently carries ads announcing Frost's new recordings. For example, in its December 1995 issue, the magazine ran an ad of the newly released album *Smile Now, Die Later*, announcing that Frost—no longer Kid Frost—was not "a kid anymore." Frost has been the featured entertainer at many shows, for example, the 1996 super lowrider show in Chicago, the 1997 super show in Denver, and the 1998 super show in Albuquerque (*Lowrider* December 1995, 21).

A Lighter Shade of Brown

The rap duo Robert Gutiérrez and Bobby Ramírez, from Riverside, California, formed A Lighter Shade of Brown in 1990. They recorded their first album, *Brown and Proud*, in 1991, and it included probably their most popular song, "On a Sunday Afternoon." They would go on to record several more albums. The lyrics from this song reveal why LSOB has remained so popular among lowriders. It describes a bunch of "homies" (homeboys from the neighborhood) spending some leisure time in a public park drinking some beer and playing some music. Young women prepare food for them, the sounds of children playing in the playground nearby are heard, and lowriders cruise slowly by the park "bumpin their funky sound" on their enhanced sound systems. A policeman shows up ready to hassle the homies for drinking illegally in public, but the beer is quickly hidden. As darkness descends, the LSOB song describes the end of a perfect Sunday afternoon as families pack up and get ready to return home in preparation for a work week and school ahead of them.

LSOB has been a popular rap group at lowrider shows. For example, it was on stage with Frost and another rap group, Slow Pain, at the 1998 Albuquerque Rollerz Only–sponsored show. In the same year, LSOB performed at the 1998 Great Salt Lake City Show, where they ripped off favorites like "A Sunday Afternoon," followed by the incomparable leader of Latin rap, Frost. Cisco, a "young gun rap group" from San Francisco, followed LSOB and Frost (*Lowrider* August 1998, 144).

LSOB was the featured performer at the 2000 *Lowrider* magazine–sponsored Phoenix show, where they shared the stage with up-and-coming rap groups including 2 Hard 2 Lift and Boulevard Posse. LSOB also made appearances at what can be described as lower-profile shows such as the 1998 La Gente (The People) in California's Imperial Valley. They were again the featured rappers at the October 2009 *Lowrider* magazine–sponsored super show in Las Vegas. Another factor that has enhanced their popularity is having their music included on the soundtracks of motion pictures such as *Mi Vida Loca* (1994), *I Like It Like That* (1994), and *Bulletproof* (1996).

Delinquent Habits

Delinquent Habits (also known as Los Delinquentes) are an East Los Angeles Chicano rap group was formed in 1991. They have performed extensively around the United States as well as in Europe, Mexico, Brazil, and Japan. Their 1996 single, "Los tres delinquents" (The Three Delinquents), sold over a million copies and helped to establish them internationally. They have recorded several albums over the past few years, and some of their music has been featured on soundtracks and video games. The group's music is distinct from most other Chicano rappers because it creatively uses traditional Mexican *mariachi* music, brass instruments, Latin piano riffs, and Latin American rhythms. The group was featured in the 2005 film *Havoc* with film star Anne Hathaway. The movie is about two wealthy, Anglo-American, young adult women who find themselves in the midst of East Los Angeles gang culture. *Lowrider* magazine carried a long story about Delinquent Habits in its December 2000 issue. The group members comment on their struggle to get signed by a major recording label. Members of the group reflect on the recording industry in general and offer advice to those musicians who are just starting out, including the advantages of striking out on their own without the support of a recording company. Delinquent Habits has appeared on stage at many lowrider shows, which has given them the opportunity to sell CDs of their songs to enthusiastic audiences (*Lowrider* December 2003, 147, 167, 170).

Li'l Rob

A popular lowrider show performer, L'il Rob was born Roberto Flores in 1975 in San Diego. He acquired his nickname, Li'l Rob, when he was in third grade and became known in his neighborhood as a break dancer who demonstrated his skill in a group of older break dancers. Early in his career he was associated with gangs, and his songs often glorified them and their violence. After a bullet shattered his jaw in 1994, he dropped his affiliation with gangs and took up a new identity as simply a Chicano rapper. Like many of the younger Chicano rappers, he imitates in his appearance—shaved head, sunglasses, loose-fitting khaki pants, Pendleton shirts or white T-shirts, tennis shoes or boots—and his demeanor—a cold, hard stare and defiant stance—the typical barrio cholo stance. Much of his music falls into the "hard" sound category, with a heavy beat and the rhythmic repetition of certain words and phrases that evoke the rough life of the barrio.

In two online interviews in 2004 and 2005 with Latinrapper.com, L'il Rob talked about his maturation as a person, the development of his music, the rejection of gang violence and barrio pride, and his desire

---

"Latinrapper.com: What does being Chicano mean to you as person? L'il Rob: Just being proud of who you are. . . . It's cool and everything to be proud of where you're from. But to kill someone you don't even know because of where you're from, that crazy. Be proud of who you are, nothing wrong with being a Chicano." (http://latinrapper.com/features16.html)

to have barrio Chicanos and the way they speak and dress become more acceptable to the mainstream.

Chicano rappers tend to be male. Relatively few female rappers have been successful among Chicano lowriders, probably because lowrider culture is itself heavily male dominated. JV, a Los Angeles–based female rapper, stands out as an exception. She has performed at lowrider events such as the 1995 Classic Lowrider Tour show and has remained popular among lowriders, probably because of her direct and confrontational style that is associated with the strong stage presence of many male Chicano rappers, who frequently depict women as mere sex objects and emphasize their physical attributes such as the size of their breasts and buttocks. JV was the first Chicana rapper to release her own album, *Naybahood Queen*, in 1994, followed by other albums including *It Gets No Reala* (1996), *Ladybug* (2002), and *Hayba' Hood Queen* (2007). Her singles "Women's Lib," "Naybahood Queen," and "Bow 2 No Man" are representative of her strongly expressed views that confront male patriarchal and sexist behaviors and attitudes toward women and serve to put her on an equal social and sexual footing with her Chicano counterparts (McFarland 2008, 53).

FURTHER READING

Guevara, Rubén. "The View from the Sixth Street Bridge: The History of Chicano Rock." In *The First Rock&Roll Confidential Report*, edited by David Marsh and the editors of *Rock&Roll Confidential*. New York: Pantheon, 1994.

Lowrider December 1977, 36; July 1981, 6; July 1982, 34; August 1988, 144; December 1995, 21; December 2003, 147, 167, 170.

Loza, Steven. *Barrio Rhythm: Mexican American Music in Los Angeles*. Urbana and Chicago: University of Illinois Press, 1993.

McFarland, Pancho. *Chicano Rap: Gender and Violence in the Postindustrial Barrio*. Austin: University of Texas Press, 2008.

Molina, Ruben. *The Barrio Guide to Low Rider Music, 1950–1975*. La Puente: Mictlan Publishing, 2002.

Peña, Manuel. *Música Tejana*. College Station: Texas A&M Press, 1999.

Reyes, David and Tom Waldman, *Land of a Thousand Dances: Chicano Rock 'n' Roll from Southern California*. Albuquerque: University of New Mexico Press, 1998.

Robb, John Donald. *Hispanic Folk Music of New Mexico and the Southwest*. Norman: University of Oklahoma Press, 1980.

Rodríguez, Luis. "Eastside Sound," *Q-Vo* 2, no. 7 (1980): 27–28.

Rodríguez, Richard T. "The Verse of the Godfather: Signifying Family and Nationalism in Chicano Rap and Hip-Hop Culture." In *Velvet Barrios: Popular Culture & Chicana/o Sexualities* edited by Alicia Gaspar de Alba, 107–122. New York: Palgrave Macmillan, 2003.

Rose, Tricia. *Black Noise: Rap Music and Black Culture in Contemporary America*. Hanover: Wesleyan University Press, 1994.

6

Women in Lowrider Culture

Women have played various but generally secondary and even subservient roles in different aspects of lowrider culture, including car clubs, media, art, and music. It is important to understand how these roles have differed from those of men and how they have evolved over the past few decades from the very beginning of lowrider culture in the post–World War II era. Essential to this understanding is our knowledge about how gender functions within the larger context of Mexican and Chicana/o society. The first part of this chapter provides this context, while the rest of the chapter examines to what extent gender roles within Chicana/o society are played out and reflected in lowrider culture itself.

MEN AND WOMEN IN MEXICAN AND CHICANA/O SOCIETY

The relationship between women and men in Mexican and in Chicana/o society is complex, and it is therefore important to clarify and better understand these gender relations before discussing the role of women in lowrider culture. The term *machismo* (hypermasculinity, maleness, manliness) is still often used in the media and even in some academic scholarship to describe the Mexican as well as the Chicano male. The term refers to what are thought to be general sexist and even misogynist behaviors and attitudes towards women ranging from a general sense of superiority, bravado, and domination to condescension and overprotectiveness, especially towards female members of one's family. The term is derived from *macho*, a word whose basic meaning refers to the male of the animal species (*hembra* being the female) and, by extension, to the human male.

A standard but oversimplified and misleading interpretation of what is considered to be a typically *machista* view of women is that women fall roughly into two categories: those who are pure in every sense, especially sexual, and those who are not. The extreme version of this dual characterization of women is that they are either (1) virginal, maternal, family oriented, and loyal and reverent like the Virgin of Guadalupe, an extremely important religious icon in Mexican and Chicana/o culture; or (2) sexually active, aggressively assertive, and disloyal to the family and the culture. In this exaggerated dichotomy, women must follow certain strict norms of behavior and manifest a specific set of attitudes in order to meet the expectations of men: humility, subservience, sexual purity before marriage and disinterest in sex after marriage, self-negation, sacrifice, long-suffering, unambitiousness, submissiveness to the desires of the man, and complete devotion to the family and the wider culture.

There are various popular theories regarding the origin of machismo and the corresponding set of female attitudes and behaviors. Many who have studied gender relations in Mexican and Chicana/o culture believe that they have their origin in Roman society, that they spread throughout the Roman Empire, and that they then have persisted over the centuries in countries of the southern Mediterranean: Italy, Spain, Portugal, and France. According to this theory, the Spanish conquerors and colonizers imported these attitudes to the New World where they imposed them on indigenous cultures such as the Mayans, the Incas, and the Aztecs. Others believe that indigenous cultures were themselves highly patriarchal and that rather than the Spanish imposing their gender values and behaviors on indigenous peoples of the New World, the gender expectations of both groups simply melded together without conflict. The two contrasting theories—the imposition of patriarchal expectations of the conquerors on the conquered, or the melding of the two patriarchal systems of the Spanish and the colonized indigenous peoples—are applicable to the Spanish Southwest. The result of both theories is in practical terms the same: patriarchy, or the dominance of males over females, was firmly established as the social norm in the Spanish colonies of the New World.

The precise history of the development of relations between Chicana women and Chicano men is difficult to trace from 1848 through the 1960s, but in general the importance of the family structure reflected in marriage, the raising of children, and the strong role of the nuclear and the extended family have persisted well into the twenty-first century. Although women continued to play subservient roles, factors such as social class, religion, and education often determined the specific character of relations between women and men. Less education and the strong belief in and the practice of traditional religious teachings translated into greater adherence to traditional male-female roles; this was particularly true of the lower economic classes, for whom education and social mobility were practically nonexistent due to lack of economic opportunity. At the same time, there are many examples in Chicana/o history of women who during the period from 1848 to the 1960s became outspoken and fearless labor and political leaders. Many women published prose and poetry and persuasive editorials on a range of relevant social topics in Spanish-language newspapers. The more historians, especially Chicana historians, have studied the period between 1848 and the 1960s, the more examples of exceptional women who have broken with traditional gender roles have come to our attention. For example, early in the twentieth century, Chicanas actively participated in the Partido Liberal Mexicano (Mexican Liberal Party), the International Ladies and Garment Workers Union, and in specific labor activities such as organizing and conducting strikes in mining and in other industries. During World War II, pachucas (see Chapter 2) carved out a distinct identity and set themselves apart from not only Anglo-American middle-class values and lifestyles but also from the aspirations of many Mexican American women to join and assimilate into that middle class (see Chapter 2). Like their male counterparts, young women also dressed up in long coats (as well as short skirts, high hair teased into rats, and excessive makeup), and adopted their own presence in the public sphere by venturing out on to the streets and into the courtrooms and police stations, thereby defying the behavioral norms and expectations for young women from traditional Mexican and Mexican American families, families who had rigid standards of feminine respectability. Their transgression of both physical and social boundaries may have provided a model for Chicana feminists of the late 1960s and 1970s who also rejected the subservient roles forced on them by a patriarchal system (Ramírez 2002, 1-35).

WOMEN AND THE BEGINNING OF LOWRIDER CULTURE

Since the World War II era, differing gender attitudes and behaviors among Chicanas/os generally have corresponded to socioeconomic status and educational level. During the war years (1941–1945), many thousands of American men, but very few women, of Mexican descent served proudly in all branches of the armed forces in both Europe and the Pacific, receiving a large number of medals and other forms of recognition for their bravery. With the sudden scarcity of men to support the massive war effort back home in the United States, many thousands of married as well as single Chicanas left their traditional roles, at least for a few years, to become employed in the factories and shipyards that had geared up to produce ships, planes, tanks, jeeps, arms, and ammunition. However, when the war ended and the men returned home once again to assume their dominant roles in families, most women also reverted to their roles as subservient wives and nurturing mothers.

On the West Coast, many Chicano veterans who had become skilled mechanics, welders, iron workers, and painters in the military went to work in the newly created and rapidly growing automobile and allied industries that had been established in the Los Angeles area even before the war had ended. As nonveterans, Chicanas were not entitled to participate in the $20 weekly benefit that Chicano veterans were able to take advantage of. Due to the combination of the skills acquired during the war, the expanded employment opportunities, and the weekly benefit program, men almost exclusively were able to buy used cars and customize them as the first lowrider cruisers. (See Chapter 1). Therefore, from the very beginning of lowrider culture, Chicanas were not afforded the same opportunities as their husbands and brothers, resulting in the very minor role they would play for decades, largely as virtually invisible and passive participants in support of the men. During the 1950s and 1960s, it was the men who continued to buy and customize cars, start lowrider car clubs that either implicitly or explicitly barred women, cruise the streets of Los Angeles and San Jose, and then eventually establish businesses such as customization, paint, hydraulics, and upholstery shops. The character of working-class lowrider culture during its formative decades was therefore distinctly male dominated and mirrored the rigidly hierarchical and patriarchal roles of women and men in the wider context of Chicana/o culture in general and more particularly in the working-class segment of the Chicana/o population.

THE RISE OF CHICANA FEMINISM IN THE 1970s

The 1960s brought about momentous changes in U.S. society with the intensification of the civil rights movement among African Americans, Native Americans, and Chicanas/os, the approval of the Civil Rights Act and Voting Rights Act by the U.S. Congress, protest against U.S. participation in the Vietnam War, and the feminist movement. The Chicano movement was a broad-based social movement characterized by protest against the historic racism and second-class citizenship manifested in disparities in the workplace, in educational institutions, and in the political life of the country. Social justice, economic and social equality, educational reforms, and political and economic self-determination for Chicana/o communities became some of the salient issues around which Chicanas/os organized their protests. César Chávez and Dolores Huerta led the United Farm Workers, which successfully unionized agricultural farm workers in California and in other states in order to improve their working conditions and pay. Rodolfo "Corky" Gonzales organized the Denver-based Crusade for Justice, which promoted urban political activities and the mobilization of young Chicanas/os. Reis López Tijerina headed up the New Mexico–based Land Grant Movement, which focused on restoring the ownership and control of Spanish land grants to their proper owners. José Angel Gutiérrez organized La Raza Unida Party, which enjoyed several successes in Texas municipal elections. The Chicano student movement was organized around establishing equality of opportunity and access at all levels of education. The Chicano Moratorium against the Vietnam War brought about the participation of Chicanas/os in the antiwar movement. Yet, despite raised political and social awareness among all segments of the Chicana/o population, most of the women active in these different aspects of the Chicano movement were not accorded the respect and the influence that they deserved—that is, until the early 1970s with the rise of Chicana feminism, which "emerged primarily as a result of the dynamics within the Chicano movement" (García, 1990, 418–431).

Chicanas played a secondary role in the Chicano movement, especially that part of it that emphasized cultural nationalism, which represented a major ideological component of the movement that stressed the importance of cultural pride and cultural survival. An essential aspect of this pride and survival dictated that men and women alike adhere to a strict code of thought and behavior that emphasized so-called traditional Mexican and Chicano values such as the family and *carnalismo* (brotherhood). Issues of gender inequality were nonexistent or, at best, low on the list of priorities for the male-led movement. According to the largely male leadership, the primary task of cultural nationalists was to combat racism and economic exploitation.

Chicanas who were active in the movement increasingly began to question the treatment that they were receiving from Chicanos, especially the expectation that the women play a supporting but unequal role in maintaining the integrity of the family and carrying out the behind-the-scenes tasks of washing, cooking, child care, and clerical work while the men in leadership positions were primarily responsible for setting the political agenda. As Chicanas began to question these roles and confront the men, they were often accused of "selling out" to Anglo-American feminism, of betraying the goals set forth by the largely male cultural nationalist leadership, and of compromising group solidarity. In the 1970s, Chicana feminists became increasingly more assertive and outspoken within the movement in advancing their agenda as independent women who rejected the explicitly sexist male attitudes towards them embodied in the belief that machismo was a form of cultural resistance and a source of cultural pride. These Chicanas were attacked, denigrated, and scorned not only by some movement men but also by so-called Chicana loyalists, who accused their sisters of betraying their cultural ideals, of being antifamily, anti-culture, antiman, and therefore anti–Chicano movement; they were accused of selling out to the middle-class Anglo-American feminist agenda.

Through their writings and in public forums, Chicana feminists forcefully rejected the criticism that cultural nationalism and feminism were irreconcilable. They founded their own publications such as the newspapers *Regeneración* and *Hijas de Cuauhtemoc*, and the journal *De Colores*, in which women contributed editorials and articles that advanced their own agenda. For example, Alma M. García, a feminist scholar, wrote: "[Chicanas] can no longer remain in a subservient role or as auxiliary forces in the [Chicano] movement. They must be included in the front line of communication, leadership and organizational responsibility. . . . The issue of equality, freedom and self-determination of the Chicana—like the right of self-determination, equality and liberation of the Mexican [Chicano] community—is not negotiable" (García 1990, 420).

THE EAST LOS ANGELES LOWRIDER COMMUNITY
AND THE CHICANO MOVEMENT

There is little documentation available that the lowrider community as a whole was active in the Chicano movement during the late 1960s and early 1970s, although individual lowriders probably participated in specific movement activities such as the public school walkouts and the protests against the Vietnam War in Los Angeles. Many lowriders across the Southwest either volunteered or were drafted into the military during the Vietnam War era, and many of them fought in Vietnam. Others left the lowriding scene to enroll in community and four-year colleges and universities, and undoubtedly there were among them those who participated in on-campus student organizations such as MEChA (Movimiento Estudiantil de Chicanos de Aztlán, or the Student Movement of Chicanos of Aztlán) and MAYO (Mexican American Youth Organization), and many past and current lowriders were involved in a wide variety of community activities.

The events surrounding the Whittier Boulevard events of the late 1960s served as the focal point for the lowrider community's involvement in political activities, at least in the Los Angeles area. Many businesses on this major street were owned by individuals who lived outside of East Los Angeles. These business owners had requested and received assistance from local law enforcement authorities to prevent lowriders from cruising on Whittier, claiming that such activity was intimidating customers and discouraging them from patronizing their businesses. The heavy presence of law enforcement personnel on the street at night and the increased participation of Chicano students—including lowriders—from area colleges and universities protesting this presence dramatically increased tensions on Whittier that finally erupted into confrontations on July 3 and 4, 1968. Many students and lowriders were arrested by members of the Los Angeles County Sheriff's Department, which probably served to politicize at least some members of the East Los Angeles lowrider community. Confrontations and arrests continued for the next three nights, resulting in the complete closure to cruising of Whittier Boulevard. Due to the support and active participation of students in these events, at least some members of the lowrider community began to be more open to the political agenda of the Chicano movement, especially the sense of cultural pride it engendered.

The intersection of the lowrider community and the Chicano movement was limited, yet what both seemed to have in common was a decidedly patriarchal and sexist view of the role of women as equal partners, especially in not encouraging women to hold positions of power, influence, and leadership in their respective organizations such as college and university student groups and lowrider clubs and publications. Many car clubs barred women from membership, and in other car clubs that allowed women to join as members their participation was limited and secondary. Much like Chicana feminists, who were not encouraged to occupy positions of leadership and influence in Chicano movement organizations, women generally played restricted support roles in male-dominated car clubs in the 1960s by doing the cooking and taking care of the children at lowrider events. And much like the young women in the early days of the movement, women, especially those who were considered physically attractive, were always welcomed at lowrider activities but as objects of desire and not as subjects with an integral part in the lowrider community's organizational leadership. Older lowrider clubs such as the Southern California-based Imperials, Lifestyle, and Klique clubs barred women from membership at least into the 1970s. Klique president Mando Estrada was perhaps representative of male attitudes towards women in their lowriding communities: "It is much easier to build a quality car because of the money and the overhead and all that is cut in half" (Penland 2003, 44–45).

Like Chicana feminists who had gone their independent way to found their own organizations in the 1970s and 1980s, women lowriders established their own all-woman car clubs such as the Lady Bugs Car Club, founded in 1974 under the leadership of sisters Yvonne and Suzie Vallego. Even today, all-woman lowrider car clubs exist, such as the UnderEstimated Low Rider Car Club of Tacoma and Oakland that specifies in its bylaws as a minimum requirement for membership: "Must be *female* [emphasis in the original] and able to participate in club functions and fund-raisers." (www.myspace.com/underestimated_tacoma)

By the late 1970s, even the more established lowrider car clubs began to accept women as members who began customizing their own cars. For example, Caroline Acosta of Salinas, California, began lowering cars for several clubs, including her own Brown Satins club as well as the Latin Pearls and Shades of Brown clubs. She and other women also began to cruise the streets and to show their cars at lowrider happenings in Northern California. In the 1980s, women began to move into positions of leadership, as Josie López did when she became director of the 24-club Arizona Lowriders Association, which was instrumental in negotiating with municipal officials to allow lowriders to continue cruising on Central Avenue in Phoenix (Penland 2003, 44–45).

LOWRIDER MAGAZINE AND THE PERPETUATION
OF SEXISM IN LOWRIDER CULTURE

The numerous men's and women's magazines, as well as automobile and motorcycle specialty magazines, that can be found in practically any large magazine display area at newsstands and in supermarkets, shopping malls, and in large chain book stores such as Borders, and Barnes & Noble display covers of women's seminude bodies in provocative poses. Lowrider publications frequently sold at these venues follow the same practice, presumably because it has proven to be an effective marketing strategy that sells more magazines.

Lowrider magazine, which was founded in 1979 by three former students at San Jose City College (see Chapter 3), has played a major role in perpetuating sexist attitudes towards women in lowrider culture. The founders had been involved in the publication of Chicano political magazines *El Machete*, *Bronze*, and *La Palabra* during their student days, and presumably they were also involved in Chicano movement activities at the same time. They are said to have founded the magazine to capture the lowrider lifestyle and to connect that lifestyle to life in Chicano barrios. Related to these twin goals was the intent expressed in the magazine's early mission statement to bring to the United States and to the world knowledge about Chicanos, especially young Chicanos, and their lifestyles. They may have achieved these goals by presenting a very select slice of this lifestyle and, in part, by presenting women in a consistently sexualized way that portrays them as one-dimensional beings whose bodies male readers are invited to gaze at and enjoy. Those editors who succeeded the magazine's original editors continued this practice.

College- and university-based movement agendas were generally progressive in terms of issues of racism, economic exploitation, and developing cultural pride, but they reflected little understanding or sympathy for women who felt excluded from meaningful leadership roles in student organizations and publications. Chicano movement publications dominated by male editors and like-minded women were often dismissive of the gender equality concerns voiced by Chicanas, but the publications were rarely demeaning of women by portraying them as objects of sexual desire, a trend that has characterized *Lowrider* magazine almost since its founding in 1977.

Roughly two years after its first issue, the editors of *Lowrider,* still the three original members of Low Rider Associates who were responsible for founding it and making it financially solvent, decided on a market strategy to make it more profitable: the display of scantily clad women in passive poses on the covers and throughout the magazine's pages, including the national beer and cigarette ads that quickly followed. Up until then, both men and women (fully clothed) had appeared on the covers. The first cover girl, Mona, who was still a high school student, posed in a white bikini to promote the first Low Rider Super Show in Los Angeles. She was supposedly expelled from her Catholic high school as a result. As reflected from the letters to the editor in forthcoming issues, the controversy that ensued among readers was divided among those, both men and women, who protested the new look and those who approved. Despite the controversy, the magazine's editors were convinced that they had discovered a successful market strategy that would increase sales. In fact, sales did soon increase by 15 to 20 percent. It is not clear to what extent *Lowrider* magazine was simply reflecting the sexism and misogyny prevalent in the lowrider community, but what seems evident is that the publication has played a major role in promoting and perpetuating these destructive attitudes over the past several decades.

No survey of *Lowrider* magazine's readership has ever been made public, nor are there any independent studies of the readership's breakdown by gender. In addition, it is difficult to arrive at a definitive conclusion based on the letters that have been published because these have been carefully selected by the editors. There is no way of learning about the content and the number of those letters that have not made it into the magazine, but judging from readers' letters that have appeared in its pages since it was founded, at least some of the letters were written by women. Some of these letters in the earlier issues of *Lowrider* magazine are "Dear Abby" letters. Chicanas would write offering advice to other Chicanas on a range of issues including man trouble involving husbands and partners who spent too much time on their cars. Rather than receiving a response from the editors, letters such as these would typically start a dialogue between readers, both men and women (Sandoval 2003, 179–196).

To the credit of the magazine's male editors, occasionally they would include a letter that would question and critique some of the sexist practices in lowrider culture itself. A good example is a letter from an anonymous reader, "La Muñeca from San Fran" (The Doll from San Francisco), published in 1979, in which a woman reader writes to complain and point out to her "macho hermanos" (macho brothers) how their "little hermanas" feel about lowriders who are overprotective of the young women in their lives and who do not let them to drive their cars for fear of having them damage their delicate hydraulics. Significantly, the reader does not complain about the magazine's masculinist discourse or about the seminude women displayed in its pages; rather, she proudly identifies herself as a model (*Lowrider* September 1979, 5).

Denise Michelle Sandoval, a scholar who has provided an analysis of the readers' letters to *Lowrider* during its first two years of publication, observes that "the issue of women's bodies within other letters demonstrates how women in turn accept codes of beauty and femininity." That is, whether it is a magazine with a largely female readership like *Latina* or one with a largely male readership like *Lowrider* and other lowrider magazines, all of which display the seminude bodies of women, their female readers take the media's standards of beauty and then objectify themselves, that is, they willingly offer images of their seminude bodies to the male gaze. This is an important observation to keep in mind in looking at the role of female models and "wannabe" models and the bikini contests at lowrider shows as well as the roles that women play in lowrider videos, movies, and music (Sandoval 2003, 190).

Despite several changes in editorship and ownership of *Lowrider* over the past several decades, the magazine continues to use female seminudity on its covers, in feature stories on lowrider vehicles, and in advertisements, presumably in order to attract and hold its largely male readership. The magazine's editors have evaded dealing directly with critiques of sexism and misogyny in editorials or letters to the editor. As the editors of other successful lowrider and nonlowrider magazines have discovered, the use of sexy females is a successful marketing strategy that sells magazines. Only *Lowrider Bicycle* magazine, which is directed at a young, pre-adult readership, has not resorted to using seminude images of women.

At the same time that editors and publishers have perpetuated images of seminude women in lowrider publications, they have also tried to emphasize the respectable community and family-friendly aspects of lowrider culture by, for example, including features and images of older lowrider owners and innovators—usually men—who have made significant contributions to lowrider culture as well as features and images of multigenerational families who continue to be involved in lowriding. It is not uncommon to find on alternating pages of recent issues of *Lowrider* or *Streetlow* magazines stories about a lowrider pioneer, an multigenerational lowrider family, or a lowrider professional like a lawyer or a doctor, only to turn the page to encounter a stunning women model posing by an equally striking lowrider vehicle. It is not clear if this strategy is designed to attract a diverse readership with different interests and tastes, but the persistence of the strategy suggests that it is effective in selling magazines.

WOMEN IN LOWRIDER FILMS AND VIDEOS

The characterization of women in lowrider films and videos (see Chapter 3 for greater detail on lowrider films and videos) varies, but it is generally contained within the narrow parameters of gender roles that are associated with patriarchal values in traditional Mexican and Chicana/o culture. Even the strong female leads in feature films such as *Boulevard Nights* and *Heartbreaker* cannot not be described as manifesting Chicana feminist attitudes and corresponding behaviors even when they are contrasted to other, less assertive women in the films

In *Boulevard Nights*, the female lead, Shady Londeros, is portrayed as an upwardly mobile young Chicana with aspirations to marry and have a family while still maintaining her middle-class career in a respectable office away from the barrio. Shady is physically very attractive but modest, even demure, in contrast to the young women who appear in lowrider scenes striving to obtain the attention of the male lowriders through flirtatious behavior and the flaunting of their sexuality. The are characterized as lacking a strong and confident self-image and a corresponding ambition to improve themselves by escaping the limiting life of sexual embellishments of the lowrider scene, of which they are an essential aspect. Shady loves Raymond but not unconditionally; she issues a quiet ultimatum that to continue their relationship he must abandon his active participation in his gang and the lowrider scene as well as his employment in a chop shop. Shady prefers that he seek to improve himself as she has done by striving to further his education and eventually find employment in a more middle-class sector of the economy. Once he demonstrates his willingness to do so, that is, to sacrifice his comfortable and nonchallenging life for one that holds more promise, Shady agrees to marry him. Her overriding goal is to start a family and to maintain a trajectory of upward economic and social mobility, not to challenge her role as a woman. Nowhere in the film is it suggested that she desires to break out of the confines of her future role as a caring mother and loyal spouse. Her aspirations are very much in line with those of U.S. women of different ethnicities who have made the successful transition from working- to middle-class life without fundamentally challenging their respective cultures' expectations that they continue to function in traditional gender roles as women.

Although she does not play as prominent role in *Boulevard Nights* as Shady, Raymond and Chuco's mother deserves comment. Their father, her husband, is absent from the family home, so it has fallen on the mother to provide parenting, guidance, and emotional support for her sons. Raymond is clearly her favorite son, whom she holds up to Chuco, a source of her deepening concern and disappointment, as a model to be emulated. The mother is depicted in a traditional role as a long-suffering woman who has sacrificed a great deal in order to provide for her sons. Her tragic death by a stray bullet at the end of the film serves to underline her long-suffering and abjectness as a traditional woman in Chicana/o culture.

Shady's counterpart in the film *Heartbreaker* is Kim, a young and beautiful blond who like Shady draws a line in the sand in her relationship to Beto, a young Chicano lowrider who seems to be in the midst of a transition away from an active lowrider life. At the beginning of the film, he expresses his preference to pass on the presidency of his lowrider car club to Angel, a younger member in whom Beto sees leadership potential. Shady is also in transition as she moves towards leaving the family home to establish her independence as a young working woman with her own apartment. Like Shady, she adheres to a set of clear expectations in her relationship with a significant man in her life. As Beto courts her, she insists that their relationship cannot continue unless he treats her with greater respect and sensibility than he and his male friends do in their casual relationships with the young women with whom they run in their lowrider group. She views these women as lacking in self-respect and in having a positive image as they throw themselves at the men in a way that demeans them as women. Unlike these women, Kim is depicted as much more modest and protective of her sexuality and more demanding in what she desires in a close relationship with a man. Like Shady, she is critical of the lowrider lifestyle, but unlike Shady, Kim is not portrayed as considering it an impediment to upward economic and social mobility. Like Shady, Kim holds a steady job and aspires to marry and have a family. Once Beto becomes aware that he must change in order to continue to develop a relationship with Kim, she also must become more open to allowing the relationship to mature. At the end of the film, Beto and Kim are portrayed as young couple committed to each other, but there is no suggestion that Kim has developed a desire to move her role as a woman beyond the cultural expectations that she will be a loyal partner committed to a traditional male. She seems content to take her place as part of the lowriding family even as she has garnered a greater deal of respect from Beto and his friends.

In Efraín Gutiérrez's comedy-of-errors film *Lowrider Weekend* (see Chapter 3), women play a decidedly secondary role to the male characters: Sonny, a small-time entertainment promoter with a gambling problem; a Chicano mafia figure; Danny de La Paz, a popular Chicano actor; Baby Marín, a friend who rescues Sonny from his own his own incompetence; and Armando, a young lowrider who is suffering from a recent breakup with his girlfriend. The women in the film play vacuous and one-dimensional characters: Sonny's receptionist, who emerges from her mousy role to discover her own considerable physical beauty; an elderly Chicana who blatantly flirts with younger men; and a young Chicana who comes to Sonny's lowrider show but who soon takes on the role as Armando's new love interest. The only female who seems to break out a proscribed role is Sonny's teenage daughter, who throughout the film is characterized as assertive and independent. It is not clear if Gutiérrez views her as representative of a new generation of confident and independent Chicanas who will refuse to conform to patriarchal expectations. He gives her a role that at least puts her on this path.

What strikes the viewer of the documentaries about lowrider culture such as *Lowriding in Aztlán: The Truth about Lowriding!* is the almost complete absence of women either as interviewees or as active participants in lowrider activities. Only *Sunday Drivers: A Look at the Guys Behind the Chrome*, a documentary about an African American lowrider car club, affords a woman, Dee Dee Girl, the opportunity to articulate her own views as the only female member of the Compton, California, club. That she was allowed to join the club as an owner of her own lowrider cruiser is in itself a significant achievement when contrasted with some of the older, established Los Angeles–area clubs who either still bar women or have only recently allowed them to have full membership. Dee Dee Girl represents herself as a strong and determined young woman who has worked hard to gain the respect of the male members of the club.

Lowrider event videos make no attempt to present a balanced view of women. Women are depicted at best as accessories to enhance for the male viewer the lowrider events that are featured in the videos. Shots of seductively posed and scantily clad models are edited into the videos almost as subliminal flashes. Women dressed in a similar fashion appear at each pause in the hopping and dancing competitions to announce the next stage in the competition, much like the women who appear in the ring to announce rounds at major boxing matches. In *Lowrider Experience*, Kitana Baker, a well-known model in the lowrider community, makes frequent appearances during several sequences that feature various categories of hopping and dancing. At one point, she lifts her tightly fitting shirt to expose her breasts, a move that elicits cheers from the both the men and women present at the competition. Such explicit nudity is generally not part of most lowrider shows, but bikini contests and wet T-shirt contests are a staple at some of the larger shows. More common are the young women dressed in provocative model outfits who roam the indoor lowrider vehicle exhibits, posing and being photographed by professional photographers. The photographs will become part of the models' portfolios and, for the lucky ones, their photographs will appear in the pages of *Lowrider* magazine accompanying a feature story on the show where they were photographed.

WOMEN IN LOWRIDER ART

The pattern of sexism towards women combined with the minor roles that women play in other aspects of lowrider culture are also found in lowrider art in lowrider magazines such as *Lowrider Arte* and in the images of women that are common as murals on lowrider vehicles. There are relatively few women who have been recognized as lowrider car painters, designers, or artists whose work is displayed either in magazines or on lowrider vehicles. The absence of women in these aspects of lowrider culture may account for the fact that most of the murals of women in magazines and on vehicles are highly sexualized and demeaning. These images seemed designed to attract and hold the male gaze.

Along with the car mural images of Mexican male historical figures such as Miguel Hidalgo, Benito Juárez, Emiliano Zapata, and Pancho Villa (see Chapter 4), 1910 Mexican revolutionary females are also popular, usually in the form of revolucionarias and soldaderas— women who either fought alongside male revolutionaries or supported them as nurses, cooks and sometimes sexual partners—who are often depicted in very seductive and provocative poses with or without their blouses. A common image is of a young female soldier with nothing but ammunition bandoleers crisscrossing her upper body.

Many murals painted on lowrider vehicles (see Chapter 4) are of the male mythic figure Popocatépetl and female mythic figure Iztaccihuatl. These are images borrowed from the images created by the Mexican popular artist Jesús Helguera and found today on wall calendars dispensed to loyal customers by Chicana/o business owners. The Aztec male is portrayed as a young muscular warrior, the Aztec maiden as a semiclad and buxom young Aztec maiden. In some renditions, she has died and he is mourning her; in others she is very much alive. When these Aztec figures are found as murals on lowrider vehicles, the woman's barely dressed physique is exaggerated, and sometimes her upper body is fully exposed.

WOMEN AND LOWRIDER MUSIC

The Eastside Sound (see Chapter 5) of the late 1950s and the early 1960s was deeply influenced by the working-class experience of young Chicanas/os growing up in the projects and barrios of East Los Angeles. It was the male singers who were largely responsible for giving Eastside rock and roll its character that emphasized working-class masculinity. Although these singers may have borrowed a feminine mod movement dress from British groups, the romantic lyrics of their songs tended to reinforce the idea that women are the objects of male desire and without their own agency. The titles of songs composed and sung by groups popular among lowriders such as Thee Midniters reflected the sentiments of males towards their former girlfriends: "My Heart Cries," "Don't Let Go," "Empty Heart," "I Need Someone," "It Still Ain't Over for Me," "That's All," and "Sad Girl." These titles and their respective lyrics cast women in secondary and passive roles in male-female relationships (Espinoza 2003, 92).

An exception to the Eastside Sound male singers of the 1960s is Ersi Arvizu, the Chicana vocalist who became best known for her rendition of the Mexican ballad "Sabor a mí" (see Chapter 5). Arvizu performed with several Chicano rock groups including El Chicano, which was very popular among lowriders. This group performed at many lowrider events during the peak years of its popularity. As the strong lead vocalist for El Chicano for many years, Arvizu found a niche in the slowly changing youth culture of East Los Angeles that in the late 1960s had become politicized as part of the social and educational agenda associated with the Chicano movement. The lyrics of her signature song, "Sabor a mí," departed from the dominant role of the male in a romantic relationship and presented in its place a relationship based more on equality between a woman and a man. In addition, the fact that the ballad was sung by a very popular female performer signaled to its listeners that women can have agency, that is, they can play an active role in a relationship. Arvizu's success as an entertainer in a male-dominated group and in an industry dominated by men was also a symbol to young women fans of the potential they could achieve in their own lives.

Rap music in general is highly sexist and misogynist, and the Chicana/o rap music popular with lowriders since the 1990s is not an exception. The Chicano movement's male activists framed the concept of *familia* (family) in patriarchal terms that relegated women to subservient and passive roles. A similar hierarchical ordering of gender is present in much Chicana/o rap music but carried to an extreme.

Produced by male rappers and directed at a working-class male audience since its earliest days, much of its content portrays women in a decidedly negative way.

Chicano Frost's song "La Raza" is representative of the negative image of women prevalent in much of Chicana/o rap music (see Chapter 5). It has been extensively played since its release in 1990 and was included in Frost's first album, *Hispanic Causing Panic*. The rapper expresses in song a deep pride in his ethnicity, his extended brown family, and its cultural traditions in a way that has been compared to the 1967 epic poem, "I Am Joaquín," by Chicano activist Rodolfo "Corky" Gonzales. Frost invokes a call to defiant opposition to forces who oppress Chicanos—the song seems to be directed at an exclusively male audience—on the streets of their own barrios. At the same time, Frost is critical of those men who are, in his view, not worthy of respect because they are not masculine enough, especially in their heterosexuality and in their masculinist behavior towards women, whom he seems to consider as sexual objects. The song's title seems to be inclusive of all Chicanas/os, but the lyrics suggest that Frost is equating "la raza" with his homeboys in the barrios whose proof of manhood comes at the expense of women; this is a deeply misogynist message. The *familia* (family) he refers to in the lyrics is exclusive, and in this sense it is inconsistent with the more inclusive message of the epic poem that Frost apparently used as his model. He continues to use the trope of the male-centered family in his later lyrics, in which he seems to expand the idea of the Chicano family to include others except perhaps gays and lesbians (Rodríguez 2003, 116).

There are few Chicano or Chicana rappers who in their songs advocate for Chicana resistance to and independence from male domination and who promote greater female agency. JV, a Los Angeles–based female rapper, is probably the best example who stands out as an exception (see Chapter 5). She has performed at lowrider events since the mid-1990s. Her direct and confrontational style is similar to the strong stage presence of many male Chicano rappers, who frequently depict women as mere sex objects and who emphasize their physical attributes such as the size of their breasts and buttocks. JV was the first Chicana rapper to release her own album, *Naybahood Queen* in 1994, followed by other albums including *It Gets No Reala* (1996), *Ladybug* (2002), and *Hayba' Hood Queen* (2007). Her singles "Women's Lib," "Naybahood Queen," and "Bow 2 No Man" are representative of her strongly expressed views that confront male patriarchal and sexist behaviors and attitudes towards women and serve to put her on an equal social and sexual footing with her Chicano counterparts (McFarland 2008, 33).

FURTHER READING

Espinoza, Dionne. "Tanto Tiempo Disfrutamos . . . ": Revisiting Gender and Sexual Politics of Chicana/o Youth Culture in East Los Angeles in the 1960s." In *Velvet Barrios: Popular Culture and Chicana/ o Sexualities*, edited by Alicia Gaspar de Alba, 89–106. Hampshire, England: Palgrave Macmillan, 2003.

García, Alma M. "The Development of Chicana Feminist Discourse, 1970–1980." *Unequal Sisters: A Multicultural Reader of U.S. Women's History*, edited by Ellen Carol DuBois and Vicki L. Ruiz, 418–431. New York and London: Routledge, 1990.

Keller, Gary. *Hispanics and United States Film: An Overview and Handbook.* Tempe, AZ: Bilingual Review Press, 1994.

Lowrider, September 1979, 5.

McFarland, Pancho. *Chicano Rap: Gender and Violence in the Postindustrial Barrio.* Austin: University of Texas Press, 2008.

Penland, Paige R. *Lowrider: History, Pride, Culture.* St. Paul, MN: MBI Publishing, 2003.

Plascencia, Luis F. B. "Low Riding in the Southwest: Cultural Symbols in the Mexican Community." In *History, Culture and Society: Chicano Studies in the 1980s*, edited by Mario T. García, 141–175. Ypsilanti, Michigan: Bilingual Press/Editorial Bilingue, 1983.

Ramírez, Catherine S. "Crimes of Fashion: The Pachuca and Chicana Style Politics." *Meridians* 2, no. 2 (2002): 1–35.

Rodríguez, Richard T. "The Verse of the Godfather: Signifying Family and Nationalism in Chicano Rap and Hip-Hop Culture." In *Velvet Barrios: Popular Culture & Chicana/o Sexualities*, edited by Alicia Gaspar de Alba 107–122. New York: Palgrave Macmillan, 2003.

Sandoval, Denise Michelle. "Cruising through Low Rider Culture: Chicana/o Identity in the Marketing of *Low Rider* Magazine." In *Velvet Barrios: Popular Culture and Chicana/o Sexualities*, edited by Alicia Gaspar de Alba, 179–196. Hampshire, England: Palgrave Macmillan, 2003.

7

Lowrider Clubs

Today, there are hundreds of lowrider clubs throughout the United States as well as in Mexico, Canada, Japan, England, Germany, and a few other countries. The majority of these clubs are located in large cities in California, Arizona, Colorado, New Mexico, and Texas, where lowrider culture itself has prospered over the past several decades. This chapter will provide an overview of the origins of lowrider clubs; their evolution, changing roles, and general characteristics; and the similarities and differences of clubs in the twenty-first century.

ORIGINS

Together with Detroit, Los Angeles in the post–World War II era had established itself as an important and dynamic automotive manufacturing and design center (see Chapter 1). The car became central to Los Angeles's middle- and working-class Anglo-American population, who were abandoning the inner city for the new suburbs. These suburbs were being built very rapidly on the periphery of the downtown area to accommodate this sector of Los Angeles's population as well as thousands of new residents from all over the United States who were flocking to Southern California in search of jobs in the area's rapidly expanding manufacturing economy. Along with the proliferation of suburbs, an extensive freeway system was designed and built to facilitate easy access by car between homes and places of employment. The car acquired a utilitarian purpose, but it also took on a recreational one as it came to be seen as a source of an owner's pride and prestige, especially when the owner invested time and energy in improving the vehicle's performance and looks.

In this rapidly expanding car culture, hot rods and hot rod culture had been very popular among Los Angeles's youth for several decades before World War II. These original hot rodders generally held liberal views towards the inclusion of minority groups such as working-class Mexican Americans, African Americans, and Asian Americans in their group activities. These attitudes changed after the war as newly formed hot rod clubs became more exclusionary and more segregated, paralleling the rapidly changing urbanization patterns in Los Angeles after the mid-1940s. Hot rod culture was after World War II much more closely associated with middle-class Anglo-American youth living in the peripheral white suburbs such as those in the San Fernando Valley as well as Glendale, Pomona, South Pasadena, and South Gate, areas where ethnic and racial integration was vigorously resisted. In the 1950s, hot rodding had become a middle-class hobby with an emphasis on the building and maintenance of high-performance hot rods designed for speed. This required an economic investment not available to most Mexican American, African American, and Asian American youth living in inner city areas such as East Los Angeles and South Central Los Angeles. In addition, their very ethnicity became a barrier to their full acceptance, recognition, and status within hot rod clubs (Ides 2009).

Along with popularity of hot rods, the custom car craze became increasingly more prominent after 1945 and particularly in the 1950s as well-known California customizers such as Harry Westergard, George Barris, "Big Daddy" Roth, and Larry Watson used their considerable artistic talents to produce cars more for show than for speed, which was central to hot rod racing and dragging. For a time in the early 1950s, custom car clubs like the Thunderbolts required in their bylaws that members' cars have a dropped suspension, which later became an essential characteristic of lowrider cruisers. Other custom car clubs such as the Honeydrippers, the Pan Draggers, the Street Scrapers, the Cut Outs, the Roadrunners, and the Renegades emphasized the low-slung look. In addition, club members enhanced their cars' appearance with first-class paint treatments, scallops, and other embellishments associated with Westergard, Barris, Roth, Watson, and others who were prominent in the custom car community (Penland 2003, 14; also, see Chapter 4).

Initially, then, the clubs that focused on customizing cars for show were inclusive in welcoming individuals from different ethnic and racial groups who shared a common interest in cars with altered suspensions combined with custom paint and other external elements. These clubs rejected the speed-focused hot rod youth culture and its development as an Anglo-American, middle-class pursuit. Gradually during the 1950s, high-end customizers such as Roth became more commercialized when they came to the attention of the automobile industry. These and other customizers were identified as a source of inspiration for the Detroit car designers who incorporated at least some of their custom elements in new models such as "muscle" cars that were targeted at young, middle-class, and largely Anglo-American buyers who could afford them. Barris also sold his name and designs to a commercial line of designs and paints and tried to market his cars directly to the Anglo-American middle-class teen market in Southern California. Roth was an exception among customizers; he rejected the middle-class hot rod culture and what he considered to be a culture of conformity in favor of nonconformist art designed to appeal to teenage male fantasy. He designed outlandish cars such as his 1959 design "Outlaw," a futuristic Ford roadster, and promoted his signature character Rat Fink (Ides 2009, 117, 157).

During the 1950s, youth car clubs in the Los Angeles area increasingly reflected the racial and the ethnic segregation of the city's neighborhoods and suburbs. In more prosperous, largely Anglo-American areas, local mechanics, custom shops, and gas stations sponsored car clubs, often providing them with a space where the young owners could draw on adult expertise and use some of the specialty tools to work on their cars. Shops and gas stations also provided places where the cars could be shown and admired at night and on weekends and where club members could plan activities such as dances, picnics, racing, and street cruising. Clubs developed distinctive identification markers such as hats, rings, and plaques that would distinguish them from other clubs, and some clubs began to focus more on the dress style of their members than on the cars themselves (Ides 2009, 141).

In the 1950s, East Los Angeles consisted of many ethnically diverse neighborhoods made up primarily of working-class Anglos-Americans, Mexican Americans, African Americans, and Asian Americans. Increasing immigration from Mexico and across California and the Southwest would gradually transform East Los Angeles into the center of Los Angeles's Mexican American population. East Los Angeles car clubs during this era—not yet known as lowrider clubs—tended to put more emphasis on the social aspects of cars rather than on the elements of speed and design that were paramount to the hot rod and custom car clubs in other areas of Los Angeles. Club members would typically scavenge for parts in auto junk yards in order to build their cars cheaply but stylishly.

Car clubs afforded Mexican American and other ethnically diverse young people the opportunity to be involved in activities that accelerated their social integration into community life and enhanced their leadership skills. Clubs like the East Los Angeles Drifters sponsored group activities such as work on cars, dances, and participation in ethnic celebrations such as the Mexican Independence Day parades. East Los Angeles community organizations such as the Catholic Youth Organization (CYO) promoted and supported affiliated car clubs as a way of discouraging teenagers from joining the gangs that were becoming more numerous. The growing number of car clubs in East Los Angeles led to the creation of the Federation of Social and Car Clubs (FSCC), a parent organization whose mission it was to enhance the image of East Los Angeles youth and provide educational and social opportunities such as dances. Some of the East Los Angeles clubs that the FSCC supported were the Coffin Cheaters, the Charmers, the Dreamers, the Playboys, the Road Knightettes, the Royal Escorts, the Valve Rockers, and Los Torredos. "Car clubs provided a social space and group on the periphery of the school, family and church, a space in which young people controlled the contours of their own culture" (Ides 2009, 150).

THE FIRST LOWRIDER CAR CLUBS

The first lowrider car clubs are part of a long tradition of Mexican Americans in the Southwest of voluntary or community *mutalistas* (mutual-aid organizations), protective societies, and social clubs that, dating as far back as the late nineteenth century, had as their purpose to provide social, cultural, and economic support to members of their communities. These societies were very popular in Mexico and Latin America and were brought to the United States by immigrant workers in areas such as mining, the railroad, and agriculture. For example, miners who came north banded together to protect members and their families from debts that they might have incurred due to illness, accidents, death, or old age (Acuña 1999, 122).

The first lowrider clubs drew on the social dimension of these traditional associations as a model in creating a place where people could gather to share common interests, sponsor dances and picnics, and engage in other community social and charitable activities. The first automotive clubs served to unite and recruit enthusiasts—mainly young Chicanos but later African Americans and other minority groups—who had a common interest in lowriding, the lowrider vehicle, custom car building, and cruising, They served to unite craftsmen—there were hardly any women at the beginning—who had a keen interest in lowrider art and culture and other forms of car modification and restoration. Once formed, car club members could then recruit like-minded enthusiasts and specialists—upholsterers, painters, muralists, mechanics, and hydraulic technicians—in building and renovating lowrider vehicles. By pooling their enthusiasm, camaraderie, access, common interests, and expertise, lowrider car clubs could then provide support to members that would normally not be available to the solo lowrider (Mendoza 2000, 9).

THE DUKES LOWRIDER CLUB

The four Ruelas brothers—Julio, Oscar, Fernando, and Ernie—started the Dukes car club, the first club with an explicit lowrider identity, in Los Angeles in 1962. They founded the club to provide themselves and their friends an alternative to belonging to a gang. There was tremendous peer pressure at the time for young adults to declare their allegiance to their barrio gang, and in fact the brothers had in the 1950s been members of 38th Street gang in East Los Angeles, the same gang that had garnered such negative media attention in 1942 when the *Los Angeles Times* and other newspapers whipped up popular condemnation of the Sleepy Lagoon defendants, who were members of this gang. (See Chapter 3)

Josefina Ruelas, their single mother, had brought the four boys to Los Angeles from Tijuana as immigrants in the mid-1950s. They all lived in the house of her Los Angeles relatives, who included Uncle Tinker and Tía Chana. The short documentary film *Low and Slow* (1997) focuses on the Ruelas brothers and on the Dukes. In the film, Fernando recalls that Uncle Tinker quickly became a father figure for the four nephews and early on taught them self-reliance, pride in their own work, ingenuity, and street savvy. He bought the four brothers a go-cart and used bicycles from local scrap yards. These became the first vehicles that they worked on to hone their mechanical skills in order to modify the vehicles to fit their own preferences. Working on and riding these and other childhood toys such as skateboards and scooters kept them off the streets (Delgado & Van Wagenen 1997; Sandoval, "Bajito y suavecito," 2003).

The brothers proved to be very precocious and attentive students, so by the age of 13 each of them had a car that they were too young to drive but old enough to learn the vehicles' mechanical complexities and intricate aspects of rebuilding a car from scratch. As a way of pooling their knowledge to work more efficiently as a family team, each brother developed an individual area of expertise in areas such as bodywork, painting, upholstery, and electrical wiring. This collective approach to building lowriders allowed them to share their successes among themselves but also with their immediate and extended family. This sense of familial bond and pride was essential when the brothers officially founded the Dukes in 1962. The object was not to get as many members as possible but for members to provide positive role models for others in their East Los Angeles community. Although there was initially some tension between Dukes members and the 38th Street gang, it largely disappeared after a few years as the lowrider club gained respect by maintaining a strict code of positive behavior and by becoming involved in numerous community charitable and social events across East Los Angeles. An example of how the Dukes provided an alternative to gangs is the 1963 defection of "Chivo" Ceniceros from his East Los Angeles gang. Ceniceros was a young barrio Chicano who had grown so disaffected with *la vida loca*, the violence and drug activity in which his gang was involved, that he and 40 other Chicanos left the gang to join the Dukes (Ides 2009, 161).

In the late 1960s, the Dukes lowrider car club played a prominent role in the proliferation of lowrider culture in the Los Angeles area. Their club cars were prominent on Whittier Avenue during the height of the cruising era, and they proudly displayed the results of their craftsmanship and artistry by parking their cars in a prime spot in the Huggy Boy parking lot on the avenue. Soon, the Vietnam War became a major disruption for lowrider culture as thousands of car

---

Families are central to some lowrider clubs. In a 1999 interview, Julio Ruelas stressed the importance of maintaining a family emphasis in the *Dukes* car club:

"A car club is a family orientated thing. We are a whole family. It is a big family and you get them together. You can invite your cousins, your brothers, your daughters, your sons, your wife, your in-laws, grandparents, whoever. We will have barbecue or dances. That is what it is all about . . . a car club" (1999 interview with Julio Ruelas in Sandoval, "Bajito y suavecito," 2003).

club members, including the Ruelas brothers, were either drafted or joined the military. Although all the brothers survived the war, the club lost many members whose deaths were commemorated by lowrider funerals where dozens of lowriders would line up their cars and trucks in the funeral procession that proceeded slowly from barrio churches to local cemeteries.

During the late 1960s and 1970s, many Dukes-affiliated lowrider clubs were formed throughout Southern California. They number over 30 today across the United States and internationally. The Ruelas brothers and their club, along with the Imperials and the Groupe lowrider clubs, played an important role in organizing the West Coast Association of Low Riders in 1978, whose main focus was to involve the lowrider community in barrio projects such as the Christmas Toys for Kids car show, whose proceeds are directed even today towards the purchase of gifts for children in low-income families. The Dukes and other lowrider clubs were for many years involved in prison projects and in fund raisers for organizations such as the United Farm Workers. The Ruelas family has continued to be central to the community commitment that the Dukes club has maintained over the decades since its founding. Denise Michelle Sandoval, a scholar who has written most knowledgeably on the Dukes car club, recounts that when the Ruelas family was first approached about making the documentary *Low and Slow*, focusing on the founding of their club, the brothers insisted that it be made available to the public schools, especially those schools that had a high concentration of young Americans of Mexican descent (Sandoval 2003).

The Dukes was among the first lowrider clubs to participate in the car show circuit, and it was a pioneer in being the first and only club to be invited to exhibit vehicles at the Trident car shows in the Los Angeles area in the mid-1960s. The invitation reflected the fact that the Ruelas brothers and other club members were fast becoming a highly respected club that demonstrated the highest standards of automotive mechanical and artistic mastery, equal to that of custom car clubs that had been formed many years before. The Dukes car club was also instrumental in helping to organize the highly successful lowrider super show at the Los Angeles convention center in 1978, an event that was cosponsored by *Lowrider* magazine and its enterprising editor, Sonny Madrid (see Chapters o3 and 8).

The Lifestyle Lowrider Club

The Dukes is an example of a lowrider club that has a distinctly family identity, and although there are others, the majority of clubs today have distinctly different characteristics, with an emphasis on club activities as a predominantly male activity. These clubs have an overriding focus on their members' complete loyalty to the club and to maintaining the highest mechanical and artistic quality of club vehicles even to the point of sacrificing family and non-club social relationships. Lifestyle, founded in East Los Angeles in the mid-1970s, provides a good example of the non–family oriented lowrider club. The all-male membership follows strict club rules, including mandatory attendance at club meetings and a dress code that requires wearing the club black-and-gold T-shirt at club meetings and in public at lowrider events. The club's membership consists of mainly young Chicano males, but Lifestyle also includes older males as honorary members whose function, along with that of the club's officers, is to set an example and mentor the younger members regarding proper behavior and attitude and especially in meeting the group's high mechanical and artistic standards for their vehicles. A club officer stressed how important these standards are in an interview with *Lowrider* magazine: "We lose sleep over what color we're going to paint our cars. . . . We live our lives like that and we bounce off each other because building a lowrider isn't just about one person, it's a unit of all our friends. So for most of us here, lowriding is a passion" (*Lowrider* August 1979, 70).

A heavy emphasis is placed on being competitive for various awards and other kinds of recognition at local and regional lowrider shows as a way of enhancing the club's stature in the lowrider community. Lifestyle has been very successful in garnering various prestigious awards at *Lowrider* magazine–sponsored and other super shows; their high standards have paid off. A club committee must evaluate and approve various aspects of a vehicle, including its paint scheme, designs, and murals. The club requires that its members own and work on only certain classic pre-1979 models such as Chevy Impalas, Buick Rivieras, and Cadillacs. The members whose vehicles fail to meet these standards or who fail to maintain standards of behavior are denied the privilege of flying the club's colors or of displaying the club plaque. Members can receive various sanctions from the club officers including fines, swats with a paddle, and as an extreme measure expulsion from the club itself (Sandoval 2003).

The Majestics Lowrider Club

An example of the first lowrider club that is predominantly African American is the Majestics, which was featured in the 2005 documentary film *Sunday Drivers: A Look at the Guys Behind the Chrome*. The club was cofounded in Compton, California, in 1978 and later expanded to include a club in Watts and eventually in other cites in California, Arizona, Colorado, New Mexico, Florida, Hawaii, Japan, and Canada. The documentary features interviews with several prominent members of the club: cofounders Craig Parker and Kevin Smith; Dee Dee Girl, the only woman in the car club at the time of the documentary; Wally Dog, a Los Angeles commodities trader; a prominent member known only as Gangster; Dr. Get Low, also known as "Doc," who is a lowrider design and paint expert; and Twin, a younger member of the club. Several of those interviewed had been involved in lowriding since the 1970s and as members of the club from its earliest days. Some members were explicit in stating that they were formerly members of gangs involved in criminal behavior. They expressed loyalty to the car club members who had provided them with an alternative to such activity. One individual recalled having been involved in a gang shootout over a disputed drug deal and doing time in a state penitentiary. The attraction of being part of a group, which initially attracted some to gangs, had become a reason for being a member of the car club. The documentary shows members participating in several activities that reinforce the sense of group cohesion, friendship, and mutual support: playing dominoes together at a weekly meeting; a car wash organized to help a member repair his damaged car; and being part of a march in support of Parents Against Violence. The club members viewed the police with a mixture of irritation and anger stemming from what some identified as harassment of club cruises on Crenshaw Boulevard. Included in the documentary is footage of the police shutting down the Boulevard in the late 1970s, an act that caused resentment among club members. The documentary includes an interview with a high-ranking member of the local police force, an African American, who presents a different take on why it is necessary to have a police presence when lowriders cruise public streets. His view was that clashes between lowriders could quickly escalate into violent confrontations that could result in the use of weapons. The officer also mentions that the police were concerned about a resurgence of gang activity among lowriders (Strong 2005).

The violent clashes between lowrider car clubs on Whittier Avenue as well as on Crenshaw Avenue in the late 1960s and early 1970s are common knowledge among older lowriders. In the January 2011 issue of *Lowrider*, Joe Ray, the editor of the magazine, wrote in his editor's letter, "In the Days of Car Club Wars Past . . . ," of open and frequent violent confrontations between members of what he identifies as "old school" clubs like the Sons of Soul, the NewWave, the

Gestapos, the Klique, the New Life, the Groupe, and the New Breed. He describes how these members would often bring their personal disputes to car club meetings where the membership was expected to support them in, for example, carrying out revenge and retaliatory attacks on members of other car clubs. Because lowrider car club membership was very robust during this period and standards were less stringent than today, it was difficult to monitor each member or to know whether they were active participants in urban gangs. Ray mentions in his letter that it was common for a group of club members to pull a member from another club out of his vehicle, beat him, smash his car, and steal his club plaque. He cites the Orpheus car club as being one that was particularly feared to the point that other clubs would clear Whittier Avenue at times when Orpheus ordered it clear for their exclusive use. Ray decries the fact that very few lowrider clubs, such as the Majestics, the Batchelors LTD, the Classics, the Imperials, and at times the Groupe, focused on pursuing a different image and direction by investing their energy in exhibiting quality lowrider cars at shows (*Lowrider* January 2011, 10–11).

Law enforcement authorities closed down Whittier Boulevard as a cruising route in 1979. Although there were many instances of police and sheriff personnel engaging in excessive force against lowriders, veteran lowriders like Jesse Valadez, president of the Imperials car club, and Joe Ray attribute the crackdown to violence on the boulevard initiated by gang members who were also members of rival lowrider clubs. Valadez commented in 1980: "Whittier was a good thing, but it got out of hand. Too much violence—the Sheriffs didn't close the Boulevard, the people did. It was our fault. The people have to pay for it now." Ray was more blunt: "Gangs stopped the cruise" (http:// blogs.myspace.com/index.cfm?fuseaction).

RECENT TRENDS IN LOWRIDER CLUBS

As lowrider culture has expanded across the United States and internationally, lowrider clubs themselves have become more diverse. For example, there are multiethnic clubs, exclusively female clubs, religiously oriented clubs, and those that closely adhere the model of the three clubs just described.

The Uso Car Club

Founded in 1992 in the Harbor Area of Los Angeles, the Uso car club (now known as the Uce car club) has as its underlying philosophy the

Jesse Valadez, longtime member of the Imperials Car Club and owner of the "Gypsy Rose" lowrider passes away in 2011. (AP Photo/ Bret Hartman)

promotion of a broad membership consisting of Samoan Americans, African Americans, Chicanos, Anglo-Americans, and individuals from other ethnic and racial groups. Its website sets forth this spirit of inclusiveness: "*Uso* prides itself on being more than a loose-knit conglomerate of individuals. The definition of the word, Uso, which means blood brother in the Samoan language, is a testament to our underlying principle. In fact, our solid communal values and interpersonal relationships reflect more of a family unit than a social club." This concept of family is different from that of the extended family linked by blood relationships that characterizes the Dukes lowrider club. (See the Uce Car Club website at http://ucefamily.com.)

Kit Lealao, the club's inspirational leader, was raised in the San Francisco Bay Area in neighborhoods known for their multiethnic and multiracial makeup. He had been a member of a lowrider club as a young adult before moving to Southern California, where he and a group of Samoan lowrider enthusiasts formed the Uso club in Carson, whose population consisted largely of Samoans, Chicanos, and African Americans. His early exposure to people from diverse cultures was key in establishing the club as a group of members who reached out to others as individuals committed to getting along and being mutually supportive even as they dedicated themselves to maintaining a high degree of automotive and artistic professionalism. As a result of its underlying philosophy, Uce now has spread rapidly, with approximately 40 chapters throughout the territorial United States and Guam as well as Canada and Sweden. In 1998, *Lowrider* selected it as the magazine's lowrider club of the year.

Lealao, who has remained a strong presence in the organization over the years, and others have at times struggled to maintain the familial aspect and the strong kinship among the members that characterized the founding club. Uso was forced to change its name because of lawsuits claiming trademark infringement; U.S.O., the United Service Organization, has for many decades provided entertainment and other services for U.S. military personnel. The new name, Uce, is also a Samoan word that is close in meaning to *Uso*. In a 2007 interview with *Lowrider* magazine, Lealao was asked about some guiding principles in starting up a lowrider club. He emphasized inclusiveness and reiterated his club's commitment to ethnic and racial diversity: "We want to let everybody know that starting up a club that you can be a White boy in lowriding, you can be a Chinese in lowriding, you don't have to be a Mexican or a Black dude. When we get together it's all about one love and we're all on the same page. As long as you love the game of lowriding that's all that should matter" (*Lowrider*).

Women's Lowrider Car Clubs

Women have tended to play a secondary role in lowrider culture (see Chapter 6), although more recently some clubs have begun to accept women as peers to the males who comprise most of the total membership. At the same time, women have formed their own clubs, some of which do not accept men as members. During the 1960s and early 1970s, women could be members of auxiliary clubs like the Bachelorettes and the Imperialettes that existed to support the all-male clubs but whose members were not considered equals. That changed in 1974 when the earliest all-woman club and all-Volkswagen club, the Lady Bugs, was founded. Stella Pérez, the founder and the club's first president, would visit lowrider gathering sites such as Elysian

Park and Whittier Boulevard to try to recruit other women. Soon, the club membership, which came from Sun Valley, Echo Park, and East Los Angeles, was meeting and cruising their Volkswagen "Beetles," a car model than lent itself to customization. The young women in the early years of the club came from diverse backgrounds; they had full-time jobs, were finishing high school, or were enrolled in college full time. There were also single parents and those who were related to or were in relationships with men in all-male lowrider clubs. Like the all-male clubs, the Lady Bugs had a tightly structured governing body and a specific set of rules for membership, including being single and at least 16 years old. The women were encouraged to meet high standards of personal behavior, to attend meetings regularly, to participate actively in club events, to look out for each other, and to strive for unity and independence (*Lowrider* November 2010, 29–30).

An example of a current all-female lowrider club is the Underestimated club with chapters in the Northwest and Oakland. Like the Lady Bugs, this club emphasizes mutual respect, support, and encouragement among its members. Its bylaws specifically disallow any gang-related activities and emphasize adherence to laws and respect for law enforcement personnel. Members must attend monthly meetings and participate in club events, including charitable and social events, in order to remain active. Members must continue to demonstrate that they have sufficient financial resources in order to pay dues, fines, and car repairs and improvements.

Religiously Oriented Car Clubs

Adding to the variety of lowrider car clubs are those that have a religious orientation. An example of such a club is the Kingdom car club, which has clubs in several cities in the Southwest. The club requires that members be believers in a Christian god, attend church regularly, contribute regularly to their church through tithing, and demonstrate "spiritual maturity." Like most other lowrider clubs, members must attend meetings and club-sponsored events. Rather than wear T-shirts with the club colors and name, the members' T-shirt must be blank. The club guidelines also specify that members' cars show a "Spirit of Excellence" before they are allowed to be exhibited at car shows or driven on the streets. This is demonstrated by maintaining a clean car, paint job, rims and tires, and interior. Adherence to the laws and respect for law enforcement personnel are considered to be essential to acceptable behavior. The Kingdom car club's ultimate mission is "to introduce God's miraculous works using our customized cars in reaching the

A religiously oriented lowrider car club participates at a lowrider show. (Courtesy Anne Tatum)

community so respect and recognition in both the streets and in the church go directly to the Lord Jesus Christ" (Kingdom Car Club website:www.kingdomcarclub.com).

Lowrider Bicycle Clubs

Lowrider bicycle clubs became popular in the early 1980s as more young adults began customizing bikes and entering them in competitions held at local and regional lowrider car and truck shows. Probably the first bicycle club was created as an affiliate of the Dukes car club when in 1979 bike builder Carlos Lima from San José approached the Dukes's Northern California president, Steve Caudillo, about starting a bike chapter. Caudillo's proposal was positively received by the club membership and the Dukes bike club was created. Other established lowrider clubs soon followed suit. Just as *Lowrider* magazine features a car and truck club in its monthly issues, *Lowrider Bike* magazine features a bike club in almost all of its recent issues. Although there are many independent lowrider bicycle clubs today throughout the United States and in a few foreign countries, many remain affiliated with well-established lowrider car and truck clubs. Lowrider club membership rules and requirements are very similar to those of car and truck clubs, although they tend to be more flexible because most of their members are teenagers and young adults who generally do not have the same financial means to invest in their vehicles (Penland 2003, 34–35).

Many lowrider car, truck, and bicycle clubs today participate actively in local, regional, and super car shows, an activity that helps establish their reputation as highly skilled craftsmen and artists. Most clubs regularly hold family and community picnics, sponsor charitable events, and participate in mentoring young adults by providing them with an alternative to dropping out of school and adopting a life of drug use and violence on the streets. *Lowrider* magazine and *Lowrider Bike* magazine do their part in maintaining this positive image by regularly featuring lowrider club social and charitable events.

FURTHER READING

Acuña, Rodolfo. *Occupied America. A History of Chicanos*. 4th ed. New York: Longman, 1999.

Delgado, Monica and Michael Van Wagenen, *Low and Slow*. 16mm, 27 minutes. Ritual Film and Publications, 1997.

Ides, Matthew Allan. "Cruising for Community: Youth Culture and Politics in Los Angeles, 1910–1970." Ph.D. dissertation, University of Michigan, 2009.

Kingdom Car Club. www.kingdomcarclub.com.

Lowrider. August 1979, 70; November 2010, 28–30; January 2011, 10–11.

Mendoza, Rubén G. "Cruising Art and Culture in Aztlán: Lowriding in the Mexican American Southwest." *U.S. Latino Literatures and Cultures: Transitional Perspectives*, edited by Francisco A Lomelí and Karen Ikas. Heidelberg: Universitatverlag, 2000.

Penland, Paige R. *Lowrider: History, Pride, Culture*. St. Paul, MN: MBI Publishing, 2003.

Sandoval, Denise Michelle. "Bajito y suavecito: The Lowriding Tradition." 2003. http://latinto.si.edu/virtualgallery/lowrider/lr_sandovalessay.htm.

Strong, Carol. *Sunday Drivers: A Look at the Guys Behind the Chrome*. 16mm, 58 minutes. Rockstar Games, Inc., 2005.

8

Lowrider Shows

The large, multiday lowrider shows that are held today throughout the Southwest contrast starkly with the small gatherings of lowriders and their cruisers on weekends that began in the 1950s. Although some of the elements of the original meetings of like-minded lowrider owners and their families and friends have been preserved over the past several decades in today's lowrider shows, the well-organized, widely publicized, and professionally promoted spectacles that draw thousands of spectators and participants bear little resemblance to the early gatherings. Today's shows dramatically reflect the evolution of lowriding from street cruising to the dominance of shows, events where lowrider owners exhibit their vehicles as examples of high-quality craftsmanship and art. This chapter will provide an overview of this evolution.

ORIGINS

Lowrider culture grew out of the overall car culture in the Los Angeles area after World War II (see Chapter 1). As the customization of cars became more popular in the 1950s, both hot rodders and lowriders were increasingly more prominent on the public streets of

Los Angeles, the fastest-growing metropolis in the United States. Both groups would show off their cars and would sometimes end up at the same venues such as restaurant parking lots and drive-ins at night so that their vehicles' customized features could be more carefully scrutinized and admired under bright lights. A local radio DJ, "Huggy Boy" Huggs, was instrumental in promoting Clock Drive-Ins across the city as welcome meeting places for all kinds of customizers, especially hot rodders and lowriders. To promote his business, the owner of the drive-ins even started sponsoring a Tuesday night event at the Bellflower site where fans could go to get Huggy Boy's autograph.

As street cruising on Whittier Boulevard and on other main streets throughout California's cities became more popular among lowriders in the 1960s, places larger than drive-ins were identified where they could gather at the end of a day or night cruise. These were typically public parks in heavily Chicana/o areas of California cities such as Elysian Park in Los Angeles, Chicano Park in San Diego, Alum Rock Park in San Jose, and Roeding Park in Fresno. Also, elsewhere across the Southwest, parks became popular sites for informal lowrider gatherings and informal competitions: Memorial Park in Houston, Ascarate Park in El Paso, Chicano Park in Austin, Encanto Park in Phoenix, and Reed Park in Tucson. Sometimes, families and friends would gather to visit during long, lazy picnics on a Sunday afternoon. Lowriders could then leisurely compare notes about their vehicles' latest features such as paint jobs, hydraulics, and interiors. Although in the beginning there were no official contests, informal bragging rights were important, especially among the many car clubs that began to spring up (see Chapter 7).

While there were no car shows exclusively devoted to lowriders, in the early 1960s lowrider owners could enter their vehicles in shows that attracted a broad range of customizers and automobile enthusiasts. For example, the Tridents car club from the Los Angeles community of Bell began organizing and promoting shows. R. G. Channing, a young and skilled promoter who had gone to high school with many Tridents car club members, also started organizing shows. Many interested lowrider owners would not qualify because they did not meet the strict requirements designed more for hot rods and street rods; however, some did. Some hot rod and street rod owners would enter the shows in their lowered vehicles with rims and chrome to try to simulate the lowrider look, but their powerful engines still clearly identified them as hot rods built for speed (Penland 2003, 20).

R. G. Channing continued to promote automotive shows in the Los Angeles area throughout the 1960s and 1970s, and although lowrider club members continued to enter a few of their cars and to attend the shows, the lowrider community was becoming progressively disenchanted with the fact that lowriders were not afforded a more prominent role at the events. Finally, Ruben "Buggs" Ochoa, a well-respected lowrider artist, began organizing a lowrider show with the help of several Los Angeles lowrider clubs including the Classics, the Imperials, New Movement, and a new club called Groupe. The show, billed as a "Lowrider Happening," was scheduled at the Great Western Exhibit Center in Long Beach on September 4, 1977. Unfortunately, five days before the show the Los Angeles Sheriff's Department cancelled it, claiming that the organizers had not provided for sufficient security. Ochoa and other organizers appealed to sympathetic members of the Los Angeles City Council who in turn requested that Mayor Sam Yorty overrule the Sheriff's Department, which he promptly did. Despite a boycott of the event by some Los Angeles lowrider clubs, cars from all over California and some from Phoenix arrived at the show, and it is estimated that approximately 15,000 fans came as well. The event was peaceful and entertaining and so successful that the Center's owner invited the lowrider show back for the next three years. The scale and unquestioned success of this first large lowrider event was a persuasive indicator of how popular lowriding had become in a few short decades. Importantly, this event spawned dozens of smaller lowrider shows,

An intricate mural design covers an entire lowrider car. (Courtesy Anne Tatum)

sometimes called "happenings," throughout California in the mid to late-1970s (Penland 2003, 72–73).

THE ROLE OF *LOWRIDER* MAGAZINE IN THE PROMOTION AND POPULARITY OF LOWRIDER SHOWS

The editors of *Lowrider* magazine played an important role in the growth and increasing popularity of lowrider shows by providing coverage of local and regional lowrider shows. The Gilroy Low Rider Happening was featured in the magazine's inaugural issue in 1977, and its first cover was of a young woman dressed in a long coat. (See Chapter 3). Coverage such as this became an essential part of the editors' growth strategy for the publication; news reports and photos of these events increased readership and the magazine's circulation, first throughout California and later across the Southwest.

The first large show, known early on as a "super show," that *Lowrider* sponsored in California was held at the Los Angeles Convention Center in 1979. It was a huge success, with over 20,000 participants and spectators in attendance. The first large show that the magazine sponsored outside of California was in the same year on the Gila River Indian Reservation close to Phoenix. Then, in the early 1980s, it sponsored super shows in San Antonio and other Southwestern cities. Although local car clubs and other organizations in California, Arizona, New Mexico, Texas, and in non-Southwestern states such as Kentucky continued to sponsor and organize lowrider shows throughout the 1980s and 1990s, often as charity and fundraising events, it was probably *Lowrider* magazine that gave these larger shows their greatest impetus and permanency.

Today, *Lowrider* magazine sponsors or cosponsors—Lugz Shoes and Pioneer Audio are frequent cosponsors—super shows as part of its *Lowrider* Tour on a regular annual schedule in cities such as Los Angeles, San Bernardino, Las Vegas, Phoenix, Pueblo, Denver, Albuquerque, San Antonio, and Tampa. In addition, it cosponsors a larger number of smaller local and regional shows and vehicle-related events that often have a charity focus. Local shows are often announced in local newspapers and on local radio stations a few weeks before they take place. Upcoming shows are also frequently publicized on websites such as www.lowridermagazine.com and www.brownpride.com.

ANATOMY OF A LOWRIDER SUPER SHOW

Each lowrider show has its own unique character, but the larger shows follow a predictable pattern in terms of venues, spectatorship,

A lowrider car competes in a hop competition in an outside area at a lowrider show. Spectators are separated from the competition area by a chain link fence. (Courtesy Anne Tatum)

times and duration, music and performances, concessions, merchandise stalls, exterior and interior vehicle exhibit areas, hopping and dancing competitions, and vehicle awards and prizes.

Larger shows, including the super shows sponsored by *Lowrider* magazine, are typically held over a weekend at urban venues that will accommodate large numbers of spectators and participants: convention centers, large-event performance centers, fairgrounds, sports stadiums, and arenas. Because the larger shows frequently attract between 10,000 and 25,000 fans, very large parking areas and easy traffic access are essential. Recent shows have been held at the Las Vegas Cashman Center, the Phoenix Convention Center, the Arizona State Fairgrounds in Phoenix, the Florida State Fairgrounds in Tampa, and the Qualcomm Stadium in San Diego. Shows usually start at midmorning on a Saturday and end late on a Sunday afternoon. There is usually an entrance fee that rarely exceeds the cost of attending a local professional athletic event such as a minor league baseball game.

Security is a major concern of the shows' sponsors and organizers as well as of the operators of the venues. Preventive measures have become both highly visible and normal. At least some uniformed police are present at large lowrider shows, and either they or clearly identified event staff closely monitor spectators as they enter the event area through gates where metal detectors and the spot searches of purses and bags are common. Because of the intense competition between car clubs who exhibit vehicles at the shows, minor skirmishes between members sometimes occur.

In addition to a large number of local car club members who attend the shows to either exhibit their cars or to support the members who do, the audiences at car shows represent a broad cross section of the urban population where the events are held, although the majority of spectators are Latina/o and African American young adults, an attendance pattern that is to be expected because urban lowriding culture continues to be most commonly practiced and popular in Latina/o and African American urban communities. Car club members and their supporters proudly wear shirts with the name of their car clubs clearly displayed. It is very common for entire families to come to the shows to enjoy a part of the weekend as an activity as carefree as going to a community sports event or to a picnic in the park.

The various activities that take place in the outside as well as the inside areas are designed to enhance the spectacle-like nature of large lowrider shows. The promoters and organizers carry out very successfully their objective to entertain spectators of all ages during their stay on the grounds of the events. To show paying customers a good time, the lowrider show grounds are pulsing with sound and alive with other sensory stimuli that appeal to sight, smell, and taste.

Temporary vendor booths displaying a variety of products are an essential part of large lowrider shows. Available for purchase are commemorative T-shirts with a large variety of lettering and decals displaying representative and figurative lowrider figures and symbols such as zoot suiters, classic drawings of pachucas and pachucos (see the Chapter 2), popular lowrider vehicles, local political issues, local car clubs, popular musical groups, and other themes. There are vendors that specialize in clothing ranging from the latest young adult fashions for women and men to classic pachuca/o and zoot clothing including suits, shirts, hats, embroidery, silk screens, and clothing for all ages and sizes. Other vendors are local and regional lowrider-related businesses such as hydraulics shops, wheel and rim retail stores, upholstery shops, paint shops, and glass etching and car mural businesses. Other vendors specialize in professionally produced music CDs and videos representing not only the most popular musical groups and individual performers among lowriders everywhere but also CDs and videos of local groups hoping to create a niche in local

Items of clothing displayed at a vendor's tent at a lowrider show. (Courtesy Anne Tatum)

markets. It is common to hear loud music coming from the powerful speakers that vendors use to attract customers. Booths representing local tattoo shops and offering onsite tattoos are increasingly common at lowrider shows as tattoo art has become an essential part of lowrider expressive art. (See Chapter 4).

Large lowrider shows have multiple sponsors ranging from local and regional car clubs to national enterprises like *Lowrider* magazine, as well as local lowrider specialty shops and vendors and sometimes multiple local radio stations. At shows where *Lowrider* magazine is the major sponsor, a semi truck and trailer with the name of the magazine emblazoned across each of the trailer's sides is parked in a highly visible location where it can be seen easily by spectators. Local radio station booths are normally located in the outside show areas close to the vehicle exhibit area and the merchandise booths. Local DJs play the latest hits popular among lowriders (see Chapter 5), and occasionally vocal performers and dancers perform in order to attract spectators to the radio booths.

Food concessions staffed by the hosting venue's personnel can usually be found in both the outside and inside show areas where a standard fare of hamburgers, hot dogs, popcorn, and nachos as well as soft drinks and water are sold. Occasionally spectators will be treated to more specialized foods on the show grounds, but local codes usually preclude much deviation from the standard food offerings.

Lowrider vehicles are exhibited at lowrider shows at both outside and inside viewing areas located in large exhibit halls. The vehicles in the outside areas are generally arranged closely together in tight groups representing car clubs, usually with barely enough room for spectators to maneuver in order to view the vehicles individually. The vehicles in the outside areas seem to fall into a secondary tier of lowrider quality in terms of their paint jobs, designs and mural art, hydraulics, interiors, upholstery, and other features in comparison to the vehicles that are exhibited in the inside viewing areas.

It is rare to find vendor booths and radio station booths in the inside viewing areas, where a high priority is placed on showing off the best lowriders and on featuring music performances. Featured music entertainers generally perform on stage within the large viewing halls with loud music blaring from powerful speakers and reverberating off the walls and ceilings of the structure. As spectators make their way among the lowrider vehicles on view—cars, trucks, bicycles, tricycles, and even strollers—they are accompanied by a steady stream of sound provided almost continuously as one performer follows another and culminating with the featured performers during peak attendance times late in the afternoon or early evening on Saturday and as the show winds down on Sunday afternoon. A common sight on the floor of the inside viewing halls—and to a lesser extent, in the outside areas—are scantily dressed young women models posing among the lowrider vehicles for professional photographers. Photos of a small percentage the more fortunate models might eventually be included in the pages of *Lowrider* magazine or on established Internet sites. Some large shows also hold bikini contests on stage, usually during periods of high spectator attendance.

The vehicles exhibited on the floor of the inside viewing areas are expected to meet a very high standard of craftsmanship and artistry. Their owners are required to pay a modest registration fee in the $50 range to the shows' sponsors. Owners may also be required to submit photos of their vehicles and provide basic information about them on the registration form: contact information; the year, make and model of car, truck, or bike; types of paint and upholstery; the owner's club affiliation; and that part of the vehicle—trunk, engine, undercarriage— that an owner wishes to display; category (the vehicles are placed in one of several categories: original, street custom, mild custom, semi-custom, full-custom, or radical); and the list of modifications that owners have made to their vehicles since they last entered them in a show by the same sponsor.

In order to assure that vehicles meet a high standard of artistry and rigorous craftsmanship, some sponsors specify in their published exhibition and safety rules that dented, damaged, unfinished, or incomplete vehicles will be refused exhibit space. These rules also lay out for exhibitors detailed information on how to display the vehicles, including compliance with applicable fire safety rules and a strict prohibition against displaying anything in or around a vehicle that the judges could consider obscene, profane, or that could be construed as a weapon, such as glass, glass bottles, or knives. Some sponsors also specify in their rules that respect for the spectators and other exhibitors must be shown, including the prohibition of profanity, excessive noise and objectionable music, and videos, artwork, or other items that show disrespect. The show judges are given absolute authority in enforcing the exhibition and safety rules, including the disqualification and expulsion of owners who are deemed not to have followed the rules (*Lowrider* magazine).

Unlike the vehicles exhibited in the outside areas, most of the vehicles displayed in the inside areas have not arrived at shows under their own power; that is, owners have not driven them to the show. Because owners have invested many thousands of dollars in their vehicles to enhance their exteriors and interiors, hydraulic systems, and other features, they must protect their investment by treating the vehicles in the same way that classic car owners treat their investment—by minimizing damage to the vehicles that could occur if they were driven on streets and highways. Many of the lowrider vehicles exhibited in the inside viewing halls are gems that display the highest standards of mechanical craftsmanship and artistic sophistication with their exquisitely prepared chrome parts, interiors, and especially the meticulously and expertly painted surfaces, often adorned with intricate designs and airbrushed murals (see Chapter 4t). They are far too valuable to be driven under their own power to the shows, and they are generally transported in covered trailers, sometimes for many hundreds of miles, for example from Los Angeles to Phoenix. However, show rules often specify that these vehicles have to pass a minimum standard to demonstrate that they are operable and complete at the time of the required inspection before the shows officially open for spectators. Inoperable vehicles can be exhibited, but they will not be allowed to compete for prizes. The following requirements are usually spelled out: the cars and trucks must be able to start under their own power; they must have an operable battery permanently positioned in the vehicle; their engines must be fueled by a fixed fuel tank and transmission; and they must demonstrate their ability to travel 20 feet of continuous motion forward, steer to the left and the right, brake to stop, shift into reverse, and travel backward 20 feet (*Lowrider* magazine).

Some of the cars and trucks exhibited in the inside viewing areas are elevated on jacks or are even mounted on rotating mechanical turntables. The rotation affords spectators a complete 360-degree view of the vehicles' exterior paint surface, the designs and murals on this surface, and their mechanical enhancements and decorative features including the chromed motors and hydraulic systems and the embellishments to the interior such as the dashboard, the steering wheel, and the upholstery. Frequently, vehicle-length mirrors are placed under both the stable and rotating cars and trucks, designed to clearly display their chromed exhaust systems and the chromed plating on their undercarriages. Local and regional lowrider clubs enter their vehicles in competitions in various categories, and they proudly display their club identifying plaques on or near the vehicles. Individual owners and club members typically stay close to their respective vehicles in order to be available to answer questions and explain the finer points about their entries.

Vehicles compete for a range of prizes and are judged in six categories: craftsmanship (quality of work, imagination, innovation, and creativity); body (modifications, paint, murals and striping, molding, glass, accessories, and craftsmanship); engine (plating, engine compartment, firewall, hinges and springs, hoses, wiring, and hood panel); undercarriage (plating, paint and striping, suspension, frame, modifications, wheels, craftsmanship, cleanliness, and detail); interior (seats, dashboard, side panels, consoles, operable audio and video or any electric accessory, detail, and workmanship); and hydraulic and air suspension (operable setup, wiring, batteries, plating, tubing, hoses, craftsmanship, detail, and cleanliness) (*Lowrider* magazine).

At the large shows, cars and trucks compete in the following classes: original (complete stock or restored vehicle but without era accessories such as hubcaps and wheels); street custom (vehicles with no more than five minor modifications); mild custom (up to two major modifications and up to four minor modifications); semi-custom (up to three major and four minor modifications); full custom (up to five major and four minor modifications); radical custom (at least seven major modifications); custom compact (compact cars usually designed for economy gas mileage); sports cars; luxury sports cars (two- or four-passenger high-performance cars); luxury cars (full-sized luxury vehicles including limousines); bombs or classic vehicles (American cars 1954 or older and American trucks 1959 or older); trucks (including open-bed trucks, sports utility vehicles, panel trucks, El Caminos, and vans); CUV/sports wagons (compact utility vehicles); and traditionals, which are American-made, full-size, 1958 through 1988 vehicles with no major modifications such as custom paint and custom interiors. The wide range of vehicle classes is designed to attract the participation in lowrider shows of the broadest range of vehicles to reflect a wide spectrum of monetary investment, craftsmanship, and artistry of the lowrider community. The traditionals category illustrates that lowrider shows are interested in attracting entry-level lowriders who may not have the interest, time, or money to invest in modified vehicles.

In the same spirit of attracting a maximum number of lowrider competitors to large shows, organizers typically give many awards that include both car- and truck-specific "outstanding" awards, including those for graphics, engines, undercarriages, hydraulics, paint jobs, interiors, murals, and audio/video accessories. Awards are also given in recognition of lowrider clubs who have the most members exhibiting vehicles. The most coveted recognition at lowrider shows are the "Best of Show" awards, including Best of Show Car, Best of Show Bomb Car and Truck, Best of Show Original, and Best of Show Traditional. Best of Show awards are usually recognized with trophies and monetary

A lowrider bicycle exhibit at a lowrrider show. (Courtesy Anne Tatum)

prizes of up to $1,000, but owners especially covet these awards as a way of enhancing their reputations among the lowrider community. At some shows, such as those included on the *Lowrider* magazine tour, a Lowrider Excellence Award is given to the vehicle "that best exemplifies the Lowrider Movement." *Lowrider* magazine also gives a Vehicle of the Year award that recognizes the cumulative recognition that a vehicle has garnered throughout a tour year. Vehicles qualify to win the award over a three-year period either consecutively or nonconsecutively as long as no major changes are made to the vehicles.

Large lowrider shows routinely have a bicycle, and occasionally a tricycle, exhibit area and competition and a set of exhibition rules that, while not as detailed as those for cars and trucks, are quite specific in areas such as registration procedures, classification of the bikes and trikes (frames, upholstery, parts, and accessories). Bikes and trikes are classified as original, street custom, mild custom, semi-custom, full custom, and radical custom depending on the number and degree of minor and major modifications made to their frames, wheels, and other parts. Bikes are also classified by tire size—12, 16, 20, and 24 to 26 inches— while trikes simply fall into a three-wheel class. A point system assigned to both bikes and trikes is used to judge the following features: frame modification, paint, craftsmanship and detail, upholstery, plating, murals, wheels and tires, accessories, display, custom parts, graphics, pinstriping, and engraving. Awards, including trophies and cash prizes, are given for each category. Just as it does for cars and trucks, *Lowrider* magazine gives a Bike or Trike of the Year award.

Very popular events at large lowrider shows are the car and truck hop and dance competitions usually held at an outdoor area within walking distance of the outdoor area and indoor exhibit halls where bleachers can be set up for spectators. Until law enforcement authorities began restricting and even outlawing even modest hopping and dancing on urban cruising routes, it was common to see a line of lowriders hopping and dancing down city streets in order to show off their hydraulics and to challenge each other in spontaneous competitions on side streets or parking lots. This was an essential part of the lowrider culture that has all but disappeared except to occasionally reappear along police-sanctioned parade routes during, for example, Cinco de Mayo celebrations. (See Chapter 3). The hop and dance competitions at lowrider shows have largely replaced the freewheeling displays common in the 1950s through the 1970s.

Hop and dance competitions are typically held at peak attendance times early in the afternoon of the second day of lowrider shows. Loud live or recorded music booms from the large amplifiers as crowds gather

A lowrider vehicle competes in a dance competition. (Courtesy Anne Tatum)

for the first in a series of competitions that can last for up to two hours. Although spectator bleachers are usually separated from the competition area by a chain-link fence or other barrier, viewers are encouraged to take photos and videos. Many amateur videos can be found on YouTube and other social sites immediately after shows have ended.

Owners who enter their cars and trucks in hop and dance competitions are specialists in developing and perfecting powerful and highly responsive lowrider hydraulic systems. These vehicles are commonly sponsored by local and regional hydraulics shops as a way to advertise their businesses. Car and trucks that are entered in hop and dance competitions are very different from the vehicles in the outside and inside exhibit areas. The have little exterior or interior adornment except for the name of the sponsor. They are built with enhanced suspension systems designed to withstand the very substantial impact when vehicles come into jarring contact with the ground after a hop or dance. It is common for part of the suspension system such as the axles or rocker arms to bend or break during the competition:

The rules for hop and dance events are almost as detailed as those described above for the exhibition vehicles, particularly the safety specifications and precautions. That these rules are laid out in such detail is understandable as a way to afford participants, judges, and spectators maximum protection. Judges are given a high level of authority in their decision making and rulings on different aspects of the hop and dance competitions. For example, the *Lowrider* magazine–sponsored events state in their rules: "Failure to comply with a . . . judge's request at any time is unsportsmanlike conduct and grounds for disqualification. Unsportsmanlike conduct by an entrant or any member of the crew in the registration, pit, staging area, show grounds or hopping area is grounds for disqualification of contestant from that show and up to two (2) following shows" (*Lowrider Magazine Car and Truck Rules*).

Cars and truck owners compete in the following classes: single pump car hop, double pump car hop, single pump truck hop, radical hop; street dance; and radical dance. The number of hydraulic pumps and batteries (including their weight and configuration) that power the pumps is specified for each class, and all pumps must be visible and available for inspection by the judges. The pumps, batteries, suspension systems, and the mounts for the pumps and batteries must follow strict and specific technical criteria in order to qualify for competition. For example, bolts that are used to mount and secure the shock absorbers must fulfill certain length and strength standards. Also, the length of the vehicles cannot deviate from factory specifications; at least in this aspect, the vehicles are not modified like the vehicles that compete in the regular show categories described above.

While a vehicle is active in the hop or dance competition, its operator or "switchman" is not allowed to be inside the car or truck but instead activates and manipulates the pumps remotely from a safe distance using a small handheld remote control panel connected to the vehicle by long cables. The object in the hop competition is to remotely elevate the front of the vehicle into the air as high as possible without falling either to the side or over backwards. The operator may make multiple attempts to elevate the vehicle, but subsequent attempts quickly drain the hydraulics system of the electrical energy generated by the batteries. Judges measure a vehicle's top height from the bottom of its front tire using a solid vertical measuring device that looks like an immense ruler. The vehicle must come back down onto its two front wheels by gravity and not by using a mechanical device or physical push.

Car and truck dancing takes place in same the area at large shows as the hop competition, and it usually takes place immediately before or after this event. The dance competition safety and other rules are as strict as those for the hopping competition. The cars and trucks must be complete vehicles with an original body, frame, complete operating engine, interior, floor and trunk or bed pans, dashboard, at least a front seat, and a maximum of four hydraulic pumps and their batteries (the placement and securing of the batteries are designed with safety in mind). As in the hop event, the operator or switchman stands outside of the vehicle and manipulates the hydraulic system by means of a handheld remote control panel, sending the car or truck through a series of five required off-the-ground moves that simulate dancing: "kick" (hop) the front of the vehicle; "kick" (hop) the back of the vehicle; dance the vehicle side-to-side; dance the vehicle front to back ("seesaw"); and bunny hop the vehicle ("pancake"). Judges assign 1 to 10 points to a vehicles' performance in the following categories: speed, height, rhythm, switch control, and overall performance (*Lowrider Magazine Car and Truck Dance Rules*).

For longstanding lowrider enthusiasts or even for the individual who would like to experience an important aspect of contemporary lowrider culture for the first time, ample opportunities to attend local as well as super shows are readily available. A current issue of *Lowrider* magazine or the magazine's and other websites usually list the dates and venues for upcoming shows. Spectators are welcome to spend a few hours or an entire day at the larger shows taking in the rich array of sights and sounds that are representative of an important aspect of American expressive culture.

FURTHER READING

Lowrider Magazine Car and Truck Dance Rules, www.lowridermazine.com/features/07_hop_and_car_and_truck_dance_rules
Lowrider magazine, http://lowridermagazine.com/lowridertour.
Penland, Paige R. *Lowrider: History, Pride, Culture*. St. Paul, MN: MBI Publishing, 2003.

9

Building a Lowrider Vehicle

This chapter is an overview of the many aspects and complexities of building a lowrider vehicle from the bottom up, including the criteria that are commonly used in selecting a vehicle and the various decisions about restoration, mechanics, interiors, and decorative elements that come into play during the building process. Building a lowrider vehicle is not for the faint of heart or for the person who is impatient or is not willing to devote time and money to the enterprise. With the help of books, rented or owned specialty tools, and knowledgeable lowrider friends, one might be able to build a vehicle in a home garage that is set up for such a task, but some of the work will have to be done in specialty shops. This may take a month or many months depending on the time available to devote to the project and budget.

The process of building a lowrider is similar to that of building a house. Generally, one individual does not possess the many skill sets and knowledge required to construct an entire structure. A house has many components requiring at a minimum the expertise of a plumber, a mason, a carpenter, an electrician, a painter, a dry waller, a roofer, and a landscaper. In like manner, a lowrider also has many facets that require the expertise of a group of individuals who know a great deal about car and truck frames, rust control, brakes, welding, suspensions, hydraulic systems, tires and wheels, engines and drive trains, exhaust systems, custom interiors, upholstery, and paint. Whether one is building a house or a lowrider, one individual many have several skills or knowledge in more that one area, but it is very rare to possess breadth and depth across all areas of expertise. Normally, a builder or a contractor oversees the construction of a house and hires or subcontracts several aspects of the building to experts in carpentry, plumbing, and other skills. Similarly, the person who wants a vehicle converted into a lowrider rarely has all the skills in the various areas required to bring the project to fruition; an exception would be a very experienced person involved in various facets of lowrider building. It is therefore more common for a person new to building lowriders to contract out to experts in the various facets of building a lowrider. Doing it yourself may save money in the short run, but like many household do-it-yourselfers, you may make costly mistakes and end up calling in a an expert to finish the task.

Having experts build a lowrider vehicle is costly, ranging from several thousand to many thousands of dollars depending on the ultimate goal and the end product desired by the would-be owner of a lowrider. This is particularly true if the owner wants to exhibit the vehicle at lowrider shows and even perhaps compete for prizes and money.

SELECTING A VEHICLE FOR CONVERSION TO A LOWRIDER

Although there are makes and models, such as 1958 to 1964 Chevy (Chevrolet) Impala cars, that experienced and knowledgeable lowriders still prefer, lowrider vehicles come in all shapes, sizes, models, years of manufacture, and price ranges. Lowrider vehicles today vary from cars manufactured by Ford, General Motors, and Chrysler to full-size trucks, mini-trucks, and compacts cars—often referred to as "Euros"—from Korean, Japanese, and European companies including Toyota, Honda, Fiat, and Volkswagen. This variety of lowrider vehicles became more popular among owners in the 1980s, particularly when lowrider shows were held more frequently in the Southwest, around the United States, and in foreign countries such as Japan. As is the case in the selection of any vehicle for purchase, the process of selecting a vehicle to be converted into a lowrider is often heavily influenced by budget and personal preference. While a newer vehicle might be more desirable, have more replacement parts readily available, and require less preparatory work, the cost may exceed what is affordable. On the other hand, selecting an older vehicle is not necessarily going to be financially more advantageous if it requires considerable restoration in order to bring it up to acceptable structural and mechanical standards. For example, if an older vehicle comes from a region that has harsh snowy and icy winters, it may have sustained considerable rust from the heavy amounts of salt and other corrosives that are typically used on streets and highways during the winter months. Even in warmer regions, an older vehicle that has sat idle and neglected for a long period of time may have sustained damage to its body from exposure to the sun, wind, and rain.

An older vehicle may require that more of its parts be replaced. It is therefore wise to determine before purchasing such a car if parts are readily available and what they will cost. Sometimes, a builder will purchase a duplicate vehicle of the same make, year, and model as the desired car to be used as a source for spare parts. This may add to an initial outlay of cash, but such a purchase may ultimately save both the money and the time required to search for replacement parts. Sheet metal, glass, and parts are sometimes available at a local motor vehicle salvage yard, but it is sometime difficult to make an exact match with what needs to be replaced without consulting a vehicle's manufacturing manual. Also, a good set of tools will be required to remove metal, glass, and parts from the salvaged vehicle. In the case of metal and glass, extreme care must be taken to prevent cuts. Heavy gloves and safety glasses are recommended to provide a safe way to transport more fragile metal and glass from the salvage yard.

Another important factor that is often taken into account in selecting a vehicle is whether it will be used as regular transportation, only occasionally for infrequent cruising on weekends and holidays, or primarily for exhibit at lowrider shows. Use not only influences the make, age, and condition of the vehicle but also the degree to which it will be modified, painted, and embellished. Generally, lowriders prefer either (1) a restored traditional custom vehicle, with stock features such as trim and emblems and with a few lowrider touches, that sits low with or without a simple hydraulics system and that features custom wheels; or (2) a full custom vehicle has a plush velour interior, a gold and chromed engine compartment, an elaborate and powerful hydraulic system, and a fully detailed undercarriage (Hamilton 1996, 6).

Many of the same guidelines that a potential buyer should follow in purchasing any used vehicle are applicable to buying a vehicle to convert into a lowrider. There are many books and websites that provide tips to the general buyer. Following is a summary of a few tips that lowrider expert Frank Hamilton offers to the lowrider vehicle buyer.

- Research the market with the aid of the latest volume of the *Kelly Blue Book*, a basic and user-friendly guide that includes price information about hundreds of cars and trucks.
- Ask the owner of the vehicle being considered questions about its condition, but do not openly express excitement or disappointment. Make a mental list of shortcomings that may help in later negotiations on price.
- Check for signs of rust. Rust in the rear quarter panels may indicate that the vehicle was involved in a collision. Rust, or what customizers refer to as "body cancer" or "body rot," can be a major and hard-to-avoid problem. Experts highly recommend that even though the vehicle may have a good paint job it is always a good idea to look underneath the surface because the exterior paint might be covering rust spots that will eventually eat through the paint unless they are eliminated. A special gauge can be used to help a buyer better determine if rust is present under the paint, even through several layers of paint. Inspecting underneath the car, especially in the inner wheel wells and trunk, might also reveal that the vehicle has a bad case of body cancer. Even if rust is discovered, it is still possible to completely strip down the vehicle to the vehicle's basic sheet metal surface to eliminate the rust or to replace parts of the sheet metal that are beyond repair.
- Check under the vehicle for signs of leakage of fluids from the engine, the transmission, and the cooling system.
- Uneven tire wear may indicate a serious problem with the vehicle's alignment caused by a front-end collision.
- Check hoses, belts, and wires under the hood that may indicate that the vehicle has not been well maintained.
- If oil is present in the radiator water, this may indicate a serious and costly repair in the engine block. Also, check for rust in the radiator.
- Pull out the "dip stick" to determine if the oil has been recently changed or if it is brown or black, a sign that the vehicle has been poorly maintained. Grit in the oil or the odor of gasoline in the oil may indicate much more serious problems.
- Check the transmission oil for color and viscosity. A burnt smell may indicate that the clutch may have to be replaced.
- Test drive the vehicle. Check the odometer for mileage and ask the owner for detailed maintenance records.
- Drive the vehicle with the windows rolled up and then rolled down listening for telltale noises like scraping, vibrations, or groans that could indicate mechanical and other problems. A test

drive can indicate problems with the suspension system and the transmission. Make sure there is no excessive play in the steering wheel when turning.

- Try all the devices in the dashboard, console, and doors to make sure the gauges, lights, radio, windshield wipers, and other features are in working order.
- After the test drive, open the hood with the engine running to check for leaks and noises. Check the radiator to determine if the coolant is circulating properly.
- If doubts arise, it is always advisable to have a reliable mechanic check out the vehicle.
- Check with the motor vehicle department to make sure there are no liens against the vehicle's title.
- Before negotiating the final price, make sure that the vehicle's registration and tags are current and in order. Check the Vehicle Identification Number (VIN) against the registration and tags. The VIN is a serial number used by the automotive industry to identify individual motor vehicles. Each vehicle should have a VIN readily visible on the vehicle for easy examination. (Hamilton 1996, 8)

TOOLS

Once the vehicle has been purchased, the proud owner can look forward to hundreds of hours of often challenging work on the new acquisition. If the work is to be done largely by the owner or by the owner with help from knowledgeable friends in a home garage or rented space, having a set of tools is essential. The tools will include what a competent mechanic considers necessary to work on any motor vehicle in addition to specialty tools required to build a lowrider. Among the specialty tools that will make building the lowrider less time consuming and less stressful are the following.

- A set of power tools, preferably air tools that are more reasonably priced and last longer than electric tools. A good set of air tools includes an impact wrench, an air ratchet, an air chisel hammer, an air blow gun, a tire inflator, several quick disconnect fittings, an air nibbler, a cut-off tool, a pistol metal shear, an air body saw, an air hammer, and different sizes of die grinders.
- Air tools require an air compressor, which comes in various sizes varying from small portable units to large ones that are bolted to the floor and have a larger storage capacity.

- A sandblaster that allows for minor rust removal from small areas of the vehicle and later for painting the vehicle.
- A 12-gallon solvent tank with dual action. This is handy for washing parts when they are removed from the vehicle.
- A heavy-duty reinforcement welding unit that is powerful enough to allow the builder to weld sheet metal and other metals up to 1/2-inch thick. An optional gun for welding aluminum is also recommended. A welding outfit that includes a welding nozzle, cutting attachment, tips, goggles, and striker is essential.
- A breaker bar and six-point socket to dislodge rusted-on bolts when replacing old and corroded parts with new ones.
- Several hammers, including a ball hammer, a soft head hammer, two types of dinging hammers to remove dents out of sheet metal, and a five-pound hammer for heavy work.
- A bolt extractor to remove bolts of all sizes when the head of the bolt breaks off when using a regular wrench.
- A flaring tool, a tubing bender, and a tubing cutter for use in bending brake lines to a vehicle frame's contours.
- Engine builder's tools including a piston ring compressor, a piston ring tool, a hydraulic lifter remover, a valve spring compressor, and heavy-duty scraper and rocker stoppers.
- A 2-1/2 ton engine crane to lift out and drop in a vehicle's engine with a minimum of physical effort.
- A heavy-duty 2-1/4 ton floor jack to lift the vehicle off the ground to, for example, remove key bolts before lifting the engine from the vehicle.
- The right torque settings, which are routinely specified in manuals on building and rebuilding engines and in replacing parts such as belts and generators, must be strictly adhered to. A click-type torque wrench is recommended.
- A trim tool to remove trim from the vehicle prior to painting it.
- For sanding and grinding a vehicle's surface prior to adding a primer and paint coats, the following air-powered tools are recommended: an in-line sander, an angle grinder, a high-speed sander, and a jitterbug sander.
- Tools needed to restore a vehicle's interior include a 90-degree angle drill, a hex wrench, a ratchet wrench with sockets, needle-nose pliers, hog ring pliers, assorted screwdrivers, and a diagonal cutter. Adding custom upholstery requires the following tools: a high-pressure paint gun to shoot adhesive, a jigsaw to cut wood, a pair of large industrial scissors, upholstery needles, an industrial sewing machine, and a heat gun to heat and stretch vinyl.

- Although it is not a tool in the strictest sense, a shop manual purchased from the dealership is indispensable to build a lowrider. It contains very specific information on parts and instructions on how to disassemble and then assemble a vehicle, usually accompanied by drawings and photographs.

DISASSEMBLY OF THE VEHICLE

Having purchased a vehicle and gathered the appropriate tools, it is now time for the next step in building a lowrider, ironically by taking it apart. The disassembly phase is usually very dirty work that is unavoidable but that can be made somewhat more pleasant by taking the vehicle to a car wash to steam clean the undercarriage and the engine. There are a few simple and helpful things to keep in mind as the disassembly phase begins:

- Have plenty of room in the garage or shed where the parts can be conveniently kept and then made accessible for the assembly phase.
- Carefully tag each part with tape and illustrate in a drawing where and how the parts go together.
- Place related parts together in a clearly labeled box; in the age of digital cameras, it is ideal to photograph the different steps in the disassembly process, especially a particularly intricate step.
- Make careful notes of parts that will need to be replaced and begin the search of where they might be available, for example, at a dealership or at a salvage yard.
- Keep a log of tasks to be performed and check them off as they are completed.
- In some cases, the vehicle may require what is called a "frame-off" restoration that involves entirely removing the vehicle's chassis from the undergirding frame; however, this is not an option that all lowrider builders choose because it is expensive, more labor intensive, and requires more space.

The disassembly phase is made more difficult if the purchased vehicle has a serious rust problem. Bolts may need to be soaked in oil for several days or even eventually broken off with a bolt extractor or cut off with an acetylene torch. It is the fortunate lowrider builder who has judiciously purchased a vehicle whose factory paint job is in good shape with little or no rust in the wheel wells, the trunk, or the undercarriage. However, if rust is found, the entire outer surface of the vehicle may have to be subjected to a method known as "media-blasting," which involves removing the paint and rust with a high-pressure air blaster using different particles such as sand, glass, or plastic beads. In extreme cases of rust, it might be less time consuming—but certainly more expensive—to take the vehicle to a facility for stripping where it can be dipped in a large vat of chemicals that will penetrate even the least visible and accessible areas of the vehicle. (The various primers and undercoating of the metal surface of a vehicle once it is ready to be painted are discussed in greater detail in Chapter 4.)

ENGINE AND DRIVE TRAIN

Normally, a first-time lowrider builder would not be so ambitious nor possess sufficient expertise to enter into the technologically and mechanically complex realm of renovating or replacing a vehicle's engine and the various components of a drive train (also referred to as a driveline), including the transmission. A cursory examination of any number of standard manuals on how to do so reveals how daunting the task would be, how risky it would be to make a simple miscalculation in, for example, finely calibrating the measurement for a bore in the process of replacing the rods, and how potentially catastrophic and costly it would be to make a mistake in the reassembly of the hundreds of engine and drive train parts. Unless a builder has had considerable experience in these areas of auto mechanics—and perhaps learned from one's mistakes—it is not recommended that building a lowrider vehicle be the first test of one's skills. An alternative would be to have an experienced mechanic consult and supervise such a project, or preferably to turn the task over to a shop that routinely renovates and replaces engines and drive train components. This would be an area where a builder's prudence and humility might prevail over bravado and self-deception. There are plenty of less difficult tasks of lowrider building that can be achieved, including the suspension system, body work, and paint (discussed Chapter 4), glass and trim removal, and installation, custom interiors, and the sound system.

EXHAUST SYSTEM

Parts of the exhaust system are very vulnerable to damage on lowered vehicles, so it is important that a lowrider builder carefully calculate how to compensate for this risk in the installation of the muffler and what is referred to as the crossover pipe and the other exhaust system components. The more powerful and the higher the performance of a vehicle's engine, the more sophisticated the exhaust system will be—a high flowing exhaust system with large-diameter tubing, a high flow muffler and a high flow catalytic converter (a vehicle's smog control device required in the United States on all post-1975 models to reduce the toxicity of emissions). It would be wise to visit a custom shop that routinely installs custom exhaust systems to meet the low cruising profile of lowrider vehicles. This is particularly important if a builder does not have access to a lift to sufficiently elevate the vehicle to snugly install components that will not drag and get damaged.

THE SUSPENSION SYSTEM AND LOWERING A VEHICLE

Once the chassis and the frame have been treated for rust, the disassembled parts cleaned and identified, and new parts acquired to replace those that could not be salvaged, the next step in the process of building a lowrider is to reassemble the vehicle, starting with the suspension system. The decision on whether to equip the lowrider with an expensive hydraulics system is determined by several factors: if the vehicle be driven daily as a commute vehicle; if it will be used occasionally on weekends and holidays; or if it will be exhibited at lowrider shows. There are other factors as well that should be taken into account. If there are local laws regarding clearance between the vehicle and the street, a hydraulic system might be desirable so that the owner can raise the car to a proper clearance level and then lower it for show when it is not being driven. Another factor is expense because a hydraulic system will cost the builder more than simpler alterations to the suspension system. Contrary to popular belief, most lowrider vehicles that are driven, as opposed to exhibited at shows, are not equipped with hydraulic systems.

Regardless of whether a lowrider builder decides to install or not install a hydraulics system, safety must be an overriding concern. Vehicle manufacturers have different safety standards on lowering or drop, and the builder is advised to be properly informed about these standards as part of the decision-making process. Related to safety is the degree to which lowering affects the alignment of the tires, the frame-to-axle clearance, and the relationship between the degree of lowering of the rear and front of the vehicle.

Generally, a lowrider builder will buy a suspension lowering kit at a local auto supply store. The desired result of lowering a vehicle's suspension is to bring the frame lower in relationship to the axle centers. Kits are designed for a variety of vehicles that have two-wheel drive and four-wheel drive. The components of the front suspension—there are different front end suspension designs such as a so-called "A-arm" or straight axle, each with its own advantages and moving parts—that come into play are the coil spring and the shock absorber, the stabilizer bar that connects the wheels to the vehicle's driving mechanism. Rear-end suspensions are either straight axle or independent with either coils or leaf springs. The basic step in lowering the front and rear ends is to replace the coil springs with low-profile, shorter coils, to remove one of the leaf springs, or preferably to replace the leaf springs with a single leaf spring especially designed for lowering.

The original reason for installing hydraulic systems in lowrider vehicles was to deal with a law passed in the 1950s in California that specified the minimum clearance between a vehicle's rear end and the street. The law was designed to discourage lowrider cruising on urban streets. (See Chapter 1 for a more detailed account of the origin of hydraulics.) In the ensuing decades, hydraulic systems have become increasingly more varied, complex, safe, sophisticated, and expensive. The component parts of these systems are no longer found in auto salvage yards or surplus stores. Today, they are readily available through mail-order catalogues and at lowrider specialty stores.

An entire hydraulics installation industry has developed since the early days of lowriding. It is common for every large urban center in

1976 Chevrolet Impala outfitted with hydraulics that allows the vehicle to jump more than foot in the air. (AP Photo/Reed Saxon)

the Southwest as well as elsewhere across the United States to have several hydraulics installation shops and for these shops to advertise online as well as in lowrider publications such as *Lowrider* magazine. Local shops sponsor vehicles at lowrider shows both in the exhibit area and in the hopping and dancing contests.

The basic components of a hydraulic system are the pumps, dumps, hydraulic cylinders, solenoids, switches, hydraulic lines, and batteries. The pumps, dumps, batteries, and solenoids are installed in a car's trunk, a truck's bed, or a station wagon's spare tire well. The switches are located in the vehicle within the driver's easy reach. The hydraulic cylinders are mounted in the vehicle's suspension system on the spring seats. The pump, which is key to the operation of the hydraulic system, produces the hydraulic pressure that is in turn fed to the cylinders on each of the vehicle's four wheels. The pump, controlled and activated by the driver who manipulates the switch, consists of a powerful electric motor sometimes made from a converted starter motor; a manifold or "block" made out of steel or aluminum that contains a gear, a tank, and the pump motor bolted to it; and a reservoir that contains oil, the essential fluid that courses through the hydraulic lines to the cylinders creating hydraulic pressure which raises the wheels. The cylinders, which are the approximate size and shape of standard shock absorbers, are mounted to the vehicle's frame. When hydraulic fluid is pumped to a cylinder, its piston rod pushes down on a suspension spring thereby lifting the vehicle at that wheel. When the pressure is released, the rod retracts and the wheel is lowered. The pump pressure and flow are controlled by the gear set and the manifold outlet size. When a system "dumps," or reverses the pressure by lowering it—again, activated by a switch controlled by the driver— the oil flows back through the block into the reservoir, pooling there to be activated again when the driver wishes to raise the front or rear end of the vehicle.

The electrical system required to operate the hydraulic system is completely separate and independent from the vehicle's regular electrical system. The hydraulics electrical system has its own set of batteries located not under the hood but elsewhere depending on the kind of vehicle. The higher the performance expectations that a lowrider builder has, the more powerful the electrical system that must be installed in a vehicle. It is not uncommon for a vehicle to have up to 10 batteries in order to generate a higher voltage, which in turn governs how fast they hydraulic system responds. The most powerful systems are found in vehicles that are entered in hopping or dancing competitions at large lowrider shows. The batteries used in such competitions are sealed so that the acid within cannot spill out during the sudden and jarring lifting and dropping that occurs as part of the competitive routines. Each battery can weigh up to 60 pounds, so the racks they are mounted on must be very sturdy.

In recent years, some lowrider builders have installed inflatable air bags rather than hydraulic systems, drawn by the superior ride that the air bags afford. The air suspension technology was originally perfected by General Motors, which installed inflatable air bags in its 1957 Cadillac models in order to better support the car's considerable weight. The failure of the technology in other GM makes temporarily delayed its widespread adoption in the automotive industry until its problems could be solved. The system operates off a lightweight air compressor mounted in a lowrider car's trunk. Like a regular hydraulics system, it is controlled by switches that activate air springs on each wheel. Because the air suspension system is not as responsive as the battery-driven system, it is not favored in lowrider show competitions; however, the superior ride it affords has made the system popular among the occasional cruiser crowd (Ganat 2001, 36–53).

GLASS REMOVAL AND INSTALLATION

An additional step that a lowrider builder can take in the restoration of the vehicle is to remove all of the glass so that the metal next to it can be thoroughly treated for rust and then painted. Because glass can easily crack and even shatter, it is always a good idea to wear heavy gloves, safety goggles, and heavy protective clothing. The rubber gasket between the lip of the window and the glass itself may also have to be replaced. On older vehicles, it is likely to be cracked and may be the source of leaks into the vehicle when it rains. Once the painting of the car is complete, the new rubber gasket and the glass can be installed. An auto glass sealant is then added around the glass to further prevent leaks (Hamilton 1996, 90).

CUSTOM INTERIORS

The lowrider builder should look forward with great anticipation to designing and installing a vehicle's interior, which comes after the arduous and sometimes tedious work of restoration that has already been described in this chapter. Along with the designs and murals painted on lowrider vehicles (see Chapter 4), interiors comprise an aspect of building a lowrider that allows for great flights of imagination that seem limited only by the tight interior spaces of cars and trucks. In addition to the fabrics and upholstering material used in interior customizing, all manner of enhancements including fish tanks, chandeliers, in-dash piano keyboards, waterfalls, roulette wheels, and garish neon lights are found in vehicles exhibited at lowrider shows.

In dealing with an older vehicle, it is possible that the interior has either been damaged or that parts of it have been replaced. If this is the case, it is important to gather information about the original interior in order to be able to replace different components of the interior with precision and also to be able to restore the interior as closely as possible to what the original interior looked like. For example, in replacing upholstery for a seat, the builder will need to know its exact contour and measurements, which must be specified in ordering the cosmetic outer upholstery as well as the seat-bottom foam set and spring mechanism, the back support, and smaller assembly parts. This and other information on the interior can be obtained from the VIN. Fortunately for the lowrider builder interested in maintaining the integrity of the original interior, there are a number of aftermarket suppliers—this refers to retailers and wholesalers who specialize in furnishing parts no longer available from the original manufacturer—that maintain large inventories of parts for older vehicles.

There are many lowrider builders who will be not interested in restoring a vehicle's interior to its authentic and original state. Some of these builders will be more interested in enhancing the interior by restoring the interior with "plush" upholstery that features, for example, wall-to-wall velour and custom-sewn seat covers done on an industrial sewing machine. This kind of specialty work is best left to an expert at a custom upholstery shop. These shops can be found in practically any large urban center in the United States.

It is common for lowrider owners to prefer swiveling bucket seats as part of a vehicle's interior customized to meet individual tastes. Because these seats are very difficult to obtain either from a salvage yard or from an aftermarket supplier, they must be made from scratch. It is common to commission a custom upholstery shop to fabricate them as part of a complete custom upholstery job. Swiveling bucket seats do not meet auto safety regulations, so they are almost exclusively restricted to show cars that are never taken out on the street and that are transported to shows on trailers.

Four basic patterns are most common in custom plush interiors: biscuit or button tuck, tuck 'n roll, diamond tuck, and coffin or wrinkle pleat. The difficult phase in installing a custom plush interior is the design of the wooden frames that will serve as the solid surface over which the foam padding and upholstery will be fitted. After tracing the desired shapes for the side panels, the dashboard, and other parts onto a sheet of pressboard, they are then cut out with a jigsaw, test fitted, tightly glued together, and secured with screws. Cardboard and foam are then used for the backing material before the outer upholstery cover of crushed velour or vinyl in one of the four patterns is fitted over the wood and padding. Velour or vinyl piping is then added. Each of these steps that should be followed in creating a custom interior requires considerable skill and patience. Similar to other aspects of building a lowrider, the beginner builder may want to have a specialty custom upholstery shop do the work. It will cost more than self-installation, but having an expert do the job can prevent costly mistakes. (Hamilton 1996, 110–112)

The audio system is an essential part of a custom interior. One of the steps in installing this system requires integrating speakers into the upholstery. While many lowrider builders will be content with a low-tech sound system that requires little technical expertise or installation experience, other builders will choose to install an expensive and highly sophisticated system. In this case, the builder might best be served by having a shop that specializes in lowrider audio systems do the installation. To underline that complexity and variety of the audio components of a lowrider, this specialization is now referred to as "mobile electronics." The terminology for sound-system components has changed over the past few decades. The 1950s-era AM/FM radio in the dashboard is now referred to as a "head unit," and is regularly installed with a single- or multi-disc changer and an equalizer to balance or enhance different elements of the sound such as the characteristic heavy, drum-like bass that is often heard booming from vehicles—not exclusively lowriders—driving down an urban street with their windows wide open. An entire audio system is controlled by the head unit. On high-end units, the volume, equalizer, disc selection, and other controls are practically hands-free because they are integrated into the steering column much like controls for the windshield wipers, lights, and cruise control. The sound is enhanced by powerful amplifiers and speakers that range from simple, inexpensive speakers with a narrow sound spectrum to very expensive speakers that can costs thousands of dollars. The more expensive sound setup requires a considerable amount of electric power, so a vehicle's electronic power system requires enhancements such as an additional fuse box and high-quality electrical wiring. The more powerful sound systems may even require a second battery and an additional alternator.

CHROME AND GOLD TRIM

Whether a lowrider builder chooses to lightly restore or fully customize a lowrider vehicle, chrome and trim are considered essential
exterior decorative elements. The vehicle's bumpers are the largest
areas of chrome, which often also includes the chrome on trunk and
door handles, the chrome trim that runs along the sides of the vehicle,
a hood ornament, spotlights, a grill, an external visor over the front
windshield, and the hubcaps. A crucial phase in the restoration of a
vehicle's exterior surface is to either strip or replace chrome from the
original vehicle. This will require removing all chrome, dipping it in
a special acid solution, and then replating it using an electric process.
Before the chrome is applied electrically, a copper plating provides
the base metal to which a thin layer of nickel is added. If a builder is
preparing a vehicle for exhibition, the entire engine compartment
and the suspension system can be chrome plated. Once the restored
or replaced chrome has been put back on the vehicle, the builder will
need to carefully maintain it. Because chrome oxidizes easily, the
vehicle's owner will have to frequently use specialty cleaning products, polishing compounds, and a special cloth. (Ganat 2001, 30)

WHEELS AND HUBCAPS

Tires, wheels, and hubcaps have been important accessories on lowrider vehicles since the beginning of lowriding itself several decades
ago. The tire and wheel combination consisted of a thoroughly cleaned
white-wall tire mounted on a stock wheel rim that was frequently
painted red to contrast with the white of the tire. In the 1950s, manufacturers started producing spinner-wheel covers for standard and custom
cars, and lowriders quickly adapted them for their own vehicles. As
aftermarket covers, hubcaps, and wheels became readily available in
the 1960s and 1970s, they became almost necessary accessories on lowriders. The most important change in wheels came with the aftermarket
availability of Daytons, spoked wire wheels, fitted in predominantly
13- and 14-inch diameters with a width of 7 inches. Daytons are different from wire wheels only in the density of spokes with which they
are laced. Today, any issue of *Lowrider* magazine or *Streetlow* carries several pages in full cover of dozens of spoked wheels that a lowrider
builder can select from. Online websites often display up to a hundred
different styles. Lowrider owners may also patronize one of the many
urban specialty stores that carry these and other lowrider accessories.

The wire wheels are chromed, although it is not uncommon to see gold-plated rims and wheels, sometimes contrasted with chrome; for example, a chromed wheel combined with a gold rim or vice versa. Some lowrider owners today prefer thin white-wall tires mounted on 13-inch wheels because the small-diameter wheel and small tire enhance the look of the vehicle while lowering it (Ganat 2001, 30, 32).

BUILDING A LOWRIDER BICYCLE

Owning a bicycle has been an important part of growing up the United States. Modifying the bike in some way to make it go faster, or at least make it look like it could go faster, has been a practice that most young owners can fondly associate with their childhood. Removing or modifying the front and rear fenders, adding streamers and mirrors to the handlebars, and attaching lights to the bike's front and rear are but a few of the ways that bikes have been enhanced in order to draw attention and admiration from peers. In the 1960s and 1970s, manufacturers began adding banana seats and featuring raised handlebars in an attempt to make bicycles look more like motorcycles. These "wheelie" bikes with smaller frames and names like "Sting Ray" and "Fastback" gave the rider greater control and maneuverability to ride on the rear wheel with the front wheel elevated off the ground and to make sharper turns. Given their size and shape, the wheelie bikes soon began to be modified as the first lowrider bikes.

Today, a child or young adult who wants to own a lowrider bicycle has a range of choices, much like the adult who wants to build a lowrider motorized vehicle. The first choice is driven by the amount of money the young lowrider has to invest in the project and whether the bike will be for street use or for show at lowrider bicycle competitions. The lowrider bicycle builder has the option of finding a used or new standard bike—mountain bikes and BMX-style bikes should be avoided—or of ordering a lowrider frame and parts from a distributor that specializes in lowrider bikes. The first option is much less costly than the second one and will have the advantage of testing and stretching the young builder's imagination and ingenuity and of developing his or her mechanical skills. In either case, the builder will need to acquire the following used or new parts that are considered essential to a top-rate lowrider bicycle: a banana seat, a "springer" fork, a front fender, a "sissy bar," a back fender, big sloping handlebars, and wire wheels with at least 100 spokes.

The tools needed to disassemble a standard bicycle to convert it into a lowrider bicycle fit well within the modest budget of most lowrider bicycle builders. The tools are inexpensive and readily available when compared to the tools required to build a lowrider car or truck: a standard set of wrenches and screwdrivers. Armed with these simple tools, the young enthusiast begins by stripping down the bike to just the frame, being careful to label all parts that might be needed later.

Once the frame has been sanded and wiped down with a wet cloth, the next step is to apply the paint. Although painting a bike is not nearly has complicated as painting a car or truck, it still requires patience and skill, especially if the builder wants to add enhancements such as metal flake, "candy" paints, and murals (See Chapter 4 for a detailed discussion of enhancements to lowrider cars and trucks.) Normally, if the bicycle is being built for street use, the builder will not invest nearly as much time and money in the paint phase of the project. Show bikes, on the other hand, can demand a great deal more of each. Builders of show bikes typically use a plastic body filler known as bondo in combination with sheet metal to fill in large open areas within the frame. A common practice is to create what looks like a small motorcycle gasoline tank out of a triangular piece of sheet metal welded together and attached just under the top frame of the bicycle. Many layers of bondo are then applied to this metal compartment. The builder adds a layer, sands it, and then adds an additional layer, shaping the bondo to achieve different effects. Other metal sheet surfaces treated with bondo can be added to attach elsewhere on the bicycle. The bondo-covered surfaces are fragile, but because the bicycles will not be driven on the street nor subjected to temperature extremes, the surfaces stand up quite well; however, they can crack if the bicycle is dropped or impacted. The designs and murals that the builder paints on the hard, finished surfaces are similar to those found on cars and trucks. An exception would be the rarity of murals of nude or semiclad women on bikes due to young age of most of the owners.

There are many other enhancements that can be added to a lowrider bicycle designed to be exhibited at a show: (1) frames can be cut down, lengthened, or have a decorative segment added; (2) the angle of the front fork mount can be changed to achieve different effects such as lowering the profile of the bike; (3) metal created from square or flat stock, heated at high temperatures, and then twisted licorice-like is shaped into handlebars, kickstands, front forks, and other components on the bike and are often chromed to bring out a brilliant reflection from artificial lighting; (4) often the wheels and the spokes, crisscrossed in intricate patterns, are chromed and even gold-plated to achieve the same reflective effect.

FURTHER READING

Editors of *Lowrider* magazine. *Lowrider's Handbook.* New York: HP Books, 2002.

Ganat, Robert. *Lowriders.* St. Paul, MN: MBI Publishing Company, 2001.

Hamilton, Frank. *How to Build a Lowrider.* North Branch, MN: CarTech, 1996.

10

Lowrider Lingo

AFICIONADO—normally meant to identity an individual who is enthusiastic or even passionate about the different aspects of lowriding

BAGGED—a "bagged" car is one with an air adjustable suspension

BAILANDO **(SPANISH)**—the motion of a lowrider vehicle in a dancing contest alternating either from front to rear or side to side

BAJITO **(SPANISH)**—a general term to described a lowered chassis on a lowrider vehicle

BLASTING—turning up a vehicle's audio system to a very high volume while cruising or parked; "blasting" can also refer to the act of cruising

BOMBA **(SPANISH)**—refers to a 1930s- or early 1940s-model lowrider vehicle

BOOTY HOPPIN'—a repeated hydraulics rear-end hop

BOUNCE—the act of jumping a car off the ground

CADDY—a Cadillac car or SUV

CAGA PALOS **(SPANISH)**—slang term for hydraulic lifts

CAR CLUBBERS—owners and operators of lowriders who are affiliated with a recognized car club or lowrider association

CARRUCHA—a caló term for "car"; cariations on *carrucha* are *carruchita* or *firme carrucha*, which a sense of class roughly equivalent to "fine"

CARAVAN (ALSO "CONVOY")—a collective and formal procession of group or club vehicles down a street or highway

CARAVANNING—the act of engaging in a caravan

CITY CRUISING—individual or group cruising down urban streets such as Whittier Avenue in East Los Angeles and Crenshaw Avenue in South Central Los Angeles

CLOWNING—the act of showing off a lowrider by hitting the hydraulic switches

COCKED UP—front-end lift on a moving or stationary vehicle

CORNERS—the act of moving an individual wheel by activating the vehicle's hydraulics

CRUISER OR CITY CRUISER—designed and equipped as a street car and generally not meant for exhibit at a lowrider show; a variation on these terms is "street cruiser"

CRUISING—a general term that refers to the act of driving lowrider vehicles for pleasure or recreation

CRUISING *BOMBITA*-STYLE—urban cruising in an older or vintage model

DANCIN' AROUND—another term for *bailando*

DAYTONS—a top-of-the-line and highly desired brand of wire wheels for a lowrider; "D's" is often used as a slang expression for Dayton wheels

DONUT OR CHAIN—steering wheels

DRIVE-BY—street "hop" or "snatch"

DUMP—a hydraulic valve that controls the downward motion of the lowrider vehicle

FIVE O—slang for a policeman

FLASHING—publicly displaying a club or group vehicle, plaque or other identifying markers; "flashing colors" is an overt signaling by one group or club to another regarding one's identity, which can be an act of pride, a warning, or a challenge

FLEXING—activating the hydraulics switches

G-RIDE—short for "great ride"

HAPPENING—a staged or formal lowrider community or corporate event in which car clubs, businesses, and individuals compete for status and rewards; examples would be a lowrider show and a hopping contest at the show

HIGH BOUNCING—high, jumping hydraulics motion

HOMEBOYS OR CLIQUE MEMBERS—family members or friends who are related to or associate with lowrider club members but who themselves do not operate a lowrider vehicle; they may, however, be members in good standing in a lowrider club

HOPPING—generally refers to front-end hydraulics motion while moving (cruising down the street) or stationary, as in a hopping competition at a lowrider show; "humping" also refers to a front-end hydraulics motion while cruising, but it is less obvious than hopping

HOP—a formal competition at a car show in which hopping and dancing events take place

HOP PIT (ALSO KNOWN AS A HYDRO PIT)—a spectator location at a lowrider show where the hopping and dancing competitions take place

HOPPER—a vehicle equipped with hydraulics that is entered in a hopping competition at a lowrider car show

HYDRAULICALLY CHALLENGED—describes a person who is not knowledgeable about lowriding

JACKED UP OR LOCKED UP—a car that can jump up and down on its hydraulic shocks

JUICED—term to describe a vehicle that has a hydraulically adjustable suspension

LAYED OR LAID—front- and rear-end lowering on a moving or stationary vehicle

LEANING ON THREE—single-wheel front- or rear-end lift on a moving or stationary vehicle

LIFT—a general term used to describe the various ways in which a vehicle's hydraulic system is manipulated to raise and lower the front and rear ends

LOCKED UP—when a car is at its highest point on its hydraulics

LOW SHOW—a lowered car designed and equipped to be exhibited at a lowrider show

LOW LOW—a lowrider

MINI-TRUCKING—the act of cruising in a lowrider truck

PANCAKING—repetitive front-end hydraulics hop while cruising or stationary

PLAQUE—a lowrider club metal logo, commonly displayed in the back window

QUEEN—generally refers to a lowrider vehicle that is not driven but is built to be exhibited a lowrider show

RADICAL—a vehicle that has been radically customized according to specific criteria set by lowrider show rules

RADICAL DANCING—rapidly alternating front- and rear-end and/or side-to-side hydraulics manipulation

RAG OR RAG TOP—usually refers to a convertible or a car model with a cloth top

RATION (SPANISH CALÓ)—a ride or cruise

RIDE—a general term that encompasses all lowrider vehicles

ROLAR (SPANISH CALÓ)—"let's roll," or get started

ROOSTER TAIL—the trail of sparks produced by a lowrider when it scrapes the street surface

SCRAPING—a hydraulics maneuver during street cruising to lower a lowrider vehicle so that its magnesium scrape-plate makes contact with the street and produces sparks; scraping at night produces the most dramatic results.

SIDE-TO-SIDE—alternating side-to-side motion of a lowrider vehicle produced by the manipulation of its hydraulics system

SLAMMING—repetitive front-end hydraulics hops while cruising or stationary

SLAMMIN' RIDE—a term of admiration that refers to an especially fine customized lowrider

SNATCHING—repetitive front-end hop while cruising or stationary

SOLO CRUISERS—lowrider vehicle owners who have no affiliation with a lowrider club or other lowrider association

SPOKES—a general term for wire wheels

TANKS, WHAMMY TANKS, VALVES AND AN O-RING—all terms referring to a complex hydraulics pump system

THREE WHEELER—a lowrider vehicle designed to be able to cruise on three wheels

TRICKED OUT—another word for "customized" or "modified" when applied to a vehicle

TROCA (SPANISH)—colloquial term for "truck" used in the Southwest and Mexico

VETERANS OR *VETERANOS*—former or current members of a lowrider club who are no longer active in building and showing lowriders

X-FRAME—a strong frame for jumping lowriders on hydraulic pumps

FURTHER READING

Mendoza, Rubén G. "Cruising Art and Culture in Aztlán: Lowriding in the Mexican American Southwest." In *U.S. Latino Literatures and Cultures: Transnational, Perspectives,* edited by Francisco Lomelí and Karin Ikas. Heidelberg: Universitatsverlag C, Winter 2000. Mendoza has compiled an excellent glossary of terms—the most complete glossary available—in both English and Spanish, including caló terms, based on his extensive research on lowrider culture.

Bibliography

Acuña, Rodolfo. *Community under Siege: A Chronicle of Chicanos East of the Los Angeles River, 1945–1975*. Los Angeles: UCLA Chicano Studies Research Center Publications, 1984.

Acuña, Rodolfo. *Occupied America: A History of Chicanos*. 4th edition. New York: Longman, 1999.

Alvarez, Luis. *The Power of the Zoot: Youth Culture and Resistance during World War II*. Berkeley: University of California Press, 2008.

Barnet-Sánchez, Holly, and Eva Sperling, eds. *Signs from the Heart: California Chicano Murals*. Venice, CA: Social Public Art Resource Center, 1990.

Barris, George, www.barris.com/history/html.

Bright, Brenda Jo. "Mexican American Low Riders: An Anthropological Approach to Popular Culture." Houston, TX: Ph.D. dissertation, Rice University, 1994.

Bright, Brenda Jo. "Nightmares in the New Metropolis: The Cinematic Poetics of Low Riders." *Studies in Latin American Popular Culture* 16 (1997): 13–29.

Bueno, Jae. "Lady Bugs C. C.: Most Influential All-Female Lowrider Car Club." *Lowrider* (November 2010): 28–30.

Cummings, Laura L. *Pachucas & Pachucos in Tucson: Situated Border Lives*. Tucson: University of Arizona Press, 2009.

Delgado, Monica, and Michael Van Wagenen, *Low and Slow*. 16mm, 27 minutes. Ritual Film and Publications, 1997.

Donnelly, Nora. *Customized: Art Inspired by Hot Rods, Low Riders and American Car Culture*. Boston: Harry N. Abrams, in association with the Institute of Contemporary Art, Boston, 2000.

Editors of *Lowrider* magazine. *Lowrider's Handbook*. New York: HP Books, 2002.

Espinoza, Dionne. " 'Tanto Tiempo Disfrutamos . . . ': Revisiting Gender and Sexual Politics of Chicana/o Youth Culture in East Los Angeles in the 1960s," in *Velvet Barrios: Popular Culture and Chicana/o Sexualities*, edited by Alicia Gaspar de Alba, 89–106. Hampshire, England: Palgrave Macmillan, 2003.

Franz, Kathleen. *Tinkering: Consumers Reinvent the Early Automobile*. Philadelphia: University of Pennsylvania Press, 2005.

Ganahl, Pat. *Custom Painting*. North Branch, MN: CarTech, 2008.

Ganat, Robert. *Lowriders*. St. Paul, MN: MBI Publishing Company, 2001.

García, Alma M. "The Development of Chicana Feminist Discourse, 1970–1980," in *Unequal Sisters. A Multicultural Reader of U.S. Women's History*, edited by Ellen Carol DuBois and Vicki L. Ruiz, 418–431. New York and London: Routledge, 1990.

García, Mario T. "Americans All: The Mexican American Generation and the Politics of Wartime Los Angeles, 1941–1945." In *The Mexican American Experience*, edited by Rodolfo O. de la Garza. Austin: University of Texas Press, 1985.

García, Mario T. *Mexican Americans: Leadership, Ideology, and Identity, 1930–1960*. New Haven, CT: Yale University Press, 1989.

García, Richard Amado. *Rise of the Mexican American Middle Class, San Antonio, 1929–1941*. San Antonio: Texas A&M Press, 1991.

Gaspar de Alba, Alicia. *Chicano Art: Inside Outside the Master's House*. Austin: University of Texas Press, 1998.

Gaytán, David Rojas. *Pachucos in the Wartime Mexican Angeleno Press*. Hayward: M.A. thesis, California State University–Hayward, 1996.

Gradante, William. "Art among the Low Riders," in *Folk Art in Texas*, edited by Francis Edward Abernethy, 71–77. Dallas: SMU Press and the Texas Folklore Society, 1985.

Grajeda, Ralph. "The Pachuco in Chicano Poetry: The Process of Legend." *Revista Chicano-Riqueña* 8, no. 4 (1980): 50–62.

Griswold del Castillo, Richard, Teresa McKenna, and Yvonne Yarbro-Bejarano, eds. *Chicano Art: Resistance and Affirmation, 1965–1985*. Los Angeles: UCLA Wright Gallery, 1991.

Guevara, Rubén. "The View from the Sixth Street Bridge: The History of Chicano Rock," in *The First Rock&Roll Confidential Report*, edited by David Marsh and the editors of *Rock&Roll Confidential*. New York: Pantheon, 1994.

Hamilton, Frank. *How to Build a Lowrider*. North Branch, MN: CarTech, 1996.

Ides, Matthew Allan. "Cruising for Community: Youth Culture and Politics in Los Angeles, 1910–1970." Ph.D. dissertation, University of Michigan, 2009.

Jackson, Carlos Francisco. *Chicana and Chicano Art*. Tucson: University of Arizona Press, 2009.

Keller, Gary. *Hispanics and United States Film: An Overview and Handbook*. Tempe, AZ: Bilingual Review Press, 1994.

Keller, Gary D, ed. *Contemporary Chicana and Chicano Art*. 2 vols. Tempe: Bilingual Press/Editorial Bilingue, 2002.

Keller, Gary D., Mary Erickson, and Pat Villeneuve, eds. *Chicano Art for the New Millennium: Collected Works from the Arizona State University Community*. Tempe: Bilingual Press/Editorial Bilingue, 2002.

Loza, Steven. *Barrio Rhythm: Mexican American Music in Los Angeles*. Urbana and Chicago: University of Illinois Press, 1993.

Madrid-Barela, Arturo. "In Search of the Authentic Pachuco: An Interpretive Essay." *Aztlán: Chicano Journal of Social Sciences and the Arts*, 4, no. 1 (Spring 1973): 31–60.

Marín, Cheech, ed. *Chicano Visions: American Painters on the Verge*. Boston: Little, Brown and Company, 2002.

Martínez, Glenn A. *Mexican Americans and Language: Del dicho al hecho*. Tucson: University of Arizona Press, 2006.

Mazón, Mauricio. *The Zoot-Suit Riots: The Psychology of Symbolic Annihilation*. Austin: University of Texas Press, 1984.

McFarland, Pancho. *Chicano Rap: Gender and Violence in the Postindustrial Barrio*. Austin: University of Texas Press, 2008.

Mendoza, Rubén G. "Cruising Art and Culture in Aztlán: Lowriding in the Mexican American Southwest," in *U.S. Latino Literatures and Cultures: Transitional Perspectives*, edited by Francisco A. Lomeli and Karen Ikas, 3–35. Heidelberg: Universitatverlag, 2000.

Molina, Ruben. *The Barrio Guide to Low Rider Music, 1950–1975*. La Puente: Mictlan Publishing, 2002.

Navarro, J. L. "To a Dead Lowrider." In *Aztlán: An Anthology*, edited by Luis Valdez and Stan Steiner, 337–339. New York: Knopf, 1973.

Nayfak, Shakina. "Que te watcha cabrones: Marking the 30th Anniversary of Luis Valdez's *Zoot Suit*." *TDR: The Drama Review* 53, no. 3

(Fall 2009). http://muse.jhu.edu/journals/the_drama_review/v053/53.3.nayfack.html.

Peña, Manuel. *The Texas-Mexican Conjunto: History of a Working-Class Music*. Austin: University of Texas Press, 1985.

Peña, Manuel. *Música Tejana*. College Station: Texas A&M Press, 1999.

Penland, Paige R. *Lowrider: History, Pride, Culture*. St. Paul, MN: MBI Publishing, 2003.

Petersen Automotive Museum website, www.petersen.org.

Plascencia, Luis F. B. "Low Riding in the Southwest: Cultural Symbols in the Mexican Community," in *History, Culture and Society: Chicano Studies in the 1980s*, edited by Mario T. García, 141–175. Ypsilanti, Michigan: Bilingual Press/Editorial Bilingue, 1983.

Ramírez, Catherine S. "The Pachuca and Chicana Style Politics." *Meridians: Feminism, Race, Transnationalism* 2, no. 2 (2008): 1–35.

Ray, Joe. "In the Days of Car Club Wars Past ..." *Lowrider* (January 2011): 10–11.

Reyes, David, and Tom Waldman. *Land of a Thousand Dances: Chicano Rock 'n' Roll from Southern California*. Albuquerque: University of New Mexico Press, 1998.

Robb, John Donald. *Hispanic Folk Music of New Mexico and the Southwest*. Norman: University of Oklahoma Press, 1980.

Rodríguez, Luis. "Eastside Sound," *Q-Vo* 2, no. 7 (1980): 27–28.

Rodríguez, Richard T. "The Verse of the Godfather: Signifying Family and Nationalism in Chicano Rap and Hip-Hop Culture," in *Velvet Barrios: Popular Culture and Chicana/o Sexualities*, edited by Alicia Gaspar de Alba, 107–122. New York: Palgrave Macmillan, 2003.

Rodríguez, Roberto. *Justice: A Question of Race*. Tempe: Bilingual Review Press, 1997.

Rose, Tricia. *Black Noise: Rap Music and Black Culture in Contemporary America*. Hanover: Wesleyan University Press, 1994.

Rosensweig, Jay B. *Caló: Gutter Spanish*. New York: Dutton, 1973.

Sandoval, Denise Michelle. "Cruising through Low Rider Culture: Chicana/o Identity in the Marketing of *Low Rider* Magazine," in *Velvet Barrios: Popular Culture and Chicana/o Sexualities*, edited by Alicia Gaspar de Alba, 179–186. New York: Palgrave Macmillan, 2003.

Sandoval, Denise Michelle. "Bajito y suavecito: The Lowriding Tradition." 2003. http://latinto.si.edu/virtualgallery/lowrider/lr_sandovalessay.htm.

Smithsonian Museum American History website, http://americanhistory.si.edu.

Stecyk, C. R. Guest curator with Bolton Colburn. *KustomKulture: Von Dutch, Ed "Big Daddy" Roth, Robert Williams and Others.* San Francisco: Laguna Art Museum and Last Gasp of San Francisco, 1993.

Stone, William Cutler. *"Bajito y suavecito* [Low and Slow]: Low Riding and the 'Class' of Class." *Studies in Latin American Popular Culture* 9 (1990): 86–126.

Strong, Carol. *Sunday Drivers: A Look at the Guys behind the Chrome.* 16mm, 58 minutes. Rockstar Games, Inc., 2005.

Suárez, Mario. "El Zopilote Kid," in *Chicano Sketches: Short Stories by Mario Suárez,* edited by Francisco A. Lomelí, Cecilia Cota-Robles Suárez, and Juan José Casillas-Núñez, 30–36. Tucson: University of Arizona Press, 2004.

Vigil, James Diego. *Barrio Gangs: Street Life and Identity in Southern California.* Austin: University of Texas Press, 1988.

Villarreal, José Antonio. *Pocho.* New York: Doubleday and Company, 1959.

Volti, Rudi. *Cars and Culture: The Life Story of a Technology.* Westport, CT: Greenwood Press, 2004.

Westergard, Harry, http://howstuffworks.com/westergard-mercury -custom-car.thm.

Index

Zapata, Emiliano, 98, 100
Zoot suiters, 29, 30, 36–49, 119–20;
    in *Lowrider* magazine, 37, 45–47,
    49, 50–51; origins of, 33–34;
    post-World War II attitudes
    toward, 41–44; resurrection
    and re-fashioning of, 44–45;

Valdez's play about, 36, 46,
    47–49, 119; World War II
    restrictions and, 36–37.
    See also Pachucas/os
Zoot Suit riots (1943), 37–41
Zoot Suit (Valdez), 37, 46,
    47–49, 119

About the Author

CHARLES M. TATUM is a professor of Spanish in the Department of Spanish and Portuguese at the University of Arizona in Tucson. Dr. Tatum has written and edited several books on Chicana/o literature and popular culture and Latin American popular culture.